A TIME TO LIVE

The *New* Christian Way Series 3

MAURA HYLAND

with the assistance of
Helena Browner
and
Máire Daly

VERITAS

Acknowledgements

The Author and Publishers are grateful to the following for permission to reproduce copyright material in this book: Editions Du Signe for extracts from *A Path through Advent for Children 1992*, F. Dolly, P. Haag, A. Hari, C. Singer, A.M. Stall; The British and Foreign Bible Society for extracts from the Good News Bible © American Bible Society, New York, 1966, 1971 and 4th edition 1976 published by The Bible Societies/HarperCollins, with permission; Darton Longman & Todd Ltd and Doubleday, a division of Bantam Doubleday Dell Publishing Group Inc. for extracts from *The New Jerusalem Bible* © 1985 and extracts from *The Jerusalem Bible* © 1966; Darton Longman & Todd Ltd for extracts from *Free to Believe* and *Where is your God?*, Michael Paul Gallagher; Saint Mary's Press, Minnesota USA, for extracts from *Love and Lifestyles*, Mary Judd, *Psalms Anew*, Nancy Schreck OSF, Maureen Leach OSF, and *The Christian Call to Justice and Peace*, Joseph Stoutzenberger; The Columban Fathers, St Columban's, Mission Education Department, Co Meath, for extracts from *The Gateway Series 1* and *The Gateway Series 3*, Tom Larkin and Pauline McAndrew SSC; The Divine Word Missionaries, Maynooth, for an extract from *Kairos* Nov/Dec 1989; Divine Word Missions, Roscommon, for an extract from *The Word*, December 1991; HarperCollins Religious for extracts from *Praise! Songs and Poems from the Bible retold for Children*, A.J. McCallan; The Columba Press for an extract from *Beginning to Pray*, Tomas O Caoimh; Resource Publications Inc., California, for the extract 'Dayenu', Michael E. Moynahan SJ, from *The Holy Week Book*, compiled by Eileen Freeman; Maryvale Department of Education, Birmingham, for extracts from *Maryvale Life Education Project*; Fr Flor McCarthy SDB for 'The Book', 'The Magi' and 'The Beatitudes'; Trócaire and Christian Aid for an extract from *It's not Fair, A Handbook on World Development for Schools and Youth Groups*; Brendan Kennelly for the poem 'A White Empty Room' from *The Book of Judas*; HarperCollins Religious/Fount Paperbacks for extracts from *Mr God, This is Anna*, Flynn, and *Jesus, The Word to be Spoken, Prayers and Meditations for every day of the year*, compiled by Brother Angelo Devananda; Robson Books Ltd, London, for extracts from *The Words of Martin Luther King*, selected by Coretta Scott King; Concordia Publishing House, Missouri, USA, for an extract from *Psalms/Now*, Leslie F. Brandt; The Mercier Press, Cork for extracts from *Stories for Preachers* and *Preaching in Stories*, Fr James A. Feehan; Weidenfeld and Nicholson for extracts from *Under the Eye of the Clock* and *Damburst of Dreams* by Christopher Nolan; St Paul's Publications, Slough, England for extracts from *Parables and Fables for Modern Man*, P. Ribes, and *Words of Comfort*, Daniel P. Cronin; The Combat Poverty Agency, Dublin for extracts from their Fact Pack, *Fair shares*; Faber and Faber Ltd for the poem 'My Parents kept me from Children who were Rough' from *The Collected Poems of Stephen Spender*; Human Development Resource Council, Inc, 3941, Holcomb Bridge Road, Norcross, GA 30092, USA, for an extract from *What They Never Told you about the Facts of Life*; Irish Commission for Justice and Peace and The Irish Council of Churches for extracts from *So Everybody Fights*, *Power to Hurt* and *Exploring Violence*; Essex Music Ltd for the words of the song 'Standing in the Rain', S. Carter; The Medical Missionaries of Mary for an extract from *Medical Missionaries of Mary*, Vol. 53 No.3 1991, Sr Teresita Donnelly MMM; SDB Media for an extract from *The Salesian Bulletin* Vol.53 No.1 1992, Brother Trevor Dean; Tullamore Travellers Movement for 'Give us a Chance' by Mary McDonnell.

Extracts from Veritas Publications are as follows: *The Calm Beneath the Storm*, Donal Neary; *The Mystery of God*, Brid Greville RSC; *Mary, A Marian Anthology*, Patrick J. Murray CSSp; *Celebrating with Mary*, Gerard McGinnity; *Dying with Love*, Patricia O'Reilly; *Priests! Telling it like it is*, Dagmar Kolata; *The Christian Way Two*, Raymond Brady; *Walk in My Presence*, Sean McEntee, Kathleen Glennon, William Murphy; *The Work of Justice*, Irish Bishops' Pastoral; *Minority Groups in Ireland*, Archbishop of Dublin; *Love is for Life*, Irish Bishops' Pastoral.

Illustrations

CYC Information Section, pp.4,12 (repeated); Robert Allen Photography, pp.6, 231; National Gallery of Ireland, pp.14, 15, 30, 33, 46, 47, 48, 111, 122, 127, 189, 215; Ger Andrews/Source, p.16; Weidenfeld & Nicolson, pp.18,19; Link-Up/John McElroy pp. 20, 21; Luke Golobitsh, pp.22, 182, 206, 207, 248, 267; HarperCollins Publishers, p.28; Les Editions du Bosquet, pp.41, 54, 55, 101, 188, 210, 264, 283; Centro Studi Russia Cristania, pp.44, 140; CIRIC, pp. 50, 62, 82, 83, 87, 88, 90, 93, 124, 150, 153, 154, 158, 166, 235, 261, 265, 274, 277, 279, 281; SDB Media, p. 61; British Museum, pp. 67, 77; ENIT, p.69; Office of Public Works, pp.71, 114, 299; Bord Fáilte, p.72; Mercier Press, p.73; Irish News Agency, p.78; KNA Bild, pp. 79, 103; British Tourist Authority, p.84; The Trustees of the Chester Beatty Library, Dublin, pp.95, 97, 147; Orthodox News, p.135; Sr Mairéad Butterly, pp.140, 293; Tretjakov State Gallery, Moscow, p.141; Patrick Peacock, p.160; Tom Kennedy/Source, p.161; Paul Peter Piech, pp.169, 175, 176, 183, 218, 220, 221, 223, 224, 225, 226, 228, 229, 232, 285, 286; United Nations Office of Public Information, p.170; Network Photographers, p.179; Age & Opportunity, p.188; Pat Langan/Source, p.185; Fr M. Collins, pp.187,241; Amnesty International, p.195; Ken Simms, p.198; The Combat Poverty Agency, pp.200-201, 208; Dr Arno Peters, Akademische Verlaganstalt, p.211; National Mission Council, pp.213, 214, 237; The Irish Times, pp.239, 275; Noeline Kelly pp.230, 245, 263; John Farragher p.255; Irish Sisters of Charity, p.257; Press Association, p.258; Rev. D. McCarthy, p.260; Mary Evans Picture Library, p.301, 304.

While every effort has been made to contact and obtain permission from holders of copyright, if any involuntary infringement of copyright has occurred, sincere apologies are offered and the owner of such copyright is requested to contact the publishers.

Reprinted 1994.

Contents

Human Life with Others

In *The Wild Boy of Aveyron* Jean Itard tells the story of a boy who, until he was aged about twelve, spent most of his childhood alone in the forest without any contact except with the animals.

The boy was discovered by three hunters while they were walking in the woods of Caine, in France, in the year 1798. When they first spied him he was moving about like an animal and when he saw them he leaped for cover among the trees. But they managed to capture him and they brought him back to the village.

The villagers named him Victor and a teacher of the deaf named Jean Itard offered to do some work with him.

Everyone in the village was amazed that Victor seemed to have none of the abilities that people use all the time as they go about their normal daily lives. He moved like an animal. He was completely without the ability to relate to others and he tried to bite and scratch anyone who came near him. He showed no sign of affection, even to those who were helping him. His eyes were without expression and he was unable to concentrate. He could not distinguish between flat or raised surfaces, between music and noise or between perfume and bad smells.

After many years of work with Jean Itard, Victor showed signs of progress. But he never developed some of the basic social, intellectual and physical skills which we take for granted in human beings.

Discuss

What do you think were the factors which caused Victor to develop as he did?

2   God's gift of life comes to us through our parents. As infants, we depend totally on our parents for survival. As we grow through the various stages of development and even into adult life, we depend on other people to help us to develop as mature, healthy, happy individuals.

With the right care and opportunities, we develop socially, we learn how to live in the world with other people; we develop physically, our bodies grow strong and healthy; we develop intellectually, we learn how to use our intelligence, we come to understand many things. For example, the physical development of four-year-olds is encouraged when they learn how to ride a bicycle; their social development is encouraged when they are taught to share their sweets with others; their intellectual development is encouraged when they take part in an activity in which they sort shapes.

In Your Religion Journal

What are the things happening in your life right now which promote your physical development, your social development, your intellectual development?

With Others at Home

9 RIGHT NOW! 12 3 6

You still have many needs which are answered by your parents and your family. You have, of course, become much more independent and you relate differently to your parents and to the other members of your family than you did when you were younger. This can sometimes cause tension at home. Adolescents can find it difficult to accept the authority of their parents. They also find it annoying to be dependent for food and clothes. On the other hand, parents often find it frustrating and confusing when their young people don't seem to understand that they, as parents, have only their good at heart.

In Your Religion Journal

List all the ways in which your needs are answered by those at home. List some situations which might cause someone of your age to be frustrated or angry at home.

(a) John arrives home from school. He's had a bad day. He got very bad marks in his maths test, and he has learned that his friends have planned to go for a cycle in the country at the weekend without including him in their plans.
His mother notices that he is not in good form and is very sympathetic.

(b) Miriam is very upset. Her friend Hilda is having a birthday party. Hilda's parents are away and Hilda has told all her friends that they can stay overnight. Miriam, who thought that this was a wonderful idea, cannot understand why her parents have told her that she does not have their permission to stay overnight.
Miriam's older brother Joe finds her sitting staring glumly at the television screen and asks what is wrong.

(c) Robert was due in at eleven o'clock. This was a new rule. When he was fourteen he'd had to be home by ten. It is now two a.m. and Robert hasn't arrived in yet. His father has been watching television, waiting for Robert to arrive. Realising what time it is and that Robert has not yet arrived home, he has decided to wake Robert's mother who had gone to bed earlier. The two of them are both worried and angry.

Find Your Group

Set up and act out these role plays.

Discuss

Do you have any experience of situations similar to those in the above role plays? What do they tell us about family life?

With others in Friendship

Find Your Group
Discuss

What are the kinds of things which you think irritate young people about their parents?
What are the kinds of things which cause most arguments in the family?
How does your list compare with the lists of the other groups?
Which of these can be solved most easily?
Which are the most difficult to solve? Why?

In Your Religion Journal

Take one of the situations mentioned in the discussion. Pretend you are a parent. Write your comments and reactions to the situation.

Discuss

What are the things which cause parents to worry about their children?
Why do these things cause parents to worry?
What could you do to help them worry less?
Do you think parents should always say 'Yes' to what their children want?
What should they say 'No' to?

In Your Religion Journal

Pretend that you are your parent, mother or father.
Is there anything in your attitudes or activities which you think you would object to if you were a parent?
Write a letter to your friend, talking about the worries and anxieties you have and asking for advice.

We also need the support and love which we experience in friendships with people outside our families.

Young people like to get together with their friends. The group they belong to, 'the gang', 'the boys', 'the girls', is like a shelter and a place of refuge.

Friendship is an adventure, a risk. It can only grow in an atmosphere where trust is exchanged. Friends share their joys and their sorrows and they trust that these are safe in the other's care. True friendship means giving and receiving rather than simply taking.

What do you think?
Is it possible for one to go through adolescence without a friend?

In Your Religion Journal

Describe your closest friend.
What characteristics does he or she have?
What is it about your friend that you like most?
What do you most enjoy about being with your friend?
What is it about your friendship that you find most helpful?
If your friend were to go away, what do you think you would miss most?
What do you think you contribute to your friend?

True Friendship

Find Your Group

Discuss

Which of the following do you agree or disagree with?

Can you rank the statements in order of importance 1—19?

Which do you think are definitely not the marks of true friendship?

Activity

In this word search find four words which you think are important marks of true friendship. Using these words make and decorate a 'friendship poster' for the classroom.

A true friend will:

___ always keep a secret;

___ cover up for you;

___ always be ready to forgive;

___ lend you money whenever you ask;

___ support and encourage you;

___ wait for you in all circumstances;

___ do anything for you without question;

___ stay with you in trouble;

___ ignore your faults;

___ tell you the truth, especially about yourself;

___ share everything possible with you;

___ listen to you when you need to talk;

___ help you to believe in yourself;

___ make you happy;

___ protect you from bullies;

___ understand you;

___ never let you down;

___ believe everything you say.

M	E	N	C	O	U	R	A	G	E	A	R	Y
P	V	O	W	A	E	R	A	L	N	O	N	T
H	I	S	H	A	R	E	A	D	E	R	E	N
A	G	O	N	Y	E	E	T	R	U	S	T	S
C	R	Y	N	Y	O	V	R	E	S	T	S	N
C	O	M	P	A	N	I	O	N	S	H	I	P
I	F	I	W	A	S	N	P	L	O	N	L	T
T	R	O	F	M	O	C	P	A	S	T	E	W
A	T	R	U	T	H	F	U	L	N	E	S	S
I	J	C	V	E	N	I	S	A	N	C	T	E

As we grow older we learn that true friendship takes into account the needs of others as well as our own needs. We therefore befriend people not only because they make us feel good or because they offer us the love and support that we need, but because we realise that we can also offer them love, care and support.

In Your Religion Journal

Think of someone whom you have befriended and who you know has benefited from your friendship.
Write a paragraph saying what you think you have offered to this person.

The Christian Understanding of Friendship

There are others outside the circle of our family and friends to whom we must relate.

As followers of Jesus we are challenged to relate to all others in a spirit of openness and love: 'Love one another as I have loved you,' is the command which he left us.

He showed us, in his own life, how to relate to others with love and care, particularly to those who are most in need.

Activity

Recall some stories from the gospels which you have already heard and which show us how Jesus related to others with love and care, particularly to those who were most in need; the poor, the sinners, the outcasts and those who were downtrodden in any way.

The following biblical references will help:
Matthew 8:5–13; 9:1–7; 9:27–31
Mark 5:21–42; 8:1–10
Luke 7:36–50; 10:38–42

Make a wall frieze entitled 'Jesus and others', using quotes from the gospels and illustrations.

In Your Religion Journal

List some of the important characteristics of the friendship which Jesus offered to others. Give reasons for your answers.

Relating to those who are different from ourselves

Sometimes we find it difficult to reach out in friendship to those who are outside our circle of friends. We often find it particularly difficult in the case of those who are different from us because they come from a different background, i.e. they were born into a different culture or they have different lifestyles etc.
Read this story:

Can They Not Taste By Themselves?

An international trading company asked an Indian producer to supply samples of mangoes which would include varieties of choice at different prices. These were accordingly prepared in five separate boxes, which the producer asked his workmen to label and with which he sent an accompanying letter to the trading company:

Dear Sirs,

In compliance with your request, I am forwarding five boxes containing 1 dozen mangoes each, selected and priced as follows:

Box No.1: Alphonso Mangoes
   @ 10 rupees each. Best quality
Box No.2: Pires Mangoes
   @ 5 rupees each. Second Best quality
Box No.3: Fernandes Mangoes
   @ 4 rupees each. Good quality
Box No.4: Malgoba Mangoes
   @ 3 rupees each. Cheap quality
Box No.5: Langda Mangoes
   @ 1 rupee each. Cheapest quality

Awaiting your order and assuring you of our prompt and efficient service.

   Yours faithfully,

Unfortunately the packers mixed up the labels, so that qualities and prices were incorrectly labelled. When the importers opened mangoes marked 'Best quality Alphonso Mangoes', they really began tasting the cheapest quality Langda.

Undeterred, however, they pronounced these deliciously sweet, despite the high price, which they considered excellent value for such quality. They would definitely place a large order.

Tasting second best quality Pires, they believed themselves to be tasting cheap quality Malgoba. They grimaced at how sour those tasted but agreed that such inferiority was reflected in the much lower price.

When the importers finally opened the box marked 'Langda...Cheapest quality', they decided not even to taste. After all, what could possibly be expected at only one rupee each! Little did they know that this box actually contained the best Alphonso mangoes, which they now threw on to a pile of rubbish.

Some crows, watching from a distance, were soon delightedly down on the best mangoes and enjoyed a feast:

'How stupid human beings are', said one of the crows. 'Can't they taste for themselves the quality of the mangoes, instead of having to rely on labels?'

'Those people pride themselves', said another crow, 'on their rationality but we, being irrational, just taste and see!'

'We trust our experience', added a third. 'We don't need labels and titles to know where good mangoes are. We can judge by ourselves where sweetness, worth and quality lie.'

Find Your Group
Discuss

What do you think of the way in which the importers judged the mangoes?

Do we ever judge people in the same way?

Talk about instances where you are aware of this happening in your own country, among your friends, or in the wider world.

Talk about situations where you would be slow or reluctant to relate to or make friends with somebody. What would be the cause of your difficulty?

Talk about a time when you have been surprised by what you found when you got to know someone whom you had not liked or not trusted at first.

Read this poem:

My Parents kept me from Children who were Rough

My parents kept me from children who were rough
Who threw words like stones and who wore torn clothes.
Their thighs showed through rags. They ran in the street
And climbed cliffs and stripped by the country streams.

I feared more than tigers their muscles like iron
Their jerking hands and their knees tight on my arms.
I feared the salt coarse pointing of those boys
Who copied my lisp behind me on the road.

They were lithe, they sprang out behind hedges
Like dogs to bark at my world. They threw mud
While I looked the other way, pretending to smile.
I longed to forgive them, but they never smiled.

Stephen Spender

Discuss

Why do you think this person's parents acted as they did?
What words would you use to describe the feelings between the writer and the children he speaks about?
Has anything like this ever happened to you?
How have things people said to you influenced the way in which you see and want to relate to others?
Can you think of any situation where a parent might have a valid reason for asking a young person to avoid friendship with a particular young person?

Destructive Friendships

Read these stories:

The Cider Party

It was lunch hour.

'What are you doing after school this evening, Paul?', asked Dave.

'Nothing much,' was the answer. 'I want to go to the football practice and then I guess I'll just watch some television if there's any time after I get my homework finished.'

'Boring,' said Dave, 'I'll be going down to the canal bank with a few of the lads. There's going to be a cider party. Why don't you come too?'

'I'm not sure that I want to,' said Paul. 'I don't think it's a very good idea. Besides, I'd be in big trouble if my parents ever found out.'

'Oh, for heaven's sake,' said Dave. 'Come on and don't be such a spoilsport.'

As Dave walked away, Paul was left wondering what he should do. He knew that what was being suggested was not right but Dave was his friend and Paul really looked up to Dave. He was so confident and Paul would hate not to be counted among his friends. He decided to go to the cider party.

The New Girl in the Neighbourhood

'She really gets on my nerves,' said Rita, 'just look at the clothes she has. Her parents must have pots of money.'

'Yes, and they must give more than her fair share of it to Linda,' added John. 'She has all the latest music and what about the way she speaks? It's as if she's talking down to everyone all the time.'

'Well, at least she's not very good in class,' Liz joined in, 'she must have got one of the worst results in the class in the last test.'

If they do it to Linda today, how do I know that it won't be me tomorrow?

'Let's take her down a peg,' suggested Peter. 'She refused to come to my house with the rest of the gang last Friday. She thinks she's too good for the rest of us. Has anyone got any ideas?'

'Well I'm sure if we tried we'd certainly be able to come up with something, something that would really make her feel small. I'm all for it,' said Rita.

'I don't think so,' said Liz. 'I know she's a real pain in the neck but I still don't think it's right to do the sort of thing you're suggesting. It's mean and cruel. Count me out.'

'Oh, don't be such a softy,' said Peter.

'We're together in this. You can't bow out. You're going to do it and you're part of our group. Besides, how would we know that we could ever trust you again?'

Liz had a sick feeling inside as she saw them exchange glances which did not include her. What should she do? She didn't want to be excluded from the group. But she knew that what they were planning was wrong. Also, she thought, 'If they do it to Linda today, how do I know that it won't be me tomorrow?'

She decided she'd better go along with the rest of the group.

Discuss

What do you think of the kind of friendship shown in these two stories?

Have you ever been put under pressure by your friends to take part in something which you knew was wrong?

How did you cope?

What feelings do you associate with that type of situation?

In Your Religion Journal

Questionnaire

Answer these questions which will help you to examine the meaning of friendship in your life right now. Do the exercise in silence, then discuss your answers with one other person.

1. Are you happier in a crowd of friends or with just one or two?

2. Do you have friends mostly of your own sex, mostly of the opposite sex, or a mixture of both?

3. Which of the following statements is true for you?

    My friends need me more than I need them.   ❑

    I need my friends more than they need me.   ❑

    It's more or less equal.   ❑

4. In what ways do you let your friends know that you care about them?

5. What qualities do you admire most in your friends?

6. Are you able to relax and be yourself with your friends or are you always trying to impress them?

7. Do you trust your friends:

    a lot?   ❑

    a little?   ❑

    not at all?   ❑

8. Do you usually follow the crowd or do you have a definite say in the things that you do with your friends?

9. Are all your friendships with people from the same background who have the same outlook on life as yourself?

10. How important do you think your present friends will be to you in the future?

What do you think?

Are there some things which you need to change?

A Time to Pray

Read the following slowly and reflectively:

God, our Creator,
Thank you for all the people in my life who have shaped me into the person I am today.

For those at home who first helped me to grow, who first gave me the feeling of being loved and cared for, who encouraged my first steps into the larger world and who continue to give me the support I need.

For those at school who give me the opportunity to learn more about myself, about others and about the world I live in, who challenge me to become aware of and to use all my gifts and talents.

For my friends who bring me happiness and fun in so many ways, who are there when I am sad or in need of support.

Thank you for all the people who love me, care for me, support me and challenge me.

Help me never to take other people for granted.
Show me how to return some of the love and care which I have been given by so many people.
Help me especially to reach out in friendship to people who are most in need of someone to care for them.

Human Life Alone

Loneliness

The things they say:

Deirdre: Sal, my best friend, has really let me down. We always did everything together. We used to have good fun. Last weekend her parents were away. She had an overnight party in her house. All the gang went. I was there, of course, though it did take a bit of persuasion before my parents allowed me to go. Everything went well and we were having a great time when Sal produced some cans of beer. I didn't want to drink alcohol. Neither did some of the others. Sal tried to persuade me. 'I never thought you'd let me down', she said. Me, let her down? To my mind I was the one who was being let down. Anyhow, I think Sal was probably afraid that I'd tell her parents or something. The end result is that she hasn't spoken to me since. In fact, she has completely ignored me. I feel very hurt that our friendship could end like this and I miss her so much. I have no one to talk to. I never thought I could be so lonely.

Christopher: My Dad was made redundant last week. Everybody was shocked. Since then there's been nothing at home except endless talk

AND I'M TOO ASHAMED TO TELL THEM WHAT I'M FEELING

about making ends meet and cutting back and making do with less and on and on it goes until everybody gets really depressed. When I hear my friends talk about new clothes and pocket money and things like that I feel out of it. And I'm too ashamed to tell them what I'm feeling. I'm not sure that they'd understand in any case. Now I know what it's like to be alone and isolated even when I'm with others.

In Your Religion Journal

Write about your most frightening experience of loneliness.
Describe the circumstances that caused you to feel lonely.
Did the experience have any lasting effect on you?
What made it possible for you to pull out of the feeling of loneliness?
OR
Draw a picture to illustrate what it felt like.

Number the following 1 to 12.

I would feel alone and afraid:

— if I was aware that there were family difficulties at home;
— if one of my parents or someone close to me was very ill;
— if I was asked a difficult or embarrassing question in class;
— if I realised that my clothes and my pocket-money compared poorly with others;
— if I was separated from home and family;
— if I was separated from my friends;
— if I was confronted by a bully who was bigger than me;
— if I had to go to hospital for painful tests because of a mysterious illness;
— if I was sitting in a dentist's waiting room;
— if I was expelled from school;
— if I had to take a decision that would go against the opinions of my friends;
— if I had an argument with my best friend;
— if I had a serious argument with my parents;
— if my friends excluded me from a group activity which I would have enjoyed.

Did Jesus experience loneliness?

Read the following:

Jesus left the city and went, as he usually did, to the Mount of Olives; and the disciples went with him. When he arrived at the place, he said to them, 'Pray that you will not fall into temptation.'
   Then he went off from them about the distance of a stone's throw and knelt down and prayed. 'Father,' he said, 'if you will, take this cup of suffering away from me. Not my will, however, but your will be done.' An angel from heaven appeared to him and strengthened him. In great anguish he prayed even more fervently; his sweat was like drops of blood falling to the ground.

Discuss

How do you think the fact that the apostles fell asleep might have affected Jesus?
How could the apostles have helped?

(Luke 4:1-13)

Discuss

Why do you think Jesus went out into the desert alone?
Does this story remind you in any way of your own experiences of loneliness?

Rising from his prayer, he went back to the disciples and found them asleep, worn out by their grief. He said to them, 'Why are you sleeping? Get up and pray that you will not fall into temptation'.

Jesus returned from the Jordan full of the Holy Spirit and was led by the Spirit into the desert, where he was tempted by the Devil for forty days. In all that time he ate nothing, so that he was hungry when it was over.

The Devil said to him, 'If you are God's Son, order this stone to turn into bread.'

But Jesus answered, 'The scripture says, "Man cannot live on bread alone"'.

Then the Devil took him up and showed him in a second all the kingdoms of the world. 'I will give you all this power and all this wealth,' the Devil told him. 'It has all been handed over to me, and I can give it to anyone I choose. All this will be yours, then, if you worship me.'

Jesus answered, 'The scripture says, "Worship the Lord your God and serve only him!"'

Then the Devil took him to Jerusalem and set him on the highest point of the Temple, and said to him, 'If you are God's Son, throw yourself down from here. For the scripture says, "God will order his angels to take good care of you." It also says, "They will hold you up with their hands so that not even your feet will be hurt on the stones." '

But Jesus answered, 'The scripture says, "Do not put the Lord your God to the test." '

When the Devil finished tempting Jesus in every way, he left him for a while.

Lonely with others

It is important to remember that we can feel lonely not only while we are alone but also when we are with others.

Everybody experiences loneliness at times. However, some groups of people are more at risk from loneliness than others. We all belong to some of these groups at one time or another in our lives:

— elderly people living alone;
— people who are sick;
— people who were married and are separated from their spouse;
— people who are unemployed;
— people who have some form of mental or physical handicap;
— people who are low in self-confidence;
— young people going through the adolescent stage of life;
— people who are in prison;
— emigrants.

Can you add to this list?

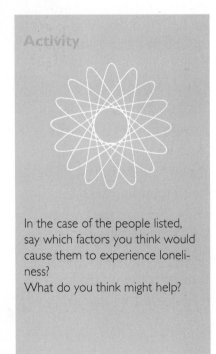

Activity

In the case of the people listed, say which factors you think would cause them to experience loneliness?
What do you think might help?

Read this poem:

Voice from the Dead

What do you see, nurses, what do you see?
Are you thinking when you are looking at me –
a crabbed old woman, not very wise
uncertain of habit with faraway eyes,
who dribbles her food and makes no reply –
when you say in a loud voice 'I do wish you'd try'.
I'll tell you who I am as I sit here so still,
as I rise to your bidding, as I eat at your will.

I'm a small child of ten with a father and mother,
brothers and sisters who love one another.
A bride soon at twenty, my heart gives a leap
remembering the vows that I promised to keep.
At twenty-five now, I have young of my own
who need me to build a secure happy home.
At fifty, once more, children play round my knee,
again we know children, my beloved and me.
Dark days are upon me, my husband is dead;
I look to the future, I shudder with dread.
My young are all busy rearing young of their own
And I think of the years and the love I have known.

I'm an old woman now, and nature is cruel:
'tis her jest to make old age look like a fool;
the body it crumbles, grace and vigour depart,
there is now a stone where I once had a heart.
But inside this old carcass a young girl still dwells,
and I'm loving and living all over again.
And I think of the years all too few gone too fast,
and accept the stark fact that nothing will last.

So open your eyes, nurses, open and see,
not a crabbed old woman; look closer – see me!

*(These verses were written by a woman who was a
patient in an old people's ward. They were found in
her locker after her death by staff who had thought
her incapable of writing.)*

Discuss

How do you think the nurses felt
when they read these lines?
In what way would they have treated her differently if they had known
how she felt?
Do you know anyone who might
write these or similar lines?
Could you do anything to help?

In the midst of our family, on a busy
street, even at a party, it is possible
to feel lonely. Loneliness in these situations comes from a sense that
others don't care about us, don't
understand us, or don't accept us
for what we are.

In Your Religion Journal

Have you ever felt lonely while you
were with others? Describe how it
felt.

Find Your Group

'Accept me for what I am and I'll
accept you for what you're
accepted as.'
(*Under the Eye of the Clock* –
Christopher Nolan)

Discuss

What do you think this statement
means?
Talk about situations when it might
influence how people relate to one
another.

Christopher Nolan

Christopher Nolan was eleven years old before anyone knew he could write. He would sit, propped in his wheelchair, staring at the grey Dublin skies, while he listened to the voices of his family and their friends, able to take part only through the unique communication he had evolved with his mother and the fierce intelligence of his blue eyes.

Christopher's handicap was caused by a difficult birth that disrupted the motor centres of his brain, leaving his body an incomplete jigsaw, with useless limbs, uncoordinated movements and a voice that is generally incoherent. But his mind was left unimpaired and the sharpness and power of his perception impeccable.

Christopher Nolan grew up a hostage to his own body, gazing out through the crystal window of his eyes, a spectator before the world, yet unable to respond, to comment, to reply. Image upon image ricocheted round his skull and burned into his consciousness. Without means of expression, the pressure to communicate was intolerable.

In his eleventh year his life was transformed by a drug, Lioresal, which relaxed the muscles of his neck sufficiently to allow him partial control of his head for short periods of time.

Discuss

What do you think were the things which caused Christopher Nolan to experience loneliness?
Can you think of other circumstances which might cause people to experience loneliness?

In his later book, *Under the Eye of the Clock,* Christopher Nolan describes some situations where people helped him to overcome his sense of loneliness and isolation. Read this extract from the book. In it, Joseph is Christopher Nolan.

Getting Ready for the Match

The lads practised each Tuesday and half-day Wednesday, but Joseph could not be there. However, he assessed how they were coming along by listening to their measuring each other's weaknesses. But now they had another match on the horizon and he heard them planning how best to close apparent gaps in their play. Paul was worried about his boots and he said he was going to buy new studs. 'I've the last class free,' he said, 'and I'm going home to get some money. Then I'll slip down to Fairview for them.' Game Joseph was first in. He looked at Paul and hinted, 'Can I come with you?' Paul smiled and said, 'Are you free for last class?' Joseph shook his head, but hinted, 'Can I come anyhow?' 'It's OK with me,' laughed Paul. Then Stephen chipped in. 'Can I come too?' 'Me too?' said Ben Simpson, and class or no class the four set off for Paul's house. Paul's mother was more than a little surprised to see the four hardies setting off for Fairview, but they all looked back at her and laughed at her seeming concern. She laughed too and shook her head before closing the front door. Delighted with his friends' loyalty, hackneyed by the strong willing hands of Stephen, Joseph felt himself being trundled along towards the sports shop. The boys chatted comradely, they hassled girls whom they encountered on their way home from school, they bought cigarettes and lit up, and they kindled anew the spark of happiness in their passenger's mind. The wind was

piercing through each of them but it was their pal in the wheelchair whom they worried about. Stephen had a brainwave, and stripping his red scarf from around his neck, he wrapped the still-warm scarf around Joseph's cold throat. Then all four, sporting only sweaters and one scarf, breasted ahead again towards Merville Avenue. The shop 'Little Sport' supplied Paul with the studs for his boots, while outside Ben, Stephen and Joseph examined the great display of new bikes. The able lads discussed the pros and cons of individual models, but on looking at the price tags they good-naturedly laughed at the futility of their appraisal. Shopping completed, they sauntered along and then suddenly Paul looked at his watch and said, 'God will you look at the time.' Looking at Joseph he said, 'Now look where you are, and your Mam is above in school searching around for you.' Joseph laughed at the thought of Nora meandering about in search of her son. He knew she would find out without bothering a teacher. She knew his friends and she'd know whom to ask. But they'd brought Joseph with them and the lads were concerned about his being absent from the school, so Paul gripped hold of the handles of the wheelchair and said to Stephen, 'Let me take a turn and we'll make tracks.' Joseph's teeth rattled as his chair bumped up and down off the footpaths. Gasfired by Paul's kindness and Stephen's heat, he gasped with mummified feelings of fortune. Racing along, they had no time to smoke or hassle girls, they were hell-bent on getting to the school before Nora got worried.

Escaping from loneliness

Discuss

Has anything similar to that described in the passage ever happened in your own experience or in the experience of anyone you know?
Have you ever been the cause of someone being able to escape from loneliness?

Find Your Group

Discuss
What kind of thing have you done in order to avoid feeling lonely?
Have you ever thought when people are lonely that all they need is a friend? Why not be that friend?

Discuss
Is there anyone among your relatives whom you think might be lonely?
What could you do to help?
Are there other people in the area where you live who are lonely?
How can you find out?
What can you do to help?

Nobody wants to be lonely. People will do extraordinary things to avoid feeling lonely. They resort to drink, drugs, feverish work, non-selective television viewing, enjoying life while the money lasts etc.

One of the worst things about being lonely is probably the feeling that you are not wanted. It's nice to be needed. On the other hand, it is also true to say that individuals have huge personal resources. Real escape from loneliness comes only when we discover these resources.

Find Your Group

Think of the following:

— fishermen who spend long lonely hours on the water;

— long-distance runners or cyclists;

— travellers or explorers;

— mountain climbers.

They spend many hours alone and often without any form of contact with other people, yet they usually don't feel lonely.

Discuss: Why do you think this is so?

A sense of isolation can also be felt by people in other situations such as:

— in times of sickness;

— when someone is unemployed.

Can you add to the list?

Discovering Personal Resources

Discuss   Have you ever felt good about being alone?
What did you most enjoy about it?

We have already discussed the many reasons why we need others. However, we also need to be aware of and to develop our own personal resources. We need to be able to live without having to cling to others at all costs.

We can do this in a number of ways. For example, we can find some interesting hobbies and develop talents in a number of areas such as fishing, painting, mountain climbing, sports, music-making, acting.

We can find ways of relaxing, for example, by listening to music, reading or taking part in physical exercise. This will help us to be more comfortable being alone.

Coping with life alone and with others

It is probably those people who are most at ease in the company of others who are also most at ease when they are alone.

Our friendships with others help us to have confidence in ourselves, to see the world as a place of possibility and hope and to approach life with an attitude of trust rather than fear or suspicion.

The more we develop our own strengths and creative talents the better we will be able to stand on our own two feet. We will be less likely to follow the trend without thinking for ourselves. We will have confidence in ourselves.

Find Your Group
Discuss

Talk about a time when you were influenced by others though it might have been better to go your own way.

Talk about a time when you made up your own mind about something in spite of what others were saying.

Research

Find out names of national organisations and voluntary groups which take care of the needs of those who are lonely for one reason or another.

Find out as much as you can about their work.

Compile a display for the class notice-board using brochures, pictures and, perhaps, accounts of interviews which you could arrange with people who work in these organisations or groups.

In Your Religion Journal

Write about one relationship in your life which helps you to approach life with a positive attitude.

Research

This could be undertaken by a small group from the class who would then make a presentation to the whole class on their findings. Do some research among your friends and classmates to find what seem to be the most common experiences of loneliness among young people of your age group in the area where you live. You could use the following or similar questions:

What are the experiences which you think are most likely to cause you to feel lonely?

— loss of a friend
— being left out of an activity
— being misunderstood
— some upset in the family
— having an argument with somebody close to you
— experiences of failure, e.g. in class, in sport etc.

Where do you think that you are most likely to feel lonely?

— at school
— at home
— with your friends
— with your family etc.

What are the things which you find most helpful at times when you feel lonely?

A Time to Pray

Read this reflection slowly and silently:

Someone I Noticed On The Pathway

He was in the ambulance, the doors
   not yet closed.
As he looked down the street I could
   see him;
He seemed lonely, downhearted,
An old man about seventy-five,
With a stoop, and a stick in his hand.

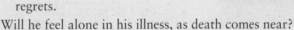

Is he alone?
Will family or friends visit him?
Maybe he'll be thinking over his life:
   its sad times,
   ambitions achieved,
   regrets.
Will he feel alone in his illness, as death comes near?

Lord, we often feel alone in the world:
   the child scared in the night when the lights are out;
   the young person whose love affair has broken up;
   the husband who thinks his wife has changed;
   the woman whose husband has died.
And I know, Lord, that even when we are communicating with one
   another,
We can feel alone,
For we are made with a desire to share life with one another.
We also desire, deep in our hearts, to be one with you;
Our longing for love and companionship
Is like our longing for union with you.

It's not only in old age, Lord, that I need your presence and your company;
It's not only in the ambulance that I need you to comfort me;
I need and want your presence every moment of my days and nights.
Help me, Lord, to know that you are near,
That you are present with me in my aloneness.
Be near that man too, Lord, in the ambulance;
He needs you, he's alone.

The Lord
Our Shepherd

The Lord is my shepherd;
I have everything I need.
He lets me rest in fields of green grass
and leads me to quiet pools of fresh water.
He gives me new strength.
He guides me in the right paths,
as he has promised.
Even if I go through the deepest darkness,
I will not be afraid, Lord,
for you are with me.
Your shepherd's rod and staff protect me.

You prepare a banquet for me,
where all my enemies can see me;
you welcome me as an honoured guest
and fill my cup to the brim.
I know that your goodness and love will
be with me all my life;
and your house will be my home as long as I live.

Let us pray,

God, our Creator, we give you
thanks for the gift of all the people
who love us. Thank you for all
those who have helped us to
grow and develop in many different ways, parents, family and
friends; for the love, the trust, the
sensitivity we experience when
we are with those who care for
us; for the fun and all the happy
times we have together.

Lesson Three

God

Find Your Group
Discuss

Each of these people had some idea in their mind about what God was like when they said what they did. In the case of each one, discuss what they thought God was like.

In Your Religion Journal

Draw cartoons to represent what they thought God was like.

What do you think God is like?

We can't see God. No one has ever seen God. But from the time when we were very young, we have heard people talk about God. And so we have built up in our minds pictures of what God is like.

When you were younger, if someone asked you to draw a picture of God you might have drawn an old man with a grey beard sitting in the midst of clouds.

What would you draw now?

Find Your Group
On a sheet of paper list all the words you would use to describe God.
Tell the others why you used the words you chose.
Listen to what the others have to say about their words.

In Your Religion Journal
Which of the words surprised you most? Why?
What did you hear anyone say about God which was very different from your own ideas about God?
Write down six things that you know about God.

Images of God

It is not possible to draw an accurate picture of God. Nobody knows what God is really like. These are some of the distorted images that people sometimes have of God:

A nice old person

God is a bit like Santa. It's nice to tell children stories about God as someone who gives them lots of gifts, but God is not terribly important. God is pleasant, kind but old-fashioned and out of touch.

Super spy

God is watching from the sky, ready to pounce on sinners and is recording all our faults and failings.

Doesn't care about Calcutta

God is self-sufficient and doesn't need or care about humanity. Therefore the suffering of people is of no concern to God.

God is serious-minded

God is very serious about everything and prefers it when people also are serious. God has no time for laughter or fun.

God is a specialist in souls

God is only interested in or knows about 'holy' things. Therefore most of the ordinary, everyday things that we do are of no concern or interest to God.

The puppeteer

God sits in the sky and is always in control of everything that happens. God the Puppeteer pulls strings to make things happen. So we must be nice to the puppeteer or the strings might be cut.

A shoulder to cry on

God is always there in time of need or trouble. However, when things are going well we have no great need for God and God has no great interest in us.

The executive

God is busy, overworked and wouldn't really have time for mere mortals.

Find Your Group Discuss: What is wrong with each of the images above?

In this extract from the book *Mister God, This is Anna*, Anna talks about how she understands God.

When you're little you 'understand' Mister God. He sits up there on his throne, a golden one of course; he has got whiskers and a crown and everyone is singing hymns like mad to him. God is useful and usable. You can ask him for things, he can strike your enemies deader than a doornail and he is pretty good at putting hexes on the bully next door, like warts and things. Mister God is so 'understandable', so useful and so usable, he is like some object, perhaps the most important object of all, but nevertheless an object and absolutely understandable. Later on you 'understand' him to be a bit different but you are still able to grasp what he is. Even though you understand him, he doesn't seem to understand you! He doesn't seem to understand that you simply must have a new bike, so your 'understanding' of him changes a bit more.

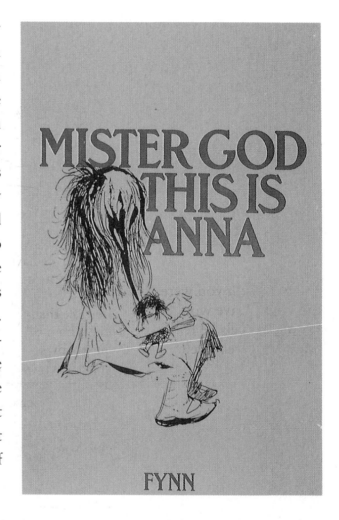

Discuss

Which of Anna's descriptions of God is closest to your own present understanding?
Does this extract remind you in any way of how your understanding of God has changed over the years?

Activity

Read Psalm 23.
Which are your favourite lines?

Activity

Read the book *I am David*, by Anne Holm.
What image of God did the boy David have?

What is God really like?

Dave has a pen-pal in Australia. He has never met Mike, though they have corresponded with each other now for over two years.

Nevertheless, if you were to ask him, Dave would tell you that he feels he really knows Mike very well.

Find Your Group
Discuss

What is Dave's knowledge of Mike based on?
Do you think Dave really does know Mike?
Have you ever felt that you knew somebody very well whom you had never met?
How did this happen?

Though we have never met God and will never in our lives see God we can still have some ideas about what God is really like.

Imagine that you have the opportunity to visit the home of someone whom you have never met and have heard very little about. Simply by being there and by taking notice of the things which are in the house, the way the house is decorated, the colours used, the pictures on the walls etc., you could get a fair idea of the kind of person who lives there.

Question: Who lives here ?

Getting to know God

In the world

When we look at the work of an artist or read the writings of a poet or novelist we also gain some insight into the kind of person the author or the artist is.

What kind of person do you think wrote this poem?

A White, Empty Room

'I'm happy to be home, I can't believe
I'm back safe and sound with my wife and children.
I was walking along High Street
When they swept me into a car
And drove to an outlying Station.
They locked me in a white, empty room
For seventy-two hours. You did it you did it
They repeated until I began to believe I was

Guilty. I'd never felt such guilt before.
You're a murderous thug, they said,
Shouting through every bone in my head,
You'll never see your family again
You'll get life you'll be hanged that's for sure.
Why did they suddenly release me then?
I was guilty no I'm not guilty now I know I'm not.
I've never even seen the place where Cassidy was shot.'

Brendan Kennelly

Roderic O'Conor, La Ferme de Lezaver, National Gallery of Ireland

God is the creator of the universe and everything in it. And so when we look around at the world we live in and see its beauty, wonder and grandeur we can get some idea of the beauty, power and creativity of God.

When we see the plan by which day follows night and season follows season, when we think of the order of the animal and plant world, we find there a work which is beyond the power of human intelligence or imagination.

In People

Above all, when we think of people, the high point of God's creation, who are, as we are told in the Bible, made in the image of God, we see most clearly reflected the love, the intelligence, the creativity of God.

Hiding God

There's a story about a tyrannical ruler who held his people in bondage but could not destroy their faith. One day he called his counsellors together and asked their advice on where they might hide God so that the people would not find him.

One suggested that they hide him behind the stars where he could not be reached. 'No,' said the ruler, 'some day they'll conquer space and find him there.'

Another suggested the bottom of the sea. 'No,' said the ruler again, 'one day science and technology will plumb the depths of the ocean and he'll be found.'

And then one wise old sage put forward his view. 'Let's hide him among the people themselves,' he advised, 'that's the last place they'll ever think of looking for him.'

Find Your Group

Discuss

Give concrete examples of things people are doing or have done which are reflections of the power and love and creativity of God.

Discuss

Can you think of any instances where people fail to see God among people?

In the Bible

What we see in the world around us can only give us a glimpse of or an insight into what God is like. However, God has invited us to get to know him and to make this possible.

God has revealed or shown himself to us in the Bible.

Read the following:

> Like an eagle teaching its young to fly,
> catching them safely on its spreading wings,
> The Lord kept Israel from falling. (Deut 32:11)

> You prepare a banquet for me,
> where all my enemies can see me;
> You welcome me as an honoured guest
> and fill my cup to the brim. (Psalm 23:5)

> You have set the earth firmly on its foundations,
> and it will never be moved.
> You placed the ocean over it like a robe,
> and the water covered the mountains. (Psalm 104:5-8)

> So the Lord answers,
> 'Can a woman forget her own baby
> and not love the child she bore?
> Even if a mother should forget her child
> I will never forget you'. (Isaiah 49:15)

> Fling wide the gates,
> open the ancient doors,
> and the great king will come in.
> Who is this great king ?
> The triumphant Lord – he is the great king. (Psalm 24:9-10)

> The voice of the Lord makes the lightning flash,
> His voice makes the desert shake. (Psalm 29:7-8)

The Bible was written many years ago by and for people who lived a very simple lifestyle very close to nature.

God is described in the Bible using simple images often drawn from the world of nature.

> The Lord is my shepherd;
> I have everything I need.
> He lets me rest in fields of green grass
> and leads me to quiet pools of fresh water. (Psalm 23:1-2)

> 'I saw the Lord. He was sitting on his throne...
> Round him flaming creatures were standing ...
> They were calling out to each other:
> 'Holy, holy, holy!
> The Lord almighty is holy!
> His glory fills the world. (Isaiah 6:1-3)

> The Lord says,
> 'When Israel was a child, I loved him
> and called him out of Egypt as my son' (Hosea 11:1).

> Who is this great king ?
> He is the Lord strong and mighty,
> the Lord, victorious in battle. (Psalm 24:8)

> His anger lasts only a moment
> his goodness for a lifetime. (Psalm 30:5)

In Your Religion Journal

Draw pictures which correspond to these images.
Which of these images of God appeals to you most?

In Jesus

Above and beyond all other ways in which we can get to know God, we can most clearly see what God is like when we look at Jesus. Jesus says, 'Whoever has seen me, has seen the Father' (John 14:9).

Jesus also helped people to understand what God was like in the stories he told.
Read the following:
Luke 15:11–32
Luke 14:16–24
Luke 8:5–8
Matthew 20:1–16
Matthew 25:14–30

Gerard David, Christ Bidding Farewell to his Mother, National Gallery of Ireland

Find Your Group

Do a quick brainstorm.
Get a sheet of paper.
What word comes most quickly to your mind when you think about the ways in which God is shown to us through Jesus?
Write down on the sheet of paper all the words mentioned by the group.

Find Your Group

God is like...

Choose one of these extracts, the one which you like most. Find a way of presenting that particular image of God to the rest of the class.

You could use drama, mime, art, poetry or any other method which appeals to you.

In Your Religion Journal

Write about a time when you felt really close to God.
Write about a time when God seemed very far away.

Write a letter to God

Read these letters:

Dear God,

In class we are taught that you have a plan for the world and for all of us who live in the world. That's all very fine but how are we supposed to find out what that plan is? And what if we never find out?

Dear God,

When things are going well I often forget all about you. Sometimes I don't even say my prayers. Then something goes wrong and I know that I need to ask you for your help and then I'm not even sure if you are there.

Dear God,

I'm confused about you. I believe that you are very powerful. Why then do you allow so much pain and suffering in the world? Every night on the television we see pictures of wars, famines, violence, oppression of all kinds. Why don't you do something about it?

Dear God,

They say you always listen to our prayers. I find that hard to believe, do you?

Dear God,

Thank you for all the good things in my life, for family and friends, all the people who love me, for health, for the world we live in. Help me always to be aware that you are with me and that I need never feel afraid.

Find Your Group Discuss

You have been asked to write a reply on behalf of God to each of these letters. What would you say?

In Your Religion Journal

Write a short letter to God expressing those things which you most want to say to God right now.

A Time to Pray

Read this translation of Psalm 139 slowly and meditatively.

O God,
    You know me inside and out,
    through and through.
Everything I do,
    every thought that flits through my mind,
    every step I take,
    every plan I make,
    every word I speak,
    You know, even before these things happen.
You know my past;
    You know my future.
Your circumventing presence covers my every move.
Your knowledge of me sometimes comforts me,
    sometimes frightens me;
    but always it is far beyond my comprehension.

There is no way to escape You, no place to hide.
If I ascend to the heights of joy,
    You are there before me.
If I am plunged into the depths of despair,
    You are there to meet me.
I could fly to the other side of our world
    and find You there to lead the way.
I could walk into the darkest of nights,
    only to find You there
    to lighten its dismal hours.

You were present at my very conception.
You guided the moulding of my unformed members
    within the body of my mother.
Nothing about me, from beginning to end,
    was hidden from Your eyes.
How frightfully, fantastically wonderful it all is!

May Your all-knowing, everywhere-present Spirit
    continue to search out my feelings and thoughts.
Deliver me
    from that which may hurt or destroy me,
    and guide me along the paths of love and truth.

Faith

A Leap in the Dark

One night while the family were asleep the house caught fire. Susan was the first to wake up. She found herself in a room full of smoke. She was terrified and immediately began shouting in fear and terror for her parents. Her parents, not sure whether they were awake or asleep, jumped out of bed. Their big worry was the children. The baby was grabbed from the cot. Susan, who was already on the landing, they told to run down the stairs saying, 'Run to the door, Susan, run as fast as you can.'

John was in the back bedroom. Already the fire was blazing on the landing. It was impossible to reach John's door.

'Climb on to the roof, John, climb on to the roof,' shouted his father.

'I'm afraid, Daddy. I'm afraid,' John shouted back.

'Climb on to the roof,' shouted his mother. 'Quickly, John. Everything will be all right. But hurry.' John climbed on to the roof. The parents and the other two children made their way outside. Neighbours had gathered. Someone took the baby into a nearby house.

'Jump, John, jump. I'll catch you,' shouted his father.

From the roof John looked over. All he could see was a wall of flames and smoke. He was petrified.

'I can't jump Dad,' he shouted. 'I can't see you.'

'But we can see you, John,' shouted back his mother. 'And that's all that matters.'

CLIMB ON TO THE ROOF, QUICKLY JOHN!

Discuss

How do you think you would have felt, had you been the boy on the roof?

Why was it so difficult for him to jump? What would have helped?

Let's presume that John did jump. What qualities did he need to enable him to overcome his immediate fear and jump?

Does this story remind you of any incident in your own life?

Small children have very few fears. They are quite likely to fall off heights, walk in front of moving vehicles or cut themselves with sharp knives. As they grow they become more aware of danger and of the need to protect themselves from harm. They begin to experience fear. Their fears often come from their experience of life.

Read the following:

Peter learns to fear

Peter loved animals. Whether they were on the pages of his picture books or in real life, he was fascinated by them. More than anything else, he wanted a pet of his own. So, for his third birthday, his parents promised that they would get him a puppy. Then, one day, as he was going into the local supermarket with his bigger sister and brother, he stopped to play with a dog which was tied to the railings.

The dog snapped at him and he was terrified. In spite of all the reassurance which his brother and sister could have given him he was still afraid.

That night he wasn't sure whether or not he still wanted a puppy for his birthday!

As people grow their experience becomes broader, they get to know more people and they understand more about the world we live in. Most people learn to have a certain confidence and trust in people and in life. They experience the goodness of people. They feel loved by their parents and by others. They enjoy the wonder of being alive.
They become more aware of the wonderful world of nature. They realise that they can trust other people.

I Believe in....

We use the word 'believe' in a number of ways, e.g.
        'I believe that Dr Smith is clever',
        'I believe in Dr Smith'.
Can you see the difference?
When we say, ' I believe that...' we are talking about facts we consider to be true.
When we say, 'I believe in ...' we are saying much more. We are talking about an attitude of trust or commitment.
Obviously, however, we will not believe in someone unless we first of all believe certain things about the person. Before you would believe in Dr Smith you would have to believe that he is a good doctor and also that he is trustworthy and caring.

In Your Religion Journal

Draw an abstract picture which describes what happened to Peter.

Find Your Group

Think back to your early childhood. Can you think of some experiences which taught you to be a little bit more cautious or even fearful about the way you approached the world and the people around you? Talk about these experiences with the others in your group.

In Your Religion Journal

Write about someone you put your trust in. What beliefs about him/her enable you to show that trust?

Faith and Life

Relationships with others

One of our experiences of faith in action in our lives is in our relationships with others.

In Your Religion Journal

Is there someone in whom you have a very deep trust, someone whom you know loves you and cares about you, someone whom you are convinced will never do anything to cause you pain or suffering?

Write about that person. Perhaps you could write about an incident which illustrates how deeply you trust the person.

What is it about that person which enables you to have such a deep trust?

Are there also people who trust you ?

What qualities do you think you have which enable people to have trust in you?

Find Your Group

Talk about a time when you knew that somebody really had faith in you. How did you feel?

Talk about a time when you knew that somebody had no faith in you. How did you feel?

Religious Faith

To say 'I believe in God' is not simply the same as saying 'I believe that God exists'. It includes it but goes much further. It means 'I put my trust in and commit myself to the God I believe exists.' In order to be able to trust God we first of all need to believe certain things about him. We believe that God is all-powerful and all-wise and so God can help us. We also believe that God is all-loving and merciful and so God wants to help us. We believe that Jesus is the Son of God who showed how much he loved us by dying for us – that he is alive and with us helping us on our journey in this life to God. These are our reasons for believing in God. The more we come to know God through Jesus, the more we are able to put our trust in God and to believe in God.

In Your Religion Journal

Write out some beliefs about God which you think help people to put their trust in God.

Describe some event from the Gospels which you think might help people to trust in Jesus or in God.

Faith and Hope

The gift of God which enables us to believe what God has revealed about himself is called faith. It leads to the further gift of hope by which we are enabled to believe in or put our trust in God's promises. Belief without trust is not true belief and hardly deserves the name of faith.

Religious faith is different from and yet similar to human experiences of trust. In religious faith we put our trust in God. We first began to know about God from the things which we heard adults say about God when we were little.

Find Your Group
Discuss

What are the first things that you can remember people saying to you about God ?
Very often as children we believe and trust in God as someone who has magical powers and who can make all our wishes come true, if, of course, we ask properly.

Which of the following children's prayers might have been yours?
Dear God
— Please make my mum better.
— Please let me get a bike for my birthday.
— Please let me get all my sums right today.
— Please make the sun shine tomorrow, so that we can have our picnic.

In Your Religion Journal

Can you add to the above list, prayers which you might have said when you were a child?

Getting to know God

As children we really know very little about God. We simply build a picture from the things we have heard. As we grow we learn to know more and more about God. We will never know all there is to know about God. That would be impossible. Our human minds are simply incapable of understanding the greatness of God. However, all through our lives we can continue to grow in our knowledge and understanding of God. God wants us to do this. God is always showing us what he is like. We call this God's revelation. In the last chapter we looked at the main ways in which God reveals himself to us. The more we come to know God the more we realise how much God loves us.

In Our Human Relationships

It is easy to be afraid that if someone knows all about us rather than just the parts that are most acceptable, they may reject us. They may think that we are silly to have certain fears, or that we are less virtuous because of certain things that we have done. However, we can be certain that God, more than anyone else, even the closest friend that we can imagine, knows us inside out and through and through. God loves us just as we are without hesitation or reservation. God's love is always available to us. God's attitude to us never changes. Sometimes, however, we are slow to believe this and to accept that it is so. Because we cannot see God it is sometimes more difficult to have faith in the love and care of God than in the love and care of a friend or person who cares for us.

Things which help me to believe in God	Things which make it difficult for me to believe in God

Faith and hope are gifts from God. They are offered to us but we are free to accept or reject them. Often we may not exactly reject them, but perhaps only partly accept them. We need to keep asking God to help us get to know him better so that we may accept his gifts of faith and hope more wholeheartedly.

God invites us to respond to his love with faith and trust in his constant love and care.

Find Your Group

What do you think these statements mean?
— Faith is like a leap in the dark.
— Faith can move mountains.

In Your Religion Journal

What are the most important questions you have about God right now?

Ways in which we can deepen our faith in God

The more we come to know God, the more we develop our relationship with God, the easier it will be to have faith in God, to believe that:
   God is always with us;
   God knows us inside out;
   God loves and cares for us more than we can imagine;
   God is always waiting to forgive us.
We can get to know God by:
   Reading the Bible;
   Spending time in prayer;

Taking time to think about our lives with others;
Celebrating the sacraments and, especially, receiving the risen Jesus in Holy Communion.
If we are serious about answering God's invitation to have faith in him we will pay attention to trying to develop our relationship with God.

Test Yourself

How often do you pray?
How often do you spend some time reflecting on God's presence in your life and in the world?
Do you ever read the Bible?
Are there areas in your life where you should try to do better?
Do you go to Mass every Sunday?

Stories of Faith

Jesus Heals a Roman Officer's Servant

When Jesus entered Capernaum, a Roman officer met him and begged for help: 'Sir, my servant is sick in bed at home, unable to move and suffering terribly.'

'I will go and make him well,' Jesus said.

'Oh no, sir,' answered the officer. 'I do not deserve to have you come into my house. Just give the order, and my servant will get well. I, too, am a man under the authority of superior officers, and I have soldiers under me. I order this one, "Go!" and he goes; and I order that one, "Come!" and he comes; and I order my slave, "Do this!" and he does it.'

When Jesus heard this, he was surprised and said to the people following him, 'I tell you, I have never found anyone in Israel with faith like this....'

Then Jesus said to the officer, 'Go home, and what you believe will be done for you.'

There was a woman who had suffered terribly from severe bleeding for twelve years, even though she had been treated by many doctors. She had spent all her money, but instead of getting better she got worse all the time. She had heard about Jesus, so she came in the crowd behind him, saying to herself, 'If I just touch his clothes, I will get well.'

She touched his cloak, and her bleeding stopped at once; and she had the feeling inside herself that she was healed of her trouble. At once Jesus knew that power had gone out of him, so he turned round in the crowd and asked, 'Who touched my clothes?'

His disciples answered, 'You see how the people are crowding you; why do you ask who touched you?'

But Jesus kept looking round to see who had done it. The woman realised what had happened to

GO BACK HOME! FROM NOW ON YOUR SERVANT WILL ENJOY THE BEST OF HEALTH!

her, so she came, trembling with fear, knelt at his feet, and told him the whole truth. Jesus said to her, 'My daughter, your faith has made you well. Go in peace, and be healed of your trouble.'
(Mark 5:25-34)

Discuss

What did Jesus mean when he spoke about Faith in these stories?

In Your Religion Journal

Write about a time when you had faith in God.
Write about a time when you found it difficult to have faith in God.

Living Faith

Belief in Jesus means belief in his teachings. It does not mean simply believing things about him or even simply putting our trust in him, but also taking him as our guide and following him. We show our faith in Jesus by living as he taught us to live. To enable us to do this we need God's greatest gift, the gift of love. It is the gift of love which enables us to express our faith in action.

What would you think of someone who said:
'I believe in human rights'–
and then kept slaves?
'I believe in honesty'–
and then cheated on his friends?
'I believe in mercy'–
and then refused to forgive others?

St James tells us that faith without good words is dead. For a living faith we need God's three gifts – faith, hope and love. All of them together give us a living faith.

In Your Religion Journal

Write in James 2:14-17.
Write about someone whose life you think expresses their faith.
Give examples of ways in which you can express or fail to express your faith in action.

A Time to Pray

In our prayers we can ask God to help us to believe and to deepen our faith.

Read the prayer on this page slowly and reflectively.

Where are you Lord?

God, I find it difficult to believe in you.
You seem so distant;
I never hear your voice,
I never see your face.
People are suffering from hunger, homelessness and violence:
Where are you?
Others seem so certain about you, so sure;
What's wrong with me?
Are you near in the world of money and power?
Where are you in a world that doesn't love or care?

Sometimes it's easy to find you in the countryside.
In the rock-like strength of the mountain,
Or the peace of the valley,
You touch us with your presence
But what about bad housing, concrete jungles, polluted air?
What about violence, murder, starvation, sickness ?
Where are you, Lord, in a world
Where babies die each day of malnutrition,
And marriages flounder from homelessness?

I know there are moments when I have found your presence.
I think you are present when someone cares and helps;
There's a glimmer in the misery.
It's a touch of your love, a sign of your presence.
I expect you to be outside the world,
But you're right in it,
You're among the starving,
Suffering with them and saving them.
You're among the homeless,
Neglected with them and consoling them.
You're within the broken marriage,
Hurting with them and healing them.

You are suffering, Lord, with those who suffer:
Not just observing it, but suffering;
Not just suffering, but courageously accepting it;
Not just accepting it, but transforming it;
Not just transforming it, but working to lessen it.

Can I believe that the glimmer in the misery is
your light,
Your risen hope,
Your eternal promise?

Lord, I believe; help my unbelief.

Donal Neary SJ

The Trinity

Mystery

Activity

1. Find a partner. You are compiling a dictionary. You must provide an explanation for the word 'mystery'. What would you write? Compare your explanation with those of others in your class.

OR

2. You are a teacher.
Choose two words from the list below which you would use if you were trying to help your students to understand what is meant when we say that something is a mystery:
puzzling; confusing; frustrating; complex; amazing; impossible to understand; exciting; challenging; just a cop-out; full of wonder.

In Your Religion Journal

Think of a time in your life when you came into contact with something which you experienced as a mystery.
Write about what happened and how you felt at the time.

OR

Illustrate your experience on a page of your religion journal.

Lots of things can seem mysterious until we learn more about them. The workings of a TV set may seem mysterious to the average television viewer, but not at all mysterious to a TV engineer. At one time lightning was considered a great mystery. Nowadays, we know that it is a discharge of electricity and, because we have learned about electricity, lightning does not seem nearly so mysterious. Detective stories are often called 'mysteries'. In order to solve them, all we need are the right clues.

When we talk about God being a mystery, this is not at all the kind of thing we mean. A real mystery is not something we could understand, if only we had some more information or the right clues. It is something we can never hope to understand fully, because aspects of it are simply beyond human understanding.

The universe is one example of a mystery. There are many things we can understand about it. We go on learning more and more all the time, but the more we learn and understand, the more questions our discoveries raise, and the more we realise how never-ending the quest to understand it is. In many ways, the more we understand about it, the more mysterious it appears.

Other people are mysteries too. Not only is there always more to learn about them, but there are always things about them we can never know or understand. We are often mysteries even to ourselves. Sometimes we don't understand why we do the things we do or why we feel the way we feel.

Find Your Group

Discuss the kind of thing in everyday life which you find mysterious, which you know you will never get to the bottom of however hard you try.
Discuss experiences you have had of being amazed by other people and what you discovered about them, even people whom you know very well.
Talk about a time when you felt that you were a mystery yourself and that you would never completely understand yourself.

The Mystery of God

God, however, is the greatest mystery of all. God does want us to get to know him and to understand him more and more. And so God has revealed himself to us. We can go on deepening our knowledge and understanding of God as we grow older and our ability to understand things increases. We gradually realise more and more what God is like. Not only is there no end to the things about God we can begin to understand, and no end to the questions we can ask about God, but we can also begin to realise that God is so infinitely great and marvellous that we could never fully understand him, even with all eternity to do so, because God is beyond our human comprehension. Only God can fully understand God.

One basic aspect of the mystery of God, revealed to us through Jesus, is the mystery of the Trinity.

Discuss

What do you think is meant when it is said of someone, 'He is very good-natured'?

Trinity Icon, Central Russia, 1800

The Trinity

Christians believe that there is one God, and that in that one God there are three persons: the Father, the Son and the Holy Spirit. We call this a Mystery. By this is meant that we can never fully understand the Trinity because it is beyond the capacity of our human minds to do so.

Christians have always believed that there is only one God. They also believe, however, not only that Jesus called his Father, God, but that Jesus himself was God, and that the Holy Spirit was God. How could all these beliefs be equally true?

Jesus said, 'I and the Father are one' (John 10:30), but at the same time he prayed to the Father, and it was clear that he was not talking to himself. How could it all be explained?

The Church explains this by pointing to the distinction between person and nature.

Each of us is a person. The nature of something is the quality which makes it what it is.

Person and Nature

Each of us possesses all that goes to make up a human being: a human body, soul, intelligence etc. As human beings we are different from all other creatures. Each of us is also individual and distinct, a separate, unique person.

Discuss

Outline some characteristics which are common to all who possess human nature.

With God the great difference is that each of the three persons in God possesses not just the same kind of nature as the others but the identical one and only divine nature. In God there is only one being, one intellect, one will, one power, one love. So, though there are three divine persons, there is only one divine being – only one God. The three powers share everything in common. They are bound together in a perfect relationship of love. They act towards creation in perfect harmony.

Find Your Group Discuss

The kind of unity described here is impossible for us to understand fully, but can you suggest examples of people who are so clearly bound together that they seem to form a unity?

Revelation

To reveal something means to make it known. God's revelation enables us to get to know God more and more deeply. This revelation comes to us most clearly through Jesus. Jesus helps us to come to know God as Father, as Son and as Holy Spirit.

Son of God

Jesus helps us to know God as Father – first of all as his Father. God is Jesus' Father in a special way, because Jesus is not just a man, but the eternal Son of God. In the Creed, we say that he is 'eternally begotten of the Father'. Jesus has existed in his divine state from all eternity.

The language in the Creed is not meant to imply that the Father 'begets' the Son in the same way as human parents beget a child. God is not a human being. But it does aim to show certain points of comparison. A human child traces its origin to the parents who 'beget' it, and through that parenthood receives a similar nature. In a similar way Jesus eternally originates from God and receives from God not merely a similar nature, but the one divine nature of God. However, there was never a time when the Son did not exist nor when the Father was not the Father.

To speak of the Son as 'begotten' is to emphasise that he is not a creature created by God, but one who actually comes forth from God's own being, someone wholly and completely divine and uncreated.

In the Nicene Creed which we say at Mass, the Church sums up its belief in Jesus, the Son of God.

> We believe in one Lord, Jesus Christ,
> The only Son of God,
> Eternally begotten of the Father,
> God from God, Light from Light,
> True God from true God,
> Begotten not made,
> of one Being with the Father.

God, Our Father

Jesus became one of us. He was conceived and born as a human being of a human mother in order to share our life and to show us, in human terms, what God is like. Simply by becoming one of us, he shows us that God, his Father, wants to be our Father too and wants us to be his children. The Son of God became a human being in order to share with us his relationship to his eternal Father. In a general sense, God is Father of all, because he is the source of all life, but Jesus wants us to know that he wants to be our Father in a more profound way, and that he loves us like a Father. He compared the love of God to the love of a loving father, but made it clear that God loves us with a love that is more perfect than that of any human parent. Human parents, even the best, are imperfect. Some human parents can be selfish, neglectful or cruel to their children. But God is the perfect Father, always caring, always ready to forgive, always wanting the best for us and knowing what that is even before we know it ourselves.

Activity

Look up the following references: Matthew 6:25-34; 7:9-11; Luke 15:11–12. Using the information you have gained, illustrate the caption 'Sons and daughters loved by God'.

Flemish French School, Provost and Aldermen of Paris in Prayer Before the Holy Trinity, National Gallery of Ireland

Our Father

We can know what the Father is like not simply by what Jesus said about him, but by looking at Jesus himself and at his actions. At the Last Supper Philip said to him, 'Lord, show us the Father; that is all we need.' He answered by saying, 'For a long time I have been with you all; yet you do not know me, Philip? Whoever has seen me has seen the Father. Why then do you say "Show us the Father"? Do you not believe, Philip, that I am in the Father and the Father is in me?' (John 14:8-10)

Lanfranco, The Last Supper, National Gallery of Ireland

Find three or four examples of Jesus' actions which you think tell us about the attitude of God towards us.

The Word-made-flesh

In his Gospel, St John calls Jesus the 'Word' of the Father. This phrase can help us to understand more clearly the relationship of Jesus to the Father.

We use words to express ourselves. Before we speak out loud to others, we first of all have those words in our minds as thoughts. In a sense we express ourselves silently to ourselves before we communicate that expression to others. The more important the words we want to say, the more time we spend forming the words in our own minds before we speak them out loud. We can never express ourselves perfectly even to ourselves, but with God it is different.

We can think of the eternal Son of God as the Father's perfect Word – his perfect self-expression of all that is in him. St John says, 'The Word became a human being and, full of grace and truth, lived among us. We saw his glory, the glory which he received as the Father's only Son' (John 1:14). Later he says, 'No one has ever seen God. The only Son, who is the same as God and is at the Father's side, he has made him known' (John 1:18). That is why Jesus can say 'Whoever has seen me has seen the Father' (John 14:9).

Discuss

Have you ever heard someone say something like, 'I couldn't find the right words'; or, 'There were no words to express what I wanted to say?'
Have you ever felt like this?

Children of God

Jesus not only shows us what the Father is like. He also shows us how to behave as God's children. As the true Son of God, Jesus is the one who can best show us what our attitude to the Father should be. Jesus also shows us how God's children should act towards one another and towards other people.

Activity

Look up Matthew 5:43-45. Put its message into your own words.
Find other incidents or sayings from the Gospels where Jesus shows us:
(a)   what our attitude to the Father should be;
(b)   what our attitudes to other people should be.

48

The Holy Spirit

But Jesus did not simply want us to act like children of God, he wanted us to become children of God. In St John's Gospel we read: 'To all who did accept him, he gave power to become children of God' (John 1:12).

He did this by the power of the Holy Spirit, who comes to us from the Father through Jesus.

The word 'Spirit' means 'breath'. The Holy Spirit is often thought of as the love between the Father and the Son – the personal bond of unity between them. The Holy Spirit is the Spirit of the Father and of the Son. As the Spirit of the Father the Holy Spirit brought about the conception and birth of Jesus from the Virgin Mary. As the Spirit of the Son, the Holy Spirit is sent to us from the Father to unite us with Jesus as his brothers and sisters. The Holy Spirit enables us to share with Jesus his relationship with God as his Father. The Spirit gives us a share in God's own life and love. That is what begins for us at Baptism. It will be

Antwerp Mannerist, The Descent of the Holy Spirit, National Gallery of Ireland

brought to perfection in the world to come. St Paul writes: 'For you did not receive the spirit of slavery to fall back into fear, but you have received the Spirit of Sonship. When we cry "Abba, Father", it is the Spirit himself bearing witness with our Spirit that we are children of God' (Romans 8:15-16).

We cannot therefore consider the doctrine of the Trinity as an abstract idea which is of no real concern to us. It is our destiny to share with Jesus as children of God in the life and love of the Trinity, through the work of the Holy Spirit within us.

The Holy Spirit in the Church

The Holy Spirit is the Father's gift to us through the Son. It is through the Holy Spirit that we are able to accept and respond to all that God has revealed to us about himself through Jesus. At the Last Supper Jesus promised to send the Holy Spirit to his followers when he would not be with them any longer: 'The Helper, the Holy Spirit, whom the Father will send in my name, will teach you everything and make you remember all that I have told you' (John 14:26). And again, 'It is better for you that I go away, because if I do not go, the Helper will not come to you. But if I do go away, then I will send him to you. When, however, the Spirit comes, who reveals the truth about God, he will lead you into all the truth. He will not speak on his own authority but he will speak of what he hears and will tell you of things to come. He will give me glory because he will take what I say and tell it to you' (John 16:7;13-14).

In the Acts of the Apostles we see the effect that the coming of the Holy Spirit had on the followers of Jesus. They had been afraid and confused. But with the Holy Spirit they overcame their fears and they had a clear message for the people. In the Acts of the Apostles we read about the way in which the Holy Spirit, the Spirit of God, worked in the early Christians.
Read *Acts 2:1-21; 5:12-16; 9:1-31.*

Discuss
What effects did the coming of the Holy Spirit have on the early Christians?
What qualities did the early Christians show which were the result of the action of the Holy Spirit?

The Holy Spirit is the Spirit of God. We often speak about the spirit of a particular team or the spirit of a particular family group. We are referring to the way in which the members relate to one another, the kind of atmosphere they create, or the way that they relate to others outside their own group. So while we can never see what we call the spirit of the group or the spirit of the team we can see the result of it in action.

Find Your Group Discuss

Have you ever heard anyone say something like, 'They have a wonderful spirit', or perhaps, 'Their spirit will keep them going,' or, 'I like the spirit of that group'. What do you think they mean by this?

The Spirit of God in the World

The Holy Spirit is at work in the world today whenever we see the fruits of the Holy Spirit in the lives of people. These are love, joy, peace, patience, kindness, goodness, trust, gentleness and self-control.

In Your Religion Journal

Write about an actual event in your local parish where you think you saw the Holy Spirit at work in the Church today.

Activity
Using pictures and clippings from newspapers and magazines make a poster illustrating the work of the Holy Spirit in the world today. You could use the caption 'By their fruits you will know them'.

In the Nicene Creed the Church sums up its belief in the Holy Spirit as the Third Person of the Blessed Trinity:

We believe in the Holy Spirit,
the Lord, the giver of Life,
Who proceeds from the Father
and the Son.
With the Father and the Son he is wor-
shipped and glorified.
He has spoken through the prophets.

God is Love

The doctrine of the Trinity teaches us, above all, that God is not some lonely, isolated, cold being who perhaps needs to create in order to find something or someone to love. The one God is a communion of persons, a communion of love. That is why St John can say 'God is Love' (1 John 4:8).

The Trinity is involved in all aspects of the Christian message. Jesus, the Son of God became a man, and therefore the actions of Jesus, in his humanity and his death for us, belong to the Son alone; but even here all that Jesus does is done in love and obedience to the Father and in the power of the Spirit. The Trinity is involved in all God's activity towards the world in a way that reflects the relations of the Persons to each other.

Andrei Roublev

Through the ages people have tried to draw images and symbols to help Christians understand the Trinity better. None of them is perfect, because it is impossible to represent a mystery perfectly. Some illustrate one aspect very well but in representing the Trinity they all fall short of a full understanding at some point. However, we can find them useful.

In the fifteenth century Russia was invaded by Mongolia. The people were terrorised and massacred. A monk named Andrei Roublev was asked by his superior to paint an icon that would help people to pray to the Trinity. It was hoped that this might help them in their sufferings. In 1410 Roublev painted a famous icon for the monastery of St Sergius near Moscow. You will often have seen this icon in textbooks and, perhaps, hanging on walls.

Before he decided what image he would use to convey the meaning of the Trinity, Roublev reflected on the story of the visit of the three angels to Abraham and Sarah which we find in Genesis 18:1-5.

The Lord appeared to Abraham at the sacred trees of Mamre. As Abraham was sitting at the entrance of his tent during the hottest part of the day, he looked up and saw three men standing there. As soon as he saw them, he ran out to meet them. Bowing down with his face touching the ground, he said, 'Sirs, please do not pass by my home without stopping; I am here to serve you. Let me bring some water for you to wash your feet; you can rest here beneath this tree. I will also bring a bit of food; it will give you strength to continue your journey. You have honoured me by coming to my home, so let me serve you.'
They replied, 'Thank you; we accept.'
Roublev painted this scene.
Rather than using words he used the figures and the colours in the scene to express the meaning of the mystery of the Blessed Trinity.

The three angels stand for the three persons of the Blessed Trinity. The rectangular table is a symbol of the earth which was created by God. The circle expresses the unity and eternity of God. The triangle is the symbol of the Trinity. The identical staffs are signs that the three persons are equal. Blue is the colour of divinity. The blue on all three angels shows that each person is God. The angel on the left represents the Father. No one has ever seen the Father so this figure has only a narrow strip of blue. Rose and gold are the colours of royalty and power. The angel in the centre represents the Son. The Son made the Father known to us and so this angel has more blue on his garments then either of the others. The red reminds us that Jesus suffered and died for us. The angel on the right represents the Holy Spirit. The green colour tells us that the Holy Spirit gives new life and growth. The chalice on the table stands for the Eucharist. There is only one opening in the circle.
This place is for each one of us who is invited to share in the life of the Trinity.

Roublev's picture gives a good representation of the three persons and their characteristics, but though it tries hard it cannot capture the total unity which makes them, in fact, only one God. This is inevitable.

Research
An ancient Irish legend tells how St Patrick used the symbolism of the shamrock when he tried to teach the people of Ireland about the Trinity.
Draw a picture showing the symbolism involved.

The shamrock is useful for giving a general idea of 'three in one', but it could be misleading if we don't realise its limitations as a symbol of the Trinity. Each leaf represents one of the persons but each leaf contains only part of the shamrock. Each of the three persons, however, possesses the whole of the divine nature.

Find Your Group
Think up a way of communicating the mystery of the Trinity to others. You could use art or music or drama.

Prayers in honour of the Blessed Trinity

Glory be to the Father

Glory be to the Father, and to the Son,
and to the Holy Spirit;
as it was in the beginning, is now and
ever shall be, world without end.
Amen.

The Apostles' Creed

I believe in God, the Father almighty,
creator of heaven and earth.
I believe in Jesus Christ, his only Son,
    our Lord.
He was conceived by the power of the
    Holy Spirit
and born of the Virgin Mary.
He suffered under Pontius Pilate,
was crucified, died, and was buried.
He descended to the dead.
On the third day he rose again.
He ascended into heaven and is seated
at the right hand of the Father.
He will come again to judge the living
    and the dead.
I believe in the Holy Spirit,
the holy catholic Church,
the communion of saints,
the forgiveness of sins,
The resurrection of the body,
and life everlasting. Amen.

The Nicene Creed

We believe in one God,
the Father, the Almighty,
maker of heaven and earth,
of all that is seen and unseen.

We believe in one Lord, Jesus Christ,
the only Son of God,
eternally begotten of the Father,
God from God, Light from Light,
true God from true God,
begotten, not made,
of one Being with the Father.
Through him all things were made.
For us men and for our salvation
he came down from heaven:
by the power of the Holy Spirit
he became incarnate from the Virgin
Mary, and was made man.
For our sake he was crucified under
Pontius Pilate;
he suffered death and was buried.
On the third day he rose again
in accordance with the Scriptures;
he ascended into heaven
and is seated at the right hand of the
    Father.
He will come again in glory to judge
the living and the dead,
and his kingdom will have no end.

We believe in the Holy Spirit, the
Lord, the giver of life,
who proceeds from the Father and the
Son.

With the Father and the Son he is wor-
shipped and glorified.
He has spoken through the Prophets.
We believe in one holy catholic and
apostolic Church.
We acknowledge one baptism for the
forgiveness of sins.
We look for the resurrection of the dead,
and the life of the world to come.
Amen.

Father
Holy Spirit
Son
Stay with us always
Trinity-in-One.

Mary be with us
Wherever we may be
On mountain peak
On wave of the sea.

May the blessing of the Father, Son
and Holy Spirit descend upon us at all
times.
May they dwell in our midst now and
forever.

The following prayer in honour of the
Trinity was written by Thomas Ken,
Bishop of Bath and Wells in South-
East England, and chaplain to King
Charles II. Under King James II he
was imprisoned in the Tower of
London with six other bishops. When
he refused to take the oath of alle-
giance to William and Mary he was
dismissed from his role as Bishop.

To God the Father, who first loved us,
and made us accepted in the Beloved;
To God the Son who loved us,
and washed us from our sins in his
own Blood;
To God the Holy Ghost;
Who sheds the love of God abroad in
our hearts be all love and all glory for
time and for eternity. Amen.

In Your Religion Journal

Write your own prayer or creed in
honour of the Trinity.

Do the Looking
Back exercises for
Unit One at the
back of this book.

LOOKING
BACK

Unit Two
Lesson Six

The Mission of the Church

The first followers of Jesus heard what he said to them. They took it as their mission. In the Acts of the Apostles we see how they put what he had said into practice. They preached the Good News of God's love to both Jews and Gentiles. They did more than that. They showed people, by the way in which they lived, how to live as followers of Jesus.

Imagine you were there in the days when the early Christian community was growing in numbers.

Read this letter:

12 The Olive Grove, Jerusalem

Dear Martha,

I thought I'd fill you in on some of the things which have been going on here in Jerusalem over the past while. As you know I had been following the progress of Jesus of Nazareth since I first heard about his teaching and preaching. When he was crucified I wasn't very surprised. Having said the kinds of things he had been saying, I didn't think it at all strange that they would want to put him to death. Naturally I thought that that would be the end of it. In fact I was glad it was all over.

I was beginning to think that there was a great deal of truth in the things he had been saying. I was even considering becoming one of his followers. And you know how the family would react to that!

Now I find that it's not over at all. There's a man called Peter, who seems to be taking up leadership of the band of followers who were closest to Jesus. He has been found preaching in the market-place. He claims that Jesus is not in fact dead, but that he has been raised from the dead. He urged the people to be baptised and to join the group of believers.

Would you believe it, that day three thousand people were baptised! Since then the leaders of the group have been seen and heard preaching and teaching all over the place. And the most unlikely people are joining the group. The latest rumour I heard is that Saul, the man who has been famous for persecuting the followers of Jesus, has in fact joined them. A lot of people are very impressed with the way they live.

They share everything they have. No one is left in need and there seems to be a great spirit among them.

So, you see, I'm back to square one. I am, once again, impressed by what I see and hear. At the first opportunity I think I'll go and talk to one of the leaders. I'm dying to hear what you think of all this. Do write soon.

With Best Wishes,

Daniel

Today the mission of the Church is the same mission which Jesus left to his followers, the same mission which Jesus had himself. Today it is our mission. We are the Church, the body of Christ in the world today.

The Mission of Christ in the Church

The role of Christ is often described as that of Prophet, Priest and King.

Prophet – Jesus Christ showed more clearly than anyone else what God is like and what God wants us to do.

Priest – Jesus Christ offers himself, the perfect sacrifice, to God the Father, for us.

King – Jesus Christ calls everyone into his kingdom of perfect love, truth, peace and justice.

The task of the Church as a whole, and of each of its members, is to cooperate with Christ in this threefold mission.

The Prophetic Role of the Church

The Church must preach the Good News brought by Jesus. The Church must help people to come to know all that Jesus has revealed about God and his mercy. The Church must show its faith in Jesus by the way its members live their lives. The Church must pass on faithfully to people in all ages the truths that Jesus revealed.

Infallibility

Jesus told his apostles to go and teach all nations. Jesus promised he would be with them always, to the end of the world (Matthew 28:19–20). Like Peter and the other apostles, their successors, the Pope and bishops, have special authority from Jesus to teach. They also have a special responsibility to safeguard the truth which Jesus gave to the Church. The Apostles had to do this in their lifetime, and their successors have had to do so on many occasions since.

Normally they do this through their ordinary teaching, through the pastoral letters which the bishops write and through the encyclicals which the Pope writes. Sometimes though, particularly when there have been serious disputes, there has been the need for a special council of bishops, called an ecumenical council, to declare once and for all whether a teaching is definitely part of the Church's faith and may not be denied, or definitely contrary to the Church's faith. A solemn definition of this kind by such a council, if it is confirmed by the Pope, is said to be infallible, i.e. free from error. This is because the Church trusts in the guidance of the Holy Spirit and in the promise which Jesus made to the apostles that he would be with them always.

Under certain conditions, the Pope alone, because of his supreme authority in the Church, can make such an infallible pronouncement. This rarely happens, however. All popes teach with authority, but the vast majority of them, including the last four popes, have never made an infallible definition.

Find Your Group

Look up Matthew 16:13—19; 18;18.

1. What authority did Jesus give both to Peter and the other Apostles in these passages?

2. Peter (whose name means 'Rock') is said to be the rock on which the Church will be built.

Why do buildings need foundations?

What happens if the foundations are not solid?

Why is rock a good foundation?

3. What do you think this tells us about Peter's role and responsibility in the Church?

4. In the Jewish kingdom the official who received 'the keys of the kingdom' was a kind of chief minister, who had the greatest authority in the kingdom after the king himself.

What do you think this tells us about the position Jesus is giving Peter?

Research

What does the most recent pastoral letter written by the bishop of your diocese deal with?
Find out what the most recent pastoral letters written by the Bishops' conference deals with.

Our Role

Popes and bishops have special tasks in the Church, but we all have to play our part in making the teaching of Jesus known through what we say and what we do. That means that we need to grow in understanding of the faith, so that we can let people know what being a Christian means. It also means that we have to be ready to stand up for the teachings and values which Jesus passed on to his followers. In this century, no less than in the past, people have been prepared to die for their faith, but even if we are not called to become martyrs, we will still often need courage to remain true to our beliefs.

Find Your Group
Discuss

Talk about a time when you felt under pressure because you insisted on staying true to your beliefs.

56

Living in the Real World

Michael is nineteen. He has just been elected to the committee of the local football club. His best pal, Dave, is the treasurer. Last week Michael attended his first committee meeting. Dave gave his financial report for the end of that particular quarter year. As he went through the figures it was obvious that the club was doing very well. There had been a good attendance at all of their home matches and the books were looking healthy. Then Dave came to a set of figures which surprised Michael. He decided that he would find out later what was going on.

On the way home he asked Dave to explain.

'Oh that,' said Dave, 'You wouldn't have heard about that before. It's the money that we give to all the committee members on the quiet. It kind of makes up for all their hard work.'

'But what would the members of the club think?' asked Michael. 'And why are they not told?'

'What would be the point in telling them?' asked Dave, 'What they don't know won't bother them. And in any case there's loads of money in the kitty.'

'That's not the point,' insisted Michael. 'It's underhand and dishonest.'

'Oh grow up,' said Dave scornfully. 'This is the way things work in the real world.'

Michael said no more. He knew that he would not win that argument. But he decided that he would bring the matter up at the next committee meeting. If they didn't listen to him there he would make known to all the members of the club what was going on. He was determined that it would not be allowed to continue.

Discuss

In what way was Michael carrying out his mission for the Church?
Have you ever seen something like this happen?
Has anything like this ever happened to you?

The Priestly Role of the Church

It is the Church's mission to join with Jesus in his offering of himself to the Father, on our behalf, and to pray in union with him for all the needs of the world.

We do this especially in the Eucharist. The Mass is the supreme way Jesus has given us of joining in offering his sacrifice. By taking part in the Mass, and especially when we receive the risen Jesus himself in Holy Commuion, we are united more closely with him, and are helped to show more clearly in our lives his attitude of love and care for others.

Getting Old

Margaret finds it a real effort now to get to Mass every morning, especially in the winter, when the pains in her joints are worse. But she wouldn't miss it for the world. She is seventy-seven and has lived alone for fifteen years.

She always sits near the front; kneeling is too difficult but she must go to the front, that's the only place where she can be sure that she'll hear what the priest is saying. When she hears the words, 'I confess...' she silently hopes that God will forgive her the wrongs she has done. 'Lord have mercy', says the priest, and Margaret repeats the words in her own mind. She loves to listen to the Gospel. There's usually something there that she can remember when she leaves the church. She prays for her children, for Paul, who always drank too much – if she keeps making the effort to come here and pray maybe some day God will give Paul the strength to stay away from drink; for Sally, happily married with four children; for Elaine, the famous one with the beautiful voice, famous for stage appearances in musicals and shows not only in this country but overseas as well; and, of course, for Andrew, her husband, who has been dead for fifteen years but who will never be forgotten.

After Mass she has words with some of the neighbours and usually agrees to visit someone in the afternoon, someone sick or one of her friends who is no longer able to get out of the house. A cup of tea and a chat are always a welcome part of Margaret's day.

Discuss

Do you think that Margaret is living out her mission for the Church?
Give reasons for your answer.

In Your Religion Journal

Make out a brochure encouraging people of your own age group to become more involved in the work of the Church.

Activity

Look at these issues:

Care of the aged
Care of the mentally handicapped
Care of the poor
Racism

Compile a report, using pictures and clippings from newspapers and magazines, stating to what extent these issues are dealt with in a Christian way in your country. You have been given the job by the Church authorities of making a poster challenging people to become more involved in work for change in the areas listed.

Every time we go to Mass and receive Holy Communion, we receive the risen Jesus who sacrificed himself for us and the whole world out of love. He comes to us in Communion to make us more like himself. Every time we go to Mass and receive Communion it is an invitation to us to imitate his love in our lives with the assurance that, if we want to, he will be with us and he will help us. When we receive the risen Jesus in Communion it can be an occasion when we renew our commitment to share his concern for all God's children, and to put that concern into action as he did, or it can be just a matter of routine.

Read this letter written to Jesus:

Jesus Christ
Heavenly Mansions
Eternal Kingdom

1 Otherside Road
Broad Way
Goatland

Dear Sir,

Thank you for your recent communication. I am, of course, very grateful for all the trouble you have gone to on my account and am perfectly content to receive the benefits you refer to, as long as this does not cause me any inconvenience. I am quite happy to attend your celebrations and to say 'Amen' to all you care to say or which others say on your behalf. I do, in fact, often remark to my friends what a good chap you are and how much I admire you. Indeed, I have written letters on this subject to various newspapers, so you can be sure that I am one of your most devoted supporters.

I feel, however, unable to accept your invitation to join in your rescue work. When I consider what you have had to go through, it occurs to me that such a course of action could seriously upset my routine and prove burdensome. It might involve me in various sacrifices, and even adversely affect my bank balance.

Since I feel so confident that you have my best interests at heart, I am sure that you cannot really expect me to do anything like that. No one is sorrier than I am if people are poor or in any distress. I am all in favour of feeding the hungry, visiting the sick and lonely, housing the homeless and helping those in trouble. I am wholly in agreement with your views on these matters, and am full of admiration for all those who, unlike myself, have the time and inclination to do these kinds of things. They can be fully confident of my moral support and I have no doubt that both you and they will be quite satisfied with that.

What do you think of O.N. Stoneyground's letter? How would you answer this letter?

In any case, I fear that any activity of the kind you suggest might interfere with the modest amount of time I feel able to devote to prayer — something I am sure you would deplore. I am having enough difficulty in that area as it is. Whenever I say, 'Give us this day our daily bread', I seem to hear a still, small voice muttering rather unpleasant things. I can only think that this is a minor psychological upset, brought on by my anxiety about the ozone layer.

Yours in the expectation of the heavenly reward I richly deserve.

O.N. Stoneyground

Building up Christ's Kingdom

Members of the Church are called not just to profess and communicate their faith, but to put it into practice; not just to celebrate Christ's sacrifice, but to imitate it in their own lives. The proclamation of the Gospel and the communication of what Christ has done for us through the sacraments always lie at the heart of the Church's mission of building up Christ's Kingdom. But, inspired by these, the Church is also called to show the love and concern of Christ for all people in all aspects of their lives through the activities of its members, and in this way also to build up Christ's Kingdom of love, truth, peace and justice.

All in the course of a day

If you were to ask Jean Anderson to tell you about herself she would probably start off by saying, 'I'm just an ordinary housewife.' Jean has five children aged five to sixteen. Sometimes she thinks she spends most of her day either taking one or other of them to or collecting one or other of them from school, or a friend's house, or the swimming pool, or the playing field or whatever.
Between times she cleans the house, does the washing, cooks the meals, helps with homework, does the ironing etc.

She belongs to the parish group 'Care of the Aged,' so she takes a turn with four others delivering dinners to five elderly people in the parish, who are no longer able to cook their own meals.
When the parish looks for volunteers, whether it is to organise the children's Christmas party or to run a stall in the sale of work for the missions, Jean is always ready to volunteer. Nobody knows where she gets her energy from but Jean seems to take it all in the course of a day's work.

Discuss

Do you think Jean carries out her mission for the Church? Give reasons for your answer.

Go Tell Everyone

Down through the ages, followers of Jesus in the Church have always taken seriously his command to preach the Good News of God's love to all peoples. St Patrick came to Ireland, Irish monks sailed to Europe, European missionaries brought the message of Jesus to America, to the Indies, to the Far East, to Australia, to Africa, to South America.
Many missionaries have suffered persecution, some have even suffered death in their work of bringing the Good News of God's love to people in all parts of the world.

The following are stories of some of the work being done by today's missionaries in many parts of the world:

Sr Teresita Donnelly is a Medical Missionary sister who works in St Luke's Hospital, Anud, Nigeria. She writes:

'I complained I had no shoes, 'til I met a man who had no leg'.

His name is Paul. He has no legs. My story is true, alas too true. Paul is one of many who have similar handicaps. I first met Paul some months after his mother had died. A young member of the St Vincent de Paul Society took me to the village one evening on the 'carrier' of his bicycle. There we met a young man who had fallen from a palm tree twelve years before. His spine was fractured and he was completely paralysed from the waist down. His only carers were his very old father and a nephew of six years old. For his bed Paul had an old mat, and when I examined him he had five bed sores, very large and deep. Ants nibbled his lifeless toes at night. From then we visited him daily taking him food, some bedding, and dressing his wounds. When these were healed and Paul was feeling stronger I took a lady surgeon to see him. She suggested that the useless legs should be amputated and then he could swing himself into a wheelchair and move about. Paul was delighted. Anything was better than lying all day on his comfortless bed. The major operation having been successfully performed, Paul was ready for discharge. The surgeon herself donated a wheelchair, propelled by hand. This was the beginning of a new life. Joyfully he drove around the village greeting all the neighbours. They thought this was a miracle. He appropriately called his wheelchair 'Christian Love', which he had inscribed on the back of it.

You could meet 'Christian Love', as he himself is now called, around the hospital daily. He is loaded down with cold minerals for the thirsty nurses to drink at breaktime. He has biscuits too and nuts, oranges and bananas and even rosaries and magazines. He is a welcome visitor around the wards and his daily income is enough to support him. Courage and determination has made the seemingly impossible possible for Paul. Please pray for him and many others not so lucky.

Discuss

What is your reaction to the work described in this story? What words would you use to describe Paul?

Touched by God

Karen Blixen, Amy Johnson and Mother Teresa — take something from each of them, roll them into one and you have a woman called Olive Allerton.

Olive spent half of her eighty-three years in England. Born in 1904, her ambition as a young woman was to learn to fly and chart unknown routes around the world. Her father had the resources which would have made this possible. However, he decided to keep Olive away from flying machines.

As a result she lived into old age, but in 1948 she did venture into the unknown. Together with her family, she went off to start a new life in Kenya so that her husband's bronchial condition would be helped by the warmer climate of Africa. Neville had been an army officer and during the evacuation from Dunkirk was in the water for four hours after the ship he was on was bombed. Neville's health was never the same again, but he coped much better in Kenya than in England.

The years after the Second World War saw the establishment of a large expatriate community in and around Kitale, just a few miles from Uganda. Dairying and mixed farming enabled many people to live prosperously through the fifties, but the Mau Mau uprising in the sixties led to virtually all expatriates selling up their farms. Financial difficulties forced the Allertons out and for the next few years they earned a livelihood by enabling visitors to experience something of the wildlife of East Africa. Lake Naivasha, Bushwackers and Seronera Lodge in the Serengeti were three places where they brought their guests into contact with the lions, cheetahs, elephants, giraffes, zebras, gazelles, wildebeeste and other animals that abound in the savannah lands of Kenya and Tanganyika, as it was then. These stimulating experiences were brought to a sudden end one day when Neville collapsed with severe internal haemorrhaging. A period of convalescence was followed by a trip to Australia where Neville and Olive intended to live out the last years of their lives near their two married children. They were both in their seventies at this stage and ready for retirement. Neville's death from cancer within six months put paid to such ideas and Olive had to support herself for the next six years by running a general store and post office in Queensland. At the age of seventy-six she *did* retire, and for twelve months followed the routine at Symesthorpe, a rest home in Toowomba.

Olive found everyone at Symesthorpe kind enough but she felt that she should be doing something constructive, not simply looking around for ways of keeping herself occupied. Eventually she became convinced that she should go off to help Mother Teresa in Calcutta, and that is where she ended up. She assisted at Nirmal Hriday, the home for the dying, and at Shishu Bavan, a hospice for babies and orphaned children.

The fact that she was on crutches and suffering from muscular atrophy did not deter her. She kept up with able-bodied people and travelled around in a rickshaw. After some months in Calcutta Olive went to Madras to help the Missionaries of Charity but, providentially, she ended up with the Salesians of Don Bosco at Vyasapardy, a suburb in the slums on the outskirts of the city.

'Beatitudes' was the name of the home provided for physically and mentally handicapped people, abandoned infants and orphaned children. Homeless people of all ages filled the crèche, the schools – infant, primary and secondary – the clinic and the infirmary which, together with dormitory blocks, craft rooms and workshops, made up the huge complex that was 'Beatitudes', serving up to 2,000 people.

Olive spent her time visiting the patients and chatting with them. Not having any nursing or administrative responsibilities, she was able to spend more time with them than the nursing staff could, and the role she played was deeply appreciated.

An annexe of 'Beatitudes' was Pope John's Garden, a home for leprosy patients about fifteen miles from the city. Coconut palms and a variety of trees, shrubs

and flowers made Pope John's Garden one of the most beautiful places in Madras. A very special effort had been made to provide beautiful surroundings for the patients, and here Olive exercised a most effective ministry. The love and empathy which she brought to them quickly led to her being dubbed 'Mummy'. More than anything else the patients appreciated her willingness to hug and embrace them – a sign of acceptance so many of them were deprived of even by family and loved ones.

Olive soon came to see as part of her mission the provision of a home for the children of these leper patients. Space had run out and 'Beatitudes' was unable to cope with the numbers. So Olive went off to Australia on two fund-raising trips and brought back $70,000 with which extensions were built at the home. The impact Olive made in Australia was remarkable. This fat, dumpy old lady would be brought into a hall or room and her wheelchair hoisted on to the stage, or she would be lifted into a chair. Then, as she began speaking, she held her audience spellbound. The usual reaction was: 'If this old lady, a semi-invalid, is doing all this in India, what am I doing?'

Olive did not live for very long after her fund-raising trips. A tumour of the brain brought on a coma and she was flown to Australia to be near her married daughter. Olive came out of the coma and was in a nursing home for some time, but she was never able to return to India as she dearly wished to do. In her lifetime Olive was an inspiration to many. Indeed, her story is still prompting people to ask themselves: 'If she did all of that, what am I doing?'

Discuss

What words would you use to describe Olive Allerton?

Activity

Think of your own parish – if there are others in your class who are also from your parish, you could do this exercise along with them:

(a)   List some of the obvious needs in your parish.

(b)   List the organisations or groups which exist in order to answer these needs.

(c)   Are there any needs which are not being answered by any of the organisations or groups which already exist?

(d)   Are there any areas where you and your friends could become involved?

Discuss

Describe some ways in which each of the following could carry out their mission for the Church in their work every day:

A doctor
A hairdresser
A farmer
A professional footballer
A secretary
A bricklayer

Belonging to the Church

Sometimes, when we think about working for the Church, the things which come to mind are going to Mass, saying our prayers, belonging to the folk group or choir, belonging to other parish groups or committees. However, we belong to the Church all the time, and this means that all through our lives, in our work, in our recreation, at home, with our friends, we are challenged to live as Jesus called his followers to live. We are challenged to work for justice, for peace and for love in our dealings with others.

Very often we look around and see the needs in our locality or country. Then we often ask why the Church isn't doing something about them. Whenever we ask a question like that, we forget that we are the Church. Ours are the eyes and ears, the hands and feet which can do the work of the Church in the world today. Remember, we are the Body of Christ.

Find Your Group

List the areas where you can be actively involved in the work of the Church right now.
Name some concrete ways in which you can carry out this work at home, at school, or in your neighbourhood.

Read the following story:

During the Second World War a little village in Bavaria was virtually wiped out by Allied air raids. Among the casualties was the parish church. The figure of Christ on a way-side Calvary beside the church was left without arms and legs. After the war the people set about restoring the church but the parish priest insisted that there be no alteration to the wayside shrine. He erected a sign at the foot of the cross which reads: 'Now I have no arms and no feet. From now on you will be my arms and feet to bring help and healing to a broken world.'

Discuss

What do you think of what the parish priest did?

Fill in this questionnaire.

Do any of these things happen in your parish?

Fundraising for the Third World _____
Football _____
Singing at Mass _____
Youth club _____
St Vincent de Paul Society _____
Sales of work _____
Care of the Aged _____
Concerts _____
Fundraising for other causes _____

Other activities: _____
_____
_____

Who takes part in these activities?

Priests _____
Parish sisters _____
Selected committee members _____
Young people _____
Married people _____

Are you involved in any of them?

Yes _____
No _____

Why/Why not? _____
_____
_____

What ways can you think of in which you can begin to become involved in something new in your parish?

_____
_____
_____
_____

Becoming Involved

Denis had belonged to the youth club now for almost five months. He had joined in the first place because all the lads were joining and he thought it might be good crack. When he found out that there was very little going on in the club which interested him he was disappointed. He didn't like snooker or badminton and he was no good at debates. So whenever he went down to the club he usually spent most of the time sitting, waiting for his friends Anne Marie, Jean and James. The best part of the night for Denis was the walk home afterwards, when he had the opportunity to talk to and have a laugh with his friends. After a few months of this he was getting a bit fed up. He decided that he could meet his friends at other times and that he'd be better off at home watching TV than sitting around the club house. He didn't really feel that he belonged to the club.

He decided to have a word with Joe, one of the leaders.

'I know you've been bored,' said Joe, when Denis told him how he felt about the club. 'What I can't understand is why you haven't thought about the kind of activity you would be interested in. Then perhaps we could see if there were others who might be interested and it might become part of the club programme.'

Denis was amazed. 'That never occurred to me,' he replied. 'I'll think about that.' That night on the way home, he asked his friends if they thought that there would be many people in the club who might be interested in bringing in their latest music tapes and spending some time listening to them. 'That way,' said Denis, 'we'd all get to hear lots of music that we'd never be able to buy for ourselves.'

'It's a good idea,' said Anne Marie. 'Next week you can see how many people would be interested. I'd bet that there will be lots'. 'Well, I'd certainly be interested for starters,' said James. 'And I'd make that two,' added Jean.

And so, Denis' idea took off in the club. Every week there was what became known as the musical hour. Denis no longer felt an outsider in the club and he looked forward to the meeting each week.

Discuss

Why do you think Denis began to feel that he was part of the club?
Has anything like this ever happened to you at school or in a group to which you belonged?

If we want to feel that we are really part of a group or an organisation we must become involved. When we have a part to play we feel that we are important and that we belong. And so it is with the Church. All of those who belong to the Church are challenged to play their part. We belong to the Church because we were baptised into it as infants. However, as we grow we can belong to the Church in more active ways. We can play our part.

In Your Religion Journal

This is the mission which Jesus left his disciples. It has been written in code, using the alphabet in reverse order. Wherever the letter Z is used it should be A, the letter Y should be B, X should be C etc. Can you decipher the message? You could start by writing the code below into your journal, which will help you to relate the letters of the code to the letters of the alphabet.

A   B   C   D   E   F . . .
Z   Y   X   W   V   U . . .

TL GSVM GL ZOO KVLKOVH

VEVIBDSVIV ZMW NZPV GSVN
NB

WRHXRKOVH: YZKGRHV GSVN
RM

GSV MZNV LU GSV UZGSVI, GSV
HLM, ZMW GSV SLOB HKRIRG,

ZMW, GVZXS GSVN GL LYVB
VEVIBGSRMT

R SZEV XLNNZMWVW BLF

(Matthew 28:19–20)

A Time to Pray

Leader: Let us listen to the challenge which Jesus left his followers.

Reader 1: A reading from the gospel according to John.

Jesus said to his disciples:

My commandment is this: 'Love one another just as I love you. The greatest love a person can have for his friends is to give his life for them. And you are my friends if you do what I command you. I do not call you servants any longer because a servant does not know what his master is doing. Instead I call you friends, because I have told you everything I have heard from my Father. You did not choose me; I chose you and appointed you to go out and bear much fruit, the kind of fruit that endures. And so the Father will give you whatever you ask of him in my name. This, then, is what I command you: love one another.'
John 15:12-17

Leader: Let us pray that we will have the courage to live as Jesus asked.

Reader 2: We pray that we will have the courage to show love always to those we live with at home. Help us, Lord, to be kind, to listen, to have consideration for the needs of others, and to put ourselves last.
     Lord, hear us.

All: Lord, graciously hear us.

Reader 3: Help us, Lord, always to show true love to our friends. Help us to do only those things which are for the good of our friends rather than those which answer our own selfish needs.
     Lord, hear us.

All: Lord, graciously hear us.

Reader 4: Help us, Lord, to show love to those whom we find it most difficult to love. Those who are different from us, who have different interests, wear different clothes, live in different neighbourhoods. Help us especially to show love to people whom we tend to look down on.
     Lord, hear us.

All: Lord, graciously hear us.

Reader 5: We pray that we will always show love to those who are most in need: those poorer than ourselves, those less able, those who are left out, those who have few friends.
     Lord, hear us.

All: Lord, graciously hear us.

Reader 6: In all our relationships help us to show qualities of generosity, patience, respect, honesty, kindness and justice.
     Lord, hear us.

All: Lord, graciously hear us.

Leader: Let us pray together:

Prayer of St Francis of Assisi
Lord, make me an instrument of your peace.
Where there is hatred, let me sow love;
Where there is injury, pardon;
Where there is despair, hope;
Where there is doubt, faith;
Where there is darkness, light;
And where there is sadness, joy.
O Divine Master, grant that I may not so much seek
To be consoled as to console;
To be understood as to understand;
To be loved as to love;
For it is in giving that we receive;
It is in pardoning that we are pardoned;
And it is in dying that we are born to eternal life.

The Church through the Ages

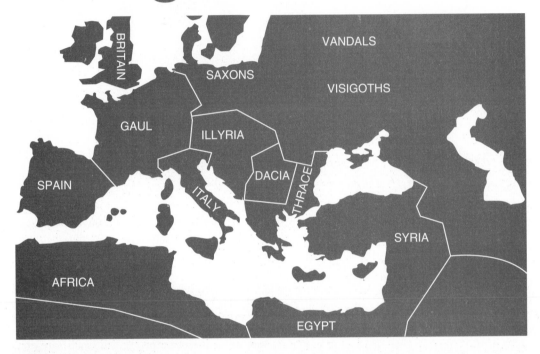

The world in which Jesus lived and died was the world of the Roman Empire. It included the Mediterranean Sea and all the lands which touched it. To the north it stretched to the Rhine and Danube, to the south to the African deserts, and to the east it included Turkey, Syria, Palestine and Egypt.

The people worshipped a number of gods of Italian, Greek and Egyptian origin. Religious practice consisted mainly of offering sacrifice to one or other or a variety of these gods, mostly in order to avoid some misfortune or other.

Jesus was born into one corner of this world, Palestine, which was the home of the Jewish religion. The Jewish religion was unique because the Jews were the only people who believed in and worshipped one single God.

Pentecost Day, when Peter preached to the Jews in Jerusalem and when three thousand of them were baptised, is regarded as the day when the Christian Church was founded. At first, Christianity was looked upon as one branch of the Jewish religion. The first Christian missionaries were all Jews who brought the Good News of the coming of the Messiah to their fellow Jews in other parts of the world. The first great Christian missionary was St Paul who preached the Good News to both Jews and Gentiles. When he set up communities of believers he kept in touch with them by writing letters. These letters were read again and again and copies were made and sent to other communities so that they also could read them. Other apostles also wrote letters to the new communities.

Thirty years after the death of Jesus the new religion had communities of believers called 'churches' in many places.

Rome had its church with St Peter as its leader. A collection of writings which would form the New Testament was gradually being built up. It included sayings of Jesus and the letters from Paul and the apostles. The Christians condemned the worship of pagan gods and this led to opposition from some people. Also, they were seen as a group who followed and even worshipped an obscure criminal who was put to death by the Imperial authorities. A clash was bound to occur.

Activity

Read the descriptions of the early Church in Acts 2:43–47 and 4:32–37.

Discuss

Name and illustrate four of the characteristics of the early Christian community.

Find Your Group

Paul made three great missionary journeys. Starting at Acts 13 read about one of these journeys.

Class Activity

Draw a map of the south-eastern Mediterranean area and trace in the routes of Paul's missionary journeys. Display it on the classroom wall.

Persecution

In the year 64 a large part of Rome was destroyed by fire. The rumour went around that the fire had been started by the Emperor Nero to clear the way for new buildings. It was even said that he had been seen singing and playing the lyre as the city went up in flames. To avoid the danger of an uprising Nero decided to put the blame somewhere else. Christians, who were already hated by many of the people, were blamed and they were cruelly punished. As an eye witness reported:

'Some were dressed in the skins of animals and torn to death by dogs; some were crucified; some were set on fire in order to light up the darkness after nightfall. The result was to arouse pity for these men, even though they deserved the severest punishment; because it was fact that they were being destroyed not for the general good but to satisfy the cruel instincts of one man.'

During Nero's persecution St Paul was beheaded and St Peter was crucified. Long after Nero's death the laws against Christians remained in force. For two and a half centuries the penalty for being a Christian in the Roman Empire was death.

In spite of the persecution, maybe even partly because of it, the Christian religion continued to grow and to spread. People greatly admired the courage of those who were persecuted and the stories of

Nero

the martyrs were written down and re-told. The system was established whereby the local churches were governed by a bishop and his council of presbyters (priests), who were assisted by deacons. At this time there were no special

church buildings because Christians had to worship in hiding so the Eucharist was celebrated in people's houses. The altar was a table and the priest did not wear vestments. The room had to look like an ordinary room to avoid suspicion. Those who wished to join the community spent

a time in preparation during which they were taught the Apostles' Creed, Christian moral laws were explained to them and they learned about the life of Jesus. During this time they were called catechumens, which means learners.

Though Christians were persecuted, there were many Christian writers during the early centuries who tried to explain the Christian faith and to defend it against attack. The greatest of these are known as the 'Fathers of the Church' and the earliest include St Clement of Rome, St Ignatius of Antioch, St Ignatius, Bishop of Lyons, St Justin Martyr, and St Hippolytus of Rome.

There is very little Christian art from the first three centuries. A picture or statue could lead to persecution or even death if seen by the wrong eyes. Obvious signs of Christianity like the cross were kept out of

sight. Instead the Christians had pictures or carvings which appeared harmless to the unbeliever but which had a special meaning for the believer.

Early Christian Illustrations

— A young man with a sheep on his shoulders stood for the Good Shepherd.
— A fish stood for Christ the Saviour since the initial letters of the Greek phrase 'Jesus Christ the Son of God' made up the Greek word for a fish.
— The catacombs, where the early Christian martyrs were buried, were also decorated with Christian symbols on the walls and on the covers of coffins.

Peace at Last

The most violent of all persecutions of Christians was carried out by the Emperor Diocletian and it began in the year 303AD. It was so vicious that he lost support even among his followers and the Emperor Constantine came to power. In his efforts to establish himself in control of the Empire, Constantine was about to lead his army against the city of Rome.
On the night before the battle he had a dream where he was told that he was to put a sign of the one true God on his soldiers before going into battle. Though he was not a Christian

Eucharistic celebration, a painting from the catacombs of St Callistus

at the time he had the Christ sign, the Chiro, put on his soldiers' shields before they went to battle.

They won the battle.

Constantine ordered the sign to be put on the banners of the army and on the coins of the Empire and soon it was everywhere to be seen. Today it remains one of the commonly used Christian symbols.

In 313 the Edict of Milan granted religious freedom to everyone in the Empire and so ended the persecution of the Christians.

Constantine supported the building of many beautiful churches, the first Christian places of worship. In Rome they were modelled on the Roman basilicas which were used as law courts and as places of public gathering. The four great churches built in Rome during the fourth century – St Peter's, St Paul's, St John Lateran's, St Mary Major – all followed the basilica pattern.

Constantine decided to move the capital of the Empire from Rome in the west to Byzantium in the east. He changed the name from Byzantium to Constantinople – the city of Constantine. Before his death, Constantine became a Christian. After Constantine,

the Roman Empire was divided into two parts, west and east, with an emperor in charge of each part. In the west, the emperor ruled from Ravenna. As Constantinople became more politically important, its bishop, who was given the title of Patriarch, began to take on a more important leadership role in the east. Since he was usually under the emperor's firm political control, successive emperors encouraged this. This sometimes led to friction with the popes in Rome, often for political reasons. Nevertheless, in both east and west, the Pope continued to be recognised as the chief bishop of the Church. He was appealed to in disputes and it was accepted that the decisions of ecumenical councils needed his approval.

This was the age of some of the great ecumenical councils, most of which were called to settle disputes which had arisen in the eastern part of the Church. The first, at Nicea (325), condemned those who denied that Christ was truly God. The second, at Constantinople (381), defended the divinity of the Holy Spirit, and gave us the Creed we now say at Mass. The Council of Ephesus (431) condemned those who seemed to be saying that Christ was really two persons, and also defended the practice of calling Mary 'Mother of God'. The Council of Chalcedon (451), called by

Basilica of St Mary Major

70 Pope St Leo the Great, finally defined the whole teaching about Christ in accurate and unambiguous language.

Among the great Fathers of the Church in this period were, in the east, St Athanasius (who vigorously defended the divinity of Christ), St Basil of Caesarea, St John Chrysostom of Constantinople and St Cyril of Alexandria. Among those in the west were St Hilary of Poitiers, St Ambrose of Milan, and the great St Augustine, whose writings have had an enormous effect on Christian thought, especially in the west. A great saint of the time was St Monica, the mother of St Augustine, through whose prayers he was converted to Christianity.

During this time many Christians decided to devote their lives totally to Christ. They did this by putting aside all worldly ambitions and going into the desert to live lives of prayer and poverty. They settled in huts and caves and supported themselves by weaving baskets and mats from palm leaves. As time went by numbers of them built their huts close to one another, they shared a common church and chose one of their number to be their leader. This is how the first convents and monasteries were formed.

One of the most famous of these early 'Desert Fathers', as they are called, was St Anthony.

Activity

Answer the following questions and complete the sentences.

Then find the answers in the wordsearch below.

Who was the first Christian emperor?

During his reign, which city became the new capital of the Empire?

How was St Paul executed?

Which emperor began the persecution of the Christians?

The catacombs are the burial places of the _____.

Who was the last emperor to take part in the persecution of the Christians?

The Roman Empire was made up of the lands around the _____ sea.

The Edict of _____ granted religious freedom to all in the Empire.

The first monks were called the ___ Fathers.

What is the Christian symbol, still used today, which Constantine had painted on his soldiers' shields?

On which Roman buildings were the earliest Christian churches modelled?

The Christian Church was born on the first _____.

St Peter was the first Bishop of _____.

C	O	N	S	T	A	N	T	I	N	E	R	O	B
O	B	E	H	E	A	M	J	E	K	E	L	A	A
N	Y	M	B	A	S	I	R	D	E	S	R	T	S
S	C	A	T	A	C	O	M	B	S	A	W	O	I
T	F	R	H	B	E	H	E	A	D	I	U	G	L
A	C	T	D	K	Y	O	R	N	M	G	L	R	I
N	J	Y	G	V	F	D	M	I	L	A	N	O	C
T	V	R	X	S	O	I	V	C	S	H	W	M	A
I	M	S	T	G	D	E	S	E	R	T	C	E	S
N	Y	Z	I	D	I	O	C	L	E	T	I	A	N
O	P	L	R	E	W	B	A	S	I	L	I	A	C
P	M	E	D	I	T	E	R	R	A	N	E	A	N
L	K	S	W	U	P	E	N	T	E	C	O	S	T
E	W	C	H	I	R	O	L	A	S	K	O	P	E
C	A	T	A	X	C	O	M	B	S	M	I	L	A

A page from the Book of Kells

where people met. They were collections of small huts which became centres of learning and of art. The Irish monks had a special reverence for the gospels and from this came the Book of Durrow and the Book of Kells.

Irish monks helped to spread Christianity to the rest of northern Europe. St Colmcille went to Scotland, St Columbanus to France, Germany, Switzerland and Italy. In 529 St Benedict founded a monastery in Italy, thus establishing the Benedictine order. Soon Benedictine monasteries were being set up all over Europe.

The Dark Ages

In the year 406 the Empire was invaded by Barbarians from the north. Wave after wave of them pressed into France, Italy, Spain and Africa. They did not set out to destroy the Empire, but they knew so little about farming that stretches of fertile land became deserts, and they were so unused to living in towns that the Roman towns and cities decayed and fell into ruins. The only institution that kept any hope alive in an empire that was falling to pieces was the Church. People looked to their local bishop for law and order.

On one occasion Pope Leo I went out of the city to plead with Attila, the leader of the Huns, who was threatening to invade the city. When Attila agreed to turn back the Pope came to be regarded as the real leader and protector of the city. Eventually, the whole of the Roman Empire in the west had been taken over and split into a collection of new kingdoms. In the east the Empire managed to survive, and even, for a time, took Italy back from the Barbarians. The Church in the west survived, however, and began to convert the invaders.

The Irish were converted to Christianity by St Patrick, who came to Ireland in 432. It seems that monastic life was taken up widely by the Irish. Monasteries for men and for women sprung up all over the country. As there were no towns these became centres

Early Irish Monasticism

Building a sixth-century monastery

Imagine a great circle of ground, perhaps more than 100 metres in diameter. Dig up the earth around it to a depth

Monks' cells on Skellig Michael

of three metres and use the clay and stone to build a wall. Fill in the ditch with water. Now you have protection against unwelcome guests and wild beasts. If the land is very rocky you can build a wall of stone. In the centre of the circle you can build a church or two. Use wood, mainly oak, and cover with a thatch of rushes. Each little church should measure about 5 x 3 metres, with enough head-room for the tallest of the monks. Better build a sacristy for storing vestments and chalices alongside the church. If the monastery becomes famous you may have to build a big cathedral church, measuring 20 x 8 metres, with enough room for well over a hundred monks. If stone is available in the locality use that for your cathedral.

Next, the monks' huts or cells. Make them about 3 metres in diameter and shape them like a beehive until they're about 2 metres high. Distribute them around the compound, out towards the great circular wall. Place the abbot's cell on its own near the principal church.

There's still more building to be done before you complete your monastic village. A kitchen and a refectory, where the monks are fed; a library and a 'scriptorium', where the manuscripts are made and stored; a guest-house, which may be placed outside the great wall. And general purpose buildings like a storehouse for provisions, a kiln for drying and a mill for grinding corn. You might also need a forge or a carpenter's shop, especially if the monastery gets much bigger and you have all that building to do!

Comgall and Ciaran were two monks of this period.

COMGALL (Bangor) From east Ulster. Was on the point of becoming a soldier when peace was made. Received his first training in St Fintan's monastery. After leaving Clonenagh he moved on to Clonmacnois and then established his own foundation at Bangor in the Ards of Ulster. Even before his death, Bangor ranked as one of the most famous monasteries in the country, especially as a centre of study. And from this monastery went two of Ireland's greatest missionaries, Columban and Gall. Comgall died around 610.

CIARAN (Clonmacnois) From the kingdom of Connacht. Became a disciple of Finnian at Clonard. Later spent some time with the community on Aran.

Back on the mainland he founded his own monastery on the banks of the Shannon just south of Athlone, on the borders of the kingdoms of Meath and Connacht. Future kings of Connacht were to make Clonmacnois their burial place. The monastery itself was to become a great centre of learning and culture.

Ciaran died in 556.

Research

Other monks of this period were Enda of Aran, Finnian of Clonard, Brendan of Clonfert, Fintan of Clonenagh, Kevin of Glendalough, Colmcille of Derry.
Find out all you can about three of them.

The monastery of Clonmacnoise

In 597, Pope St Gregory sent a group of Benedictine monks, led by a monk called Augustine, to re-introduce Christianity to the southern part of England. Augustine, who eventually became St Augustine of Canterbury, was very successful. He was made a bishop and established the centre of his diocese at Canterbury.

Some kind of order was restored in the west when Charlemagne established control over large parts of what had been the Western Empire. He was crowned Emperor by the Pope in Rome in 800, and his empire became known as the Holy Roman Empire, which survived, at least in theory, until the end of the eighteenth century.

In 1054 a great tragedy occurred. Because of the difficulties caused by the fall of the Roman Empire in the west there had been for some time less and less communication between the Church in the west and the east and, in addition, especially since the foundation of the Holy Roman Empire, strong political rivalries had grown up. In consequence the Church in the east and in the west had tended to drift apart. A dispute arose because Rome had introduced a new phrase into the text of the Creed (*see* Lesson 12) and Constantinople objected. Very unwisely and quite illegally, since the Pope he was representing had just died, the chief of the papal legates went to Constantinople and excommunicated the Patriarch, who thereupon excommunicated the legates from Rome. The split that occurred then has never been healed. Most of the Church in the east rejected the authority of the Pope, and since then has become known as the Orthodox Church.

Activity

Make a wall frieze of pictures which illustrate the spread of Christianity to your country; early monastic settlements; manuscripts; high crosses; metalwork etc.

The Middle Ages

During the time from 1000 to 1500 the Church dominated every aspect of life in Europe: art, architecture, music, education, even recreation. Great cathedrals were built in cities all over Europe. Statues of Christ and of scenes from the Bible stood in the porches, and stained glass windows were used for the first time.

St Francis of Assisi was born in 1182. He was the son of a wealthy cloth merchant but he gave up the riches and comforts of his home to go and live among the poor. He is remembered for his gentleness and for his great love and reverence for everything in the world of nature.

Francis did not intend to form a religious order but many people asked to join him. He could not turn them away, and when he died in 1226 he had hundreds of followers in many countries. So began the Franciscan Order of Friars. Other religious orders were formed during this period also, e.g. the Augustinians, the Carmelites and the Dominicans. Unlike monks, who were expected to stay in their monasteries and to confine their ministry to their immediate neighbourhood, these new friars wandered all over the country begging for their food and preaching the Gospel.

The Middle Ages saw the emergence of many people of great sanctity whose lives have had a lasting influence on the Church, including St Anselm of Canterbury, St Albert the Great, St Thomas Aquinas, St Bonaventure, St Elizabeth of Hungary, St Bridget of Sweden and St Catherine of Siena.

In 1453 the Turks captured Constantinople and put an end to the old Roman Empire in the east.

Carving of St Francis in Askeaton Friary

74 In the west many abuses crept into the Church. Christian kings and emperors professed loyalty to the Church, often because they wanted to use it for their own ends. They were particularly interested in the riches of the monasteries and the cathedrals and they often insisted on having their supporters appointed as bishops or abbots.

Statue of Thomas à Becket in Canterbury Cathedral

The Popes had to wage a constant struggle against the attempts of emperors and kings to dominate the Church. In England Thomas à Becket, Archbishop of Canterbury, was murdered in Canterbury Cathedral because of his opposition to the king's attempts to control the Church.

However, in these circumstances some Church leaders were more interested in money than in religion and in being servants of the king rather than in being servants of God. There were many attempts to reform the Church, some by individuals or groups, others by councils. At this time some movements arose which propagated doctrines which were contrary to the accepted teaching of the Church, sometimes on quite basic matters. To combat this the Church set up the Inquisition in various countries. This was meant to win heretics (as these people were called) back to the Church, but it often behaved in an oppressive manner and caused many injustices. In Spain, particularly, the Inquisition became very powerful and was greatly feared. Worst of all, the Inquisition was sometimes used by kings and governments to oppress their opponents. In some cases it was also used to persecute people who were not heretics, but who were merely making justifiable protests against abuses and corruption in the Church.

In the Middle Ages, when religious belief and the whole life of society were so closely intertwined, an attack on belief was seen as an attack on society as a whole. But even so, and even when one realises that general attitudes towards individual freedom were very different then, it is impossible to justify the oppressive measures often used by the Inquisition.

Research

There are many stories which illustrate the kindness and gentleness of St Francis of Assisi. Find some of these. Make your own class magazine about St Francis.

Renaissance and Reformation

The word renaissance means rebirth and it refers to the new interest in the culture of ancient Greece and Rome which developed in Italy towards the end of the fifteenth century. Two of the most famous people of the period are Leonardo da Vinci, who is famous for his painting of the Last Supper, and Michelangelo,

Michelangelo

who is famous for many works of painting, architecture and sculpture.

One of the great projects started in Rome at the time was the rebuilding of St Peter's. Christians all over Europe were called to give money for the project. Preachers were sent out to encourage people to

Leonardo da Vinci

make contributions. They promised people that they would be rewarded for their contributions by being granted indulgences, that is a lessening of the punishment which they would have to undergo in purgatory.

While it was right to preach that giving money or other goods to the poor or to the Church was a good deed and that it would be rewarded by God, it was also right to preach that the Church can and does grant indulgences. This means that the Church, by her prayer and authority, opens the treasures of grace which are the fruit of Christ's life and of the lives of faithful Christians, to people who carry out certain prayers and actions in a proper frame of mind. It was, however, wrong to suggest, as some preachers did, that God's favour or forgiveness could be bought. On 31 October 1517 Martin Luther, a young German Augustinian friar, nailed a document which attacked the doctrine of indulgences to the church door at Wittenberg. That action marked the beginning of the Protestant Reformation.

There were many people who were unhappy with the abuses which existed in the Church at the time. The truth of many of Luther's criticisms won him a large number of followers. However, many of his teachings were contrary to the teachings of the Church and so, what started off as a movement to reform the Church from within, actually became a Church of its own. Henceforth there would be two Christian traditions in western Europe: Catholicism and Protestantism. There are a number of strands within the Protestant Churches which you will already have examined in detail in last year's course.

The Council of Trent was held by the Catholic Church beginning in 1545 to deal with the abuses in the Catholic Church and to re-affirm the traditional teachings of the Church. The result of the council was the first ever general reform of the Catholic Church from within.

The Council of Trent

Research

Find out about some of the developments in art or architecture which took place during the Renaissance;
OR
Write a biographical note on Michelangelo.

The Jesuits

One of the great names of this period is St Ignatius of Loyola. He was born in Loyola in Spain in 1491. He became a soldier and at the age of thirty he was the commander of a garrison in the town of Pamplona when it was besieged by the French. He suffered severe leg wounds which made him an invalid for quite a while. While he was ill he passed the time by reading. He read every novel he could lay his hands on and when these were finished he started reading the lives of the saints and the life of Christ. To his own amazement he found himself deeply influenced by what he was reading. He eventually spent a long time in prayer and meditation in the Spanish town of Manresa. He resolved to spend the rest of his life serving God.

First, he finished his education in Paris. There he met a number of men who shared his ideals, among them Francis Xavier, also a Spaniard. They made their way to Rome and offered their service to the Pope. In 1540 they began a new religious order, the Society of Jesus, generally known as the Jesuits. Ignatius' new order became a great force for advancing in the Church the reforms of the Council of Trent and for promoting the Catholic faith. The Jesuits were great educators, setting up schools in many countries, and they were also great missionaries. In particular they took the Gospel to India, Japan and the East Indies. St Francis Xavier was one of their greatest missionaries.

St Teresa of Avila

Research

Find out more about the lives of St Ignatius of Loyola and St Francis Xavier. St Teresa of Avila was born in 1515. She became a Carmelite nun and was one of the great mystics of her time. Find out more about her life.

The Age of Enlightenment

In 1643 Louis XIV became King of France and ruled for seventy-two years until his death in 1715. He surrounded himself with pomp and splendour and built immense palaces which were meant to show the world the greatness of France. Vincent de Paul became captain at the royal court of Louis XIV. Soon he decided that he did not want to live his life in a palace while the world outside was full of people living in poverty and ignorance. There were many parts of France where there were few priests. Vincent de Paul thought that these were almost like mission territories. He organised a group of priests to go around and give 'missions' in these areas. Eventually these priests were formed into a new religious order, the Vincentians.

They also set up seminaries around France for the training of future priests. In 1625 France entered the Thirty Years War. As the armies swept across France they left behind them poverty, famine and disease. Starving, penniless refugees flooded into the rest of the country. Vincent set about organising help. He set up hospitals and orphanages. He sent wagon-loads of food and clothing to the worst-hit areas. He begged and borrowed from anyone who had anything to give. His most valuable helpers were a group of women whom he formed into the Sisters of Charity. They lived and worked among the poor, visiting them in their homes and nursing them in hospitals. Today they are known as the Daughters of Charity.

After the French Revolution in 1789 there followed a century when monarchs were overthrown all over Europe. In Ireland, Daniel O'Connell won Catholic Emancipation in 1829, which meant that from that time on Catholics in Ireland and Great Britain were no longer persecuted for the practice of their religion. Irish

religious orders which had been established to educate young people, the Christian Brothers, founded by Edmund Ignatius Rice, and the Presentation Sisters, founded by Nano Nagle, were able to

Louis XIV

expand. Irish sisters, brothers and priests went abroad in great numbers to work as missionaries, to Britain, to the United States, to Australia, to New Zealand, to British colonies in Africa and Asia.

In 1738 John Wesley, an English Anglican priest, began a new movement within the Church of England which eventually led to the foundation of the Methodist church.

Thérèse Martin was born in 1873, the youngest of five girls, into a middle-class family who

lived in the small town of Lisieux in northern France. All five sisters became nuns, four of them at the Carmelite convent of Lisieux. Thérèse entered there at the age of fifteen and took the name Sister Thérèse of the Child Jesus. Nine years later she died of tuberculosis. During the last years of her life she was asked by her superiors to write an account of her life, which was published after her death. Almost overnight she became world famous. Her life had been dedicated to prayer, taking part in the Eucharist and doing housework. She had devoted herself to doing 'ordinary things extraordinary well.' In 1925 she was canonised.

In 1812, with Napoleon's invasion of Russia, the west, for the first time, became aware of what life there was really like. It had been ruled over by the Tsar with absolute power. The peasants lived in poverty and near slavery. It was not only in Russia that the poor were oppressed. Many of the peasants in eastern Europe also lived in poverty.

In 1870 the First Vatican Council was called. One of the most important declarations of the council concerned the infallibility of the Pope. The council taught that when he was speaking in his official capacity as leader of the Church, and he solemnly defined a doctrine concerning faith or morals as something which had to be accepted as part of the Catholic faith by the whole Church, his teaching would be free from error. The Church believes this because it relies on the promises of Christ and the guidance and protection of the Holy Spirit to keep it from falling into error concerning the faith it teaches.

Leo XIII was Pope from 1878 to 1903. He saw the many problems facing the people, particularly the poor, and put forward a Christian solution. He wrote many encyclical letters, the most notable of them, *Rerum Novarum*, dealing with the situation of the poor. 'A small number of rich men,' said Pope Leo in *Rerum Novarum*, 'have been able to lay upon the teeming masses of the labouring poor a yoke little better than that of slavery itself'. He demanded a 'living wage' for working people and defended their right to protect themselves through trade unions.

Discuss

In what way is Pope Leo XIII's statement still true in our world today?
If you were Pope today, what issue would you choose to write an encyclical letter on?

Research

Other religious orders founded during this period were the Sisters of Mercy in Ireland and the Salesians in Italy. Find out as much as you can about these.

The Twentieth Century

Pope St Pius X became Pope in 1903. He urged people to receive Holy Communion frequently. In the early Church people received Holy Communion whenever they went to Mass. In the Middle Ages, however, this practice changed. Because of an added emphasis on reverence people very seldom received Holy Communion. Pius X recommended that Catholics should, once again, receive Holy Communion frequently, even daily, so long as they did so worthily.

The First World War, 1914–1918, and the Second World War, 1939–1945, caused great upheaval throughout Europe.

In 1917 the Bolsheviks, who were atheistic communists, came to power in Russia. Persecution of all Christian Churches began. The Soviet leader, Stalin, attempted to suppress completely the Ukrainian Catholic Church, and thousands of clergy and lay people from all churches, Catholic, Orthodox and Protestant, were sent to work camps. No practising Christian had a chance of going to university or obtaining any kind of responsible or well-paid job.

After the Second World War the Soviet Union took over a number of Eastern European countries, and the communists who were put in power imitated the Soviet persecution of religion. However, the Church kept going under persecution, and in some countries, like Poland, even seemed to grow stronger. There were people who betrayed their faith, but many others resisted persecution heroically. Similar persecutions also took place in China and other Asian countries taken over by the Communists.

The Pope after the Second World War was Pius XII. He was a fierce opponent of communism and a great reformer. He began reforms of the liturgy, particularly regarding the celebration of Easter. He relaxed the Eucharistic fast, so that people were no longer obliged to fast from all food and drink from midnight before receiving communion, and he encouraged Catholics to study the Scriptures.

When the atomic bomb was first used in the Second World

Pope Pius XII

War it resulted in a type of destruction that the world had never known before. Millions of people were killed and millions of others were left starving and homeless.

Hitler's campaign took the lives of most of Europe's Jews and many of its leading Christians. Two great martyrs of the time were the Catholic priest Maximilian Kolbe and the Lutheran pastor Dietrich Bonhoeffer. In a world which seemed to be moving away from Christianity, one effect of Hitler's persecution was to bring Christians of different persuasions closer together. Bonhoeffer conducted a service for Catholic and Protestant prisoners on the day before his death and the same thing happened in many other prison camps.

Research

Find out as much as you can about the lives of St Maximilian Kolbe and Dietrich Bonhoeffer.

The man who brought the Church to meet the modern world was Pope John XXIII who was Pope from 1958 to 1963. His parents were Italian peasants. He was almost seventy-seven when he was made Pope and no one expected him to live very long or to do very much. Everyone was amazed when he decided to hold a general council of the Church, known as the Second Vatican Council, starting in autumn 1962.

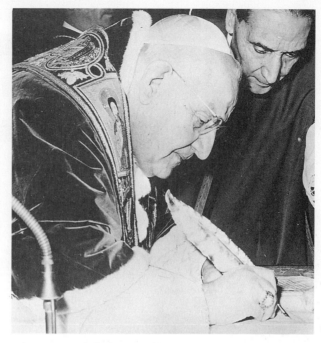

The aims of the Council were:

— To proclaim to the world again the true teachings of Jesus Christ;
— To work for unity among all Christians and for greater understanding among followers of all religions.

The documents issued by the Council fill a book of 700 pages. They are the guidelines for many advances which have taken place in the Church since the council.

Some of these are:

— People who lived in countries where Latin was the language used in the Mass and other parts of the liturgy were allowed to use the language of their country as well as Latin.
— New rites were developed which made it possible for the people to be more actively involved in the celebration of the sacraments.
— Churches were designed so that the priest faced the people.
— People were encouraged to spend more time reading and reflecting on the word of God in the Bible.
— Lay people were encouraged to play a greater part in the life and work of the Church.
— The Christian community was challenged to put greater effort into working for peace and justice.
— Catholics began to take a greater part in the ecumenical movement which works for unity among Christians.

Meanwhile the Church continued to grow vigorously in Asia, Africa and South America.

Find Your Group

Choose one of the countries from Asia, Africa or South America. Find out as much as you can about the Church in that country.

Research

Mother Teresa of Calcutta and Archbishop Oscar Romero of El Salvador are two outstanding people from this era. Choose one of them. Find out as much as you can about that person.

In Your Religion Journal

Imagine that the Third Vatican Council is about to be held. Where do you think it should be held? What do you think should be on the agenda?
Give reasons for your answers.

Across

1 St Thérèse of Lisieux became noted for doing _____ things extraordinary well.
2 The Second _____ Council was called by Pope John XXIII.
3 In the encyclical *Rerum Novarum* Pope Leo XIII urged people to take account of the needs of the _____.
4 St Benedict founded the _____.
5 The Jesuits were founded by St Ignatius of _____.
6 Pope _____ XII relaxed the Eucharistic fast so that people no longer had to fast from midnight.
7 The language once used in the rite of the Mass was _____.

Down

8 St Maximilian _____ was one of those who suffered martyrdom under Hitler's regime.
9 St _____ of Siena was one of the great saints and writers of the Middle Ages.
10 Leonardo da _____ was one of the artists of the Renaissance.
11 Pope John XXIII was born in _____.
12 Franciscan order of _____.

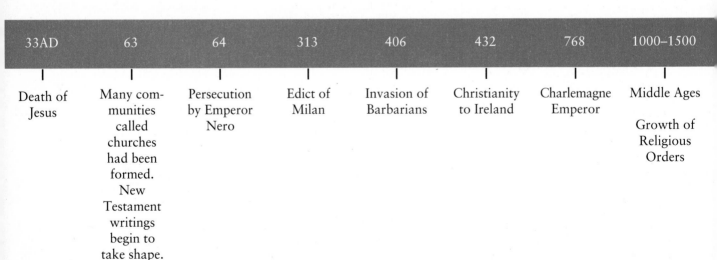

33AD	63	64	313	406	432	768	1000–1500
Death of Jesus	Many communities called churches had been formed. New Testament writings begin to take shape.	Persecution by Emperor Nero	Edict of Milan	Invasion of Barbarians	Christianity to Ireland	Charlemagne Emperor	Middle Ages — Growth of Religious Orders

A Time to Pray

Leader: God has promised to look after the Church. Let us listen to the following reading from the prophet Ezekiel *(34:11-16)*.

The Lord God says this: I am going to look after my flock myself and keep all of it in view. As a shepherd keeps all his flock in view when he stands up in the middle of his scattered sheep, so shall I keep my sheep in view. I shall rescue them from wherever they have been scattered during the mist and darkness. I shall bring them out of the countries where they are; I shall gather them together from foreign countries and bring them back to their own land. I shall pasture them on the mountains of Israel, in the ravines and in every inhabited place in the land. I shall feed them in good pasturage, the high mountains of grazing ground; they will browse in rich pastures on the mountains of Israel. I myself will pasture my sheep, I myself will show them where to rest — it is the Lord who speaks. I shall look for the lost one, bring back the stray, bandage the wounded and make the weak strong. I shall watch over the fat and healthy. I shall be a true shepherd to them.

Leader: Let us pray that God will guide all of us who belong to the Church as we try to live out the Gospel in our daily lives.

All: Amen.

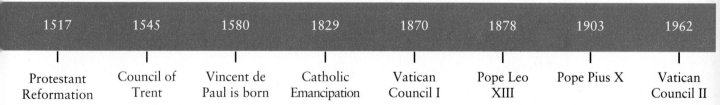

1517	1545	1580	1829	1870	1878	1903	1962
Protestant Reformation	Council of Trent	Vincent de Paul is born	Catholic Emancipation	Vatican Council I	Pope Leo XIII	Pope Pius X	Vatican Council II

Mary

All ages shall call me blessed

You already know the story in St Luke's Gospel about how Mary, after she learned she was to be the mother of Jesus, visited her cousin Elizabeth. Read it again in Luke 1:39-56.

In her words to Elizabeth, Mary says that:
> God has looked upon the humiliation of his servant.
> Yes, from now onwards all generations will call me blessed,
> For the Almighty has done great things for me *(Luke 1:48-49)*.

This really sums up Mary's life. She was, to all appearances, an ordinary young Jewish woman – not from a rich or powerful family, but the wife of a carpenter, living in an unimportant village. She lived the same kind of life as those around her, and had the same kind of joys and hardships, but at the same time God had chosen her for the greatest honour he could give to anyone. That is why Elizabeth says, 'Blessed are you among women', and why all ages thereafter have called her blessed.

Her Early Life

Mary was the most unlikely of people to have been given a role that was to make her known and remembered by people down through the generations. Mary, so far as we know, was born in Nazareth, in the region of Galilee, a province of Palestine which was then under the control of Rome. We know very little about Mary's early childhood, but that is not unusual since she probably lived in a very ordinary family who were known only to a small circle of friends.

When we first hear of Mary in the Gospel she is about to become an unmarried mother. For a girl at that time living in a small Jewish village in a strict, male-dominated society this would have been very difficult. Mary was betrothed to Joseph. He too must have been worried and confused. Had Mary been unfaithful to him? Why? Mary must also have been distressed to see Joseph become the victim of gossip and unanswered questions. It must have been very difficult for Mary to continue to believe, though she could not have fully understood, that God had chosen her for the unique honour of becoming the mother of his Son. She must have been tempted to ask God to find somebody else. But Mary persevered and in the midst of difficulties and pain showed tremendous courage, commitment and faithfulness. More than anything else Mary wanted to respond to God's call and to fulfil the mission which she had been given.

The Virgin of Tenderness, icon

84

In Your Religion Journal

Read Luke 1: 26-38.
Write a poem or draw a picture depicting the feelings
which you think Mary would have experienced.

Immaculate Conception

God had prepared Mary for the great task
he wanted her to perform. When we are
baptised, we receive the reconciliation with
God that Jesus won for us. Before that,
though loved by God, we are not united
with him by the gift of his Spirit. It is that
lack which we call the state of original sin.

Epstein, Madonna and Child

But Mary came into existence already specially chosen by God, already blessed with
his favour on account of the Son she would
bear and the redemption which he would
win. From the first moment of her existence,
therefore, she is consecrated for her task.
The Holy Spirit dwelt within her at all times
and she was never at any time deprived of
God's grace. That is what is meant by the
doctrine of the Immaculate Conception, and
that is what is meant by prayers which refer
to Mary as 'conceived without (original) sin.'

Mary is redeemed through Christ, as we
all are, but more perfectly. What we receive
in Baptism to fit us to become children of
God, she received from the first moment of
her existence to fit her to be God's mother.

Research

1. In a missal find the Preface for the Feast of the
   Immaculate Conception or the Opening Prayer of
   the Mass for that feast.
   Copy it into your journal and underline the words
   which explain what the feast is about.
2. There is a popular article of devotion called the
   'miraculous medal'. Can you find out about it? If you
   can find one, draw a picture showing both sides of it.

Birth of her first child

Many Christmas cards present a fairy-tale
picture of the nativity. The reality, however,
must have been quite different. Childbirth is
a time of great joy and happiness for a
mother but also a time of pain and discomfort. The days immediately before the birth,
particularly of a first child, can be stressful
and uncomfortable. For Mary, these were
days spent travelling on the back of a donkey from Nazareth to Bethlehem. The only
place available where her baby could be

born was in the starkness of a stable. Not only that, but shortly after the birth she and Joseph had to take the baby and flee because someone wanted to kill him.

Activity

Make a poster using clippings and headlines from newspapers and magazines which show situations in today's world where people have to endure difficulties and hardships similar to those endured by Mary.

Virgin and Mother

In St Luke's Gospel, Mary wonders how she can have a child, since she is not yet married. She is told that this will be brought about by the Holy Spirit.

Jesus Christ was born of a human mother, Mary. It was from her that he took his humanity. The Son of God came among us as a true human being, one of our human family. He was born of a human mother, and Mary was that mother. God the Father brought about his conception by the power of the Holy Spirit.

This has two important messages for us:

Firstly, it is a sign of who Jesus really is. The fact that he is conceived and born of a human mother makes it clear that he is truly one of us, but the fact that his conception is brought about directly by God is a sign for us that the one who is born as the son of Mary is also truly the eternal Son of God.

Secondly, it makes clear that the salvation which Jesus brings comes to us all as a gift from God. It is God who takes the initiative and brings it about. It is not something which human beings bring about by themselves.

Read Matthew 1:18-25.
Write out the words which make it clear that Joseph was not the father of Jesus.
Write out the words which tell us why the child is to be called Jesus.
What does the name 'Jesus' mean?
Why is the title 'Emmanuel' a good one for Jesus?

Mary: woman of faith, symbol of the Church

Will you bring Christ into the world?

The question that God asked Mary through the angel was: 'Will you bring Christ into the world?' Mary's answer was 'Yes', in the words which we repeat in the Angelus:

'Behold the handmaid of the Lord.

Be it done unto me according to your word.' God asks the Church and each individual Christian the same question: 'Will you bring Christ into the world?' Mary represents the whole human race when she, on their behalf, accepts and promises to cooperate with God. Mary is the living model and symbol of what we all should be. The rest of her life was spent living out that 'Yes'. Many of the days in Mary's life were spent doing the ordinary things which other women at that time living in her country did also. She was the wife of a craftsman and the mother of a travelling teacher. The family was not wealthy so Mary probably spent some of her time doing chores to help them to maintain some form of dignified existence. She probably spent time spinning, weaving and grinding wheat for bread. She probably dressed like the other women of Galilee of that time – in colourful clothes, perhaps

86

with ear-rings, gold rings and bracelets. She would have experienced the tensions of living in a land ruled by an occupying power, and would have been constricted just as much as anyone else by the shortcomings of the society in which she lived, particularly as these affected women. On the other hand, Mary's experience of life had in it the greatest joys and the deepest sorrows. She had the joy of knowing that she was doing the will of God and that her son was God's Son. She experienced fear, inadequacy, anxiety, loneliness, pain and bereavement.

'Will you bring Christ into the world?' That question is today addressed to the Church and to each one of us as individuals. In the Church, Mary is looked upon as the one who shows us how to answer that call. Her life shows us what we can expect if we answer 'Yes' – the joy of knowing that we are answering God's call and that God is with us, and the pain and suffering that will result from the fact that we are living in a world which does not want to receive or know Christ today, no more than it did at the time of Jesus.

Activity

Make a poster to illustrate the caption 'Bringing Christ into the World today'.

Imagine that you are a private investigator. Some followers of Jesus of Nazareth have called upon your services. They want to know more about Jesus, and about his relationship with God. You have decided that the first and best way to start is by finding out all you can about his mother, Mary. There are many sources of information for your investigation but you are going to start with what the gospel writers, Matthew, Mark, Luke and John, have said about her.

The first piece of information that has been uncovered is already in the beginning of your report.

Report Sheet from ———————————————— P.I.

Information you have found: Your sources:

Mary was engaged to Joseph (a carpenter in the   Mt 1: 18;
town of Nazareth) when she became pregnant.   Lk 1: 26-33

Conclusion and other comments:

Signed: ————————————————————————————

Statue of the Virgin by an Indian artist

Your employers have requested some specific information:

1. Information on Mary's own family.

2. How did she know that her son was the Son of God?

3. What role did Mary play in the life of Jesus?

4. Were there any specific events in the life of Jesus where Mary was mentioned by any of the gospel writers?

In Your Religion Journal

Please file all your findings in your religion journal.

Find Your Group

Compare your findings with those of your group.

Activity

Make a wall chart showing all the information that your group has collectively found out about Mary.

Mary's Faith

Mary put her faith in God. However, when she started on her journey of faith, she did not know all the situations through which she would have to travel. Like us, she did not always immediately understand everything that happened on the way.

When she found the child Jesus in the Temple in Jerusalem after he had been lost, St Luke tells us that she did not understand his reply when she asked him why he had caused her and Joseph so much worry. But we are also told that afterwards 'she pondered all these things in her heart.' She put her trust in God, knowing that he would gradually help her to understand more and more.

Find Your Group

Read Luke 2:41-51.
How do you think Mary might have felt when she discovered that Jesus was missing?
What do you think Jesus meant by his reply to her question?
What message do you think Mary's final reaction has for all Christians?

Do whatever he tells you

Read the account of the wedding feast in John 2:1-11.

When Mary tells Jesus that the wine has run out, his reply is rather mysterious, but it certainly doesn't sound encouraging. However, Mary doesn't appear discouraged, because she immediately tells the waiters, 'Do whatever he tells you'.

It is then that Jesus performs his first miracle, and afterwards we are told that because of this his disciples believed in him. What is

Virgin and child from Madagascar

clear, however, is that Mary believed before the miracle took place. Unlike the disciples, she did not need miracles. She just knew that if people do as Jesus tells them, the most wonderful and unlikely things can happen.

We need faith like Mary's to do what Jesus tells us. Sometimes everything seems to be going wrong, and we can't see how acting as Jesus tells us to can do any good. If someone offends or injures you, your reaction might be to get your own back. That might teach him or her a lesson, and stop them annoying you in future. But Jesus tells us to return good for evil.

In Your Religion Journal

Write about an occasion when to follow what Jesus says might seem difficult or pointless.

The Death of Jesus

The time of greatest trial and suffering for Mary must have been Good Friday and the days which led up to Good Friday. She watched her son as he was humiliated, rejected, beaten, tortured, stripped and cruelly killed.

The image presented by Mary on Good Friday is not one of glory and power but one of unbearable pain, sorrow and suffering. Imagine the fear that she felt as she followed her son, wondering how long his strength would last and how soon his body would become unable to bear the pain and give in to death. As we look at Mary on Calvary we see a woman in pain and anguish but we also see a woman sustained in spite of all her suffering because she believed that God was with her.

Activity

From newspapers and magazines find headings and pictures which depict situations in today's world where people experience pain similar to that of Mary as she followed Jesus to Calvary.

Any mother watching her child suffer shares in the pain. Mary on Calvary shares in Christ's suffering and is united with him as he offers his life for our salvation.

The figure of Mary at the foot of the Cross is a symbol of the Church and of every faithful Christian. Like Mary, the Church, and every individual Christian, must remain faithful to Jesus Christ even when all seems dark and desperate.

We stand at the foot of the Cross with Mary whenever we take part in the celebration of Mass and, with real faith in the risen Jesus, join with him in offering his sacrifice.

We also stand at the foot of the Cross with Mary, whenever we remain true to Jesus and his teachings, even when that costs us something; when we are ready to stand up for our faith or against injustice; when we make sacrifices to help those in need; when we are ready to share in another's pain and sorrow.

To be able to do all this we need a faith like Mary's.

Activity

There is a special feast day – the Feast of Our Lady of Sorrows – which highlights Mary's share in her son's sufferings. An ancient hymn (originally in Latin) called the 'Stabat Mater' is often sung at this feast. In most hymn books the first line of the English version is: 'At the Cross her station keeping'. Look up this hymn, and copy into your religion journal one or two verses which you think best express the sorrow of Our Lady on Calvary.

Give some examples of how Christians may be called on to share Christ's sufferings.

Mother of the Church

In St John's Gospel we read that Jesus, from the Cross, saw his mother and John, who is called 'the beloved disciple'. He says to Mary, 'Woman, this is your son', and then to the disciple, 'This is your mother' (John 19:26-27).

In this incident, John represents all of us who are followers of Jesus. In giving him Mary to be his mother, Jesus is in reality making her the mother of all Christians, and calling on all members of the Church to regard themselves as her children. Mary, therefore, is called the Mother of the Church.

By giving us his mother to be our mother also, Jesus is confirming that we are indeed, through Baptism, his brothers and sisters. It

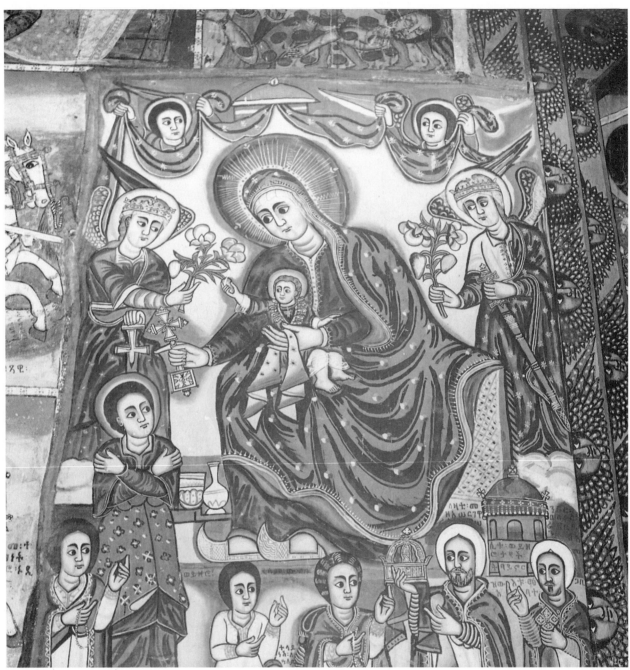

Virgin from an Orthodox monastery in Ethopia

is also an invitation to us to relate to Mary as our mother, to trust her and ask her with confidence to pray for us, her children. Throughout the ages Christians have honoured Mary and prayed to her, confident of her kindness and compassion.

Activity

What qualities do you associate with a good mother? Find a number of prayers or hymns which refer to Mary as our mother. What kind of things do they say about her which you would associate with a mother?

The Assumption

Christ promises that at the end of time all the faithful will share in the glory of the resurrection when they will be with God in heaven for all eternity. The Church believes that what Christ promises to all the faithful has already been granted to Mary. Because of her special holiness and her unique role in Jesus' work of redemption, she already, here and now, enjoys in her complete humanity the fullness of the resurrection which is the future hope of all the Church. This is called the doctrine of the Assumption.

It is an added assurance to all Christians that Christ's victory over death is meant for them too. In her life on earth Mary, who is without sin, is the living sign of what the Church on earth is meant to be; in heaven she is the living sign of all that the Church hopes for, when all its faithful members will share in the glory of the resurrection. In the person of Mary, the Church has already experienced the goal which is offered to all.

Activity

Because of her special position in heaven, Mary has been given a great number of titles, such as 'Queen of Heaven'. Look up the litany in honour of Mary to find similar titles which point to her heavenly glory.

Pilgrimages

Many Christians go on pilgrimages to places where Mary is believed to have appeared to people. Some of the reasons why people go to these special places are:

— particular devotion to Mary the Mother of God;
— to thank Mary for helping them through a time of suffering in their lives or in the life of someone close to them;
— to pray for the courage to bear the suffering of a particular situation in life.

You have probably heard of many of the places of pilgrimage in honour of Mary – Lourdes, Knock, Walsingham, Fatima, Medjugorje.

Activity

Find all of these places on a map of the world. Choose one of them and find out when and to whom Mary is believed to have appeared.

Images of Our Lady

Find Your Group

When you think about Mary the mother of Jesus what images come to mind?
Check out the images which the other people in your group had.
Where do you think these images come from?

There are all kinds of pictures and statues of Mary. Some try to show her as she might have looked in Nazareth or at the foot of the Cross. Others want to convey the impression of Mary in heaven. Many of them show her with the infant Jesus, to remind us why she is so important, but are still aiming to show her in glory rather than as she was in her earthly life. Some are connected with particular apparitions, for example, statues of Our Lady of Lourdes; others are trying to express something about her attitude to us. All of these can be helpful in different ways.

Find a number of examples of pictures/statues of Our Lady, and say in each case what message you think the artist was trying to convey.

Some statues of Our Lady show her with one foot on a serpent's head. Do you know, or can you find out, what this means?

Feast days in honour of Mary

8 December:	The Immaculate Conception
1 January:	Solemnity of Mary, Mother of God
11 February:	Our Lady of Lourdes
25 March:	The Annunciation of the Lord (*Strictly speaking, this is a feast day in honour of Our Lord, but it also com memorates a great moment in the life of Mary when she consented to be the Mother of God.*)
31 May:	The Visitation of the Blessed Virgin Mary
16 July:	Our Lady of Mount Carmel
15 August:	The Assumption of the Blessed Virgin Mary
22 August:	Mary, Queen of Heaven and Earth
8 September:	The Birthday of Our Lady
15 September:	Our Lady of Sorrows
7 October:	Our Lady of the Rosary
21 November:	The Presentation of the Blessed Virgin Mary

Activity

Pick three of the feasts from this calendar and explain the event that is being remembered and why this event is important to us.

Example:
1 January: The Solemnity of Mary, Mother of God

Through Mary, God gave his Son Jesus to the world for its salvation. On this day we celebrate Mary's role as the one chosen to be the mother of Jesus.

This day has also become the World Day of Peace. Pope John Paul II prayed, in his homily during the Mass in St Peter's Basilica on 1 January 1979:

Mother, you who know what it means to clasp in your arms the dead body of your Son, of him to whom you gave birth, spare all mothers on this earth the death of their children, the torments, the slavery, the destruction of war, the persecutions, the concentration camps, the prisons! Keep for them the joy of birth, of sustenance, of the development of people and of their lives. In the name of this life, in the name of the birth of the Lord, implore with us peace and justice in the world! Mother of Peace, in all beauty and majesty of your motherhood, which the Church exalts and the world admires, we pray to you: Be with us at every moment! Let this New Year be a year of peace, in virtue of the birth and the death of your Son! Amen.

A Time to Pray

Virgin and child from Zimbabwe

Discuss

Which of the images of Mary used in this lesson do you prefer? Why?

Leader: Let us begin by examining how we are living as Christians by reflecting on some phrases from Mary's Magnificat:

Reader 1: **My soul glorifies the Lord.**

Do I live my life for God's glory? Is the living God the centre of my life? Are the false gods of money and pleasure more important to me? Do I feel the need for God? Do I live as if God did not exist? Do I pray to God from time to time during the day? Do I turn to God in trust and praise? Do I thank God for his love and goodness?

Reader 2: **My spirit rejoices in God my Saviour.**

Do I thank God for sending Jesus to save me? Do I genuinely try to change by avoiding situations of temptation and situations in which I know that I am likely to commit sin?

Reader 3: **He looks on his servant in her lowliness; henceforth all generations will call me blessed.**

Do I accept God's will in illness and in suffering? Do I allow myself to be humbly guided by Christ's teaching through his Church?

Reader 4: **The Almighty works marvels for me: holy his name.**

How do I respond to God's holiness? Do I use God's holy name with respect? Do I live up to the name of Christian? Am I ready to stand by my Christian principles? Is my Sunday an expression of my Christian faith? Am I careless about Mass on Sundays and holy days? Do I put Sunday to good use or do I waste it in self-indulgence?

94 **Reader 5:** **His mercy is from age to age, on those who fear him.**

Do I reflect the mercy, tolerance and tenderness of God? Do I try to bring happiness to my family and to those around me? Do I give way to anger? Do I indulge in selfish moods? Do I seek revenge? Do I refuse to forgive? Do I use or condone violence, intimidation, threats or bullying? Do I lead others into sin?

Reader 6: **He puts forth his arm in strength and scatters the proud-hearted.**

Do I live a pretence? Do I tell lies? Have I been truthful in my dealings with others – with members of my family and with my friends? Do I keep my promises? Do I respect confidential information? Do I avoid pretence in my conversation and style of life? Have I tried to overcome prejudice, resentment and dislike of others? Have I injured my neighbour by malicious gossip and slander?

Reader 7: **He casts the mighty from their thrones and raises the lowly.**

Do I condone and bolster unfair structures? Do I work for fair play, harmony and reconciliation?

Reader 8: **He fills the starving with good things, sends the rich away empty.**

Have I stolen? Have I deliberately damaged property by vandalism, waste, neglect? Have I been selfish in refusing my time to those who look to me for help? Have I been jealous of another's possessions or success? Do I contribute to causes and organisations which work for a world where everyone will have enough?

Leader: For all that we have done wrong we are truly sorry. We pray to Mary the mother of God to help us as we try to live our lives as Jesus taught us.

All: Mary the dawn, Christ the perfect Day;
Mary the gate, Christ the heavenly Way;
Mary the root, Christ the Mystic Vine;
Mary the grape, Christ the Sacred Wine;
Mary the wheat, Christ the Living Bread;
Mary the stem, Christ the Rose, Blood Red;
Mary the font, Christ the Cleansing Flood;
Mary the cup, Christ the Precious Blood;
Mary the temple, Christ the Temple's Lord;
Mary the shrine, Christ the God Adored;
Mary the beacon, Christ the Haven's Rest;
Mary the mirror, Christ the Vision Blest;
Mary the mother, Christ the Mother's son;
By whom are all things blessed while endless ages run.

Leader: Let us pray that through Mary we might see the will of God more clearly.

All: Hail Mary, full of grace,
The Lord is with you.
Blessed are you among women
and blessed is the fruit of your womb, Jesus.
Holy Mary, mother of God,
Pray for us sinners,
Now and at the hour of our death.
Amen.

Do the Looking Back exercises for Unit Two at the back of this book.

LOOKING BACK

Unit Three
Lesson Nine

Matthew's Gospel

The Development of the Gospels

Where does Matthew's Gospel fit in?

Stage One

AD 30   33

Public Life, Death and Resurrection of Jesus

Stage Two

AD 40   50   60

The early Church gathers. The first missionary work of the Church takes place when St Paul and the other apostles preach the Good News to people around the Mediterranean. Stories and sayings of Jesus are recalled, retold and collected.

Stage Three

AD 70   80   90   100

Mark's Gospel, the first gospel, is written. Matthew's Gospel and Luke's Gospel are gradually put together during this period. The last of the four gospels, John's Gospel, is written.

Matthew's Gospel was written for Jews who converted to Christianity. Matthew himself grew up in the Jewish faith and this background had a great influence on his writings. He set out in his Gospel to show that Jesus fulfilled the teachings of Moses and the Prophets. The Jewish converts for whom he was writing were familiar with the Old Testament and with the teachings of Moses and the prophets. In chapter 5:17 of Matthew's Gospel Jesus says: 'Do not think that I have come to do away with the Law of Moses and the teachings of the prophets. I have not come to do away with them but to make their teachings come true.'

He set out to show that Jesus was the promised Messiah, whom the Jews had been waiting for. His gospel is written for people who were familiar with and believed in the Jewish hopes and expectations that God would send them a saviour.

Matthew, then, is careful to link important events in the life of Jesus with Old Testament prophecies.

In *Matthew 2:15*, speaking of the return from Egypt, he says, 'This was done to make what the Lord had said through the prophet come true,' and in *Matthew 2:18*, speaking about the slaying of the infants, he says, 'In this way what the prophet Jeremiah had said came true.'

Matthew's Gospel was written at Antioch. The author used Mark's Gospel, which had already been written as a reference, but when he retold some of the incidents which are recorded in Mark's Gospel, he adapted them for a different audience.

Jesus is presented in Matthew's Gospel as a teacher. He teaches the people about the Kingdom of God or the Kingdom of Heaven.

Find in the wordsearch the words which fill in the blanks.

Matthew's Gospel was written for Jewish ___ to Christianity.
He set out to show that Jesus was the promised ___.
Matthew grew up in the ___faith.
The first gospel was written at ___.
___ wrote the last of the four gospels.
The first Christian missionary was St ___ .
Matthew's Gospel was written at ___.
Jesus is presented as a ___ in Matthew's Gospel.
Matthew linked events from the life of Jesus with the Old Testament_____ .

M	E	S	S	I	A	H	T	R	E	E
A	P	A	U	L	N	G	O	O	S	J
R	T	J	A	M	T	H	B	U	E	O
K	B	E	D	S	I	L	Y	W	C	H
O	G	S	A	F	O	K	I	L	B	N
J	Q	W	A	C	C	S	U	R	F	G
J	E	W	I	S	H	U	V	F	R	U
L	P	R	O	P	H	E	C	I	E	S
O	I	C	O	N	V	E	R	T	S	Y

Structure of Matthew's Gospel

There are three main parts in Matthew's Gospel:

The introduction 1

The main body of the gospel 2

The conclusion 3

The Introduction

This part includes chapters 1 and 2 and tells the story of the birth of Jesus.

The Body of the Gospel

This includes chapters 3 to 25. This section is itself divided into five parts which call to mind the first five books of the Old Testament, the Pentateuch. In the Pentateuch, the Law of the Jewish religion is outlined as the 'Old Law'. Matthew presents Jesus, again and again, as the one who teaches the 'New Law'. Jesus refers to the Old Law as it was written and taught and then sets out the new expectations of the 'New Law', for example, 'You have heard that people were told in the past, "Do not commit murder; anyone who does will be brought to trial," But now I tell you: whoever is angry with his brother will be brought to trial' *(5:21-22)*.

Later he teaches 'You have heard that it was said, "An eye for an eye, and a tooth for a tooth." But now I tell you: do not take revenge on someone who wrongs you. If anyone slaps you on the right cheek, let him slap your left cheek too' *(5:38-39)*.

The Kingdom of God

The content of the body of Matthew's Gospel is Jesus' teaching about the Kingdom.

Chapters 3 to 7

Jesus announces the Kingdom of God or the Kingdom of Heaven. Jesus teaches about the nature of the Kingdom.

Chapters 8 to 10

The Kingdom is preached.

Chapters 11 to 13

Exploring the Kingdom in parables

Chapters 14 to 18

Living in the Kingdom

Chapters 19 to 25

The Kingdom and conflict

The Conclusion

This part includes the passion, death and resurrection of Jesus.

The Kingdom of God or the Kingdom of Heaven

When the Jewish people thought about the coming of the Kingdom, they had in mind a time when they would be free from Roman rule. They longed for the time when they would be free to build up a kingdom which would be powerful and independent. In Matthew's Gospel Jesus teaches the people about the Kingdom of God. He helps them to understand that the Kingdom of God will come about when people live according to certain values and attitudes. In chapters 5, 6 and 7 he challenges the people to take a new look at their lifestyles and to revise their ideas about how to live good lives.

He teaches them about several different areas of their life and, in each case, he starts by reminding them of what the Law of Moses says and then goes on to point out that the New Law makes even greater demands on them.

At the beginning of this teaching he points out to them that they are to be like salt and light for the world.

Read Matthew 5:13-16.

Discuss

What does salt do for food ?
What would Jesus have meant when he said 'You are like salt for all mankind'?
What do you think Jesus meant when he said 'You are like light for the whole world'?

In Your Religion Journal

Draw two images, one to illustrate verse 13 and the other to illustrate verses 14-16.

Jesus went on to teach the people about how they should act in specific areas of their lives.

Read Matthew 5:21-7:6. Match the following references with the headings.

Anger	7:1-6
Adultery	6:19-21
Divorce	5:21-26
Vows	6:5-15
Revenge	6:24-34
Enemies	5:27-30
Charity	5:38-42
Prayer	5:31-32
Fasting	5:33-37
Riches	5:43-48
Possessions	6:1-4
Judging others	6:16-17

Find Your Group

Choose two of these teachings of Jesus. Make posters to illustrate the message of each one of them.

The Kingdom:

— has small beginnings;
— grows to huge proportions;
— is worth giving up everything for;
— demands commitment from those who belong;
— has within it good people and bad people;

Those who do not measure up to the demands of the Kingdom will be severely judged at the end of time.

Match the statements above with the parables contained in Matthew 13.

In Your Religion Journal

Write your own parable to help people to understand what the kingdom is like.

Listening without hearing!

How well do we listen?
How much do you usually remember after a class in school?
How much do you usually remember after being at Mass on Sunday?
What are the things which make you want to hear and remember what is being said?
What are the things which make you careless about listening and remembering?

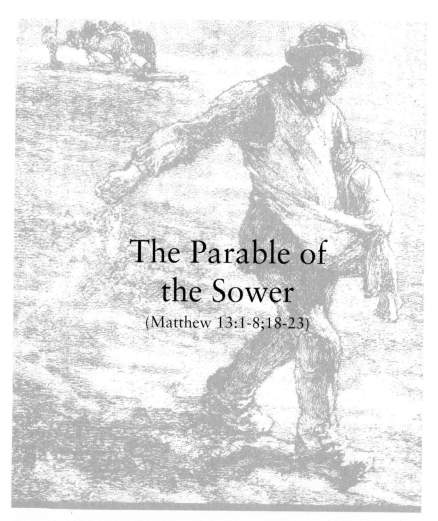

The Parable of the Sower
(Matthew 13:1-8;18-23)

That same day Jesus left the house and went to the lakeside, where he sat down to teach. The crowd that gathered round him was so large that he got into a boat and sat in it, while the crowd stood on the shore. He used parables to tell them many things. 'Once there was a man who went out to sow corn. As he scattered the seed in the field, some of it fell along the path, and the birds came and ate it up. Some of it fell on rocky ground, where there was little soil. The seeds soon sprouted, because the soil wasn't deep. But when the sun came up, it burnt the young plants; and because the roots had not grown deep enough, the plants soon dried up. Some

100

of the seed fell among thorn bushes, which grew up and choked the plants. But some seeds fell in good soil, and the plants produced corn; some produced a hundred grains, others sixty, and others thirty.'

Listen, then, and learn what the parable of the sower means. Those who hear the message about the Kingdom but do not understand it are like the seeds that fell along the path. The Evil One comes and snatches away what was sown in them. The seeds that fell on rocky ground stand for those who receive the message gladly as soon as they hear it. But it does not sink deep into them, and they don't last long. So when trouble or persecution comes because of the message, they give up at once. The seeds that fell among thorn bushes stand for those who hear the message; but the worries about this life and the love for riches choke the message, and they don't bear fruit. And the seeds sown in the good soil stand for those who hear the message and understand it: they bear fruit, some as much as a hundred, others sixty and others thirty.

Discuss

If a seed is planted in fertile soil, if it has enough moisture, light and heat it will probably grow into a mature, healthy plant. On the other hand, if it is deprived of any one of these it probably will not grow or its growth may be impaired.

Talk about places you know of where seeds grow well.

Talk about places you know of where seeds do not grow well.

Where do you usually hear the word of God?

Do you think that you want to be the kind of person who does what God wants?

Do you think that you can make an effort to be that kind of person?

Talk about times when you find it easy and times when you find it difficult.

Which kind of soil do you usually provide for the word of God – like the path, the rocky ground, the thorn bushes or the good soil?

Why do you think that this is so?

The Kingdom of Heaven is like...

Jesus searched through the ordinary everyday life of the people to find images and happenings which he could use to help them to understand what the Kingdom was like.

He then told parables using the images he had chosen. The parables were stories which helped the people to understand the messages he wanted them to hear. Stories help people to pay attention to what is being said and they also help people to understand.

In Your Religion Journal

Read Matthew 13:24-50. Draw or write down some of the images used by Jesus in these passages to help people understand more about the Kingdom of Heaven. What have you learned from each of these images?

Who belongs to the Kingdom?

Different Responses

John has just got a Christmas present from his sister. He is delighted. It's just what he wanted. He throws his arms around her and gives her a big hug to say 'Thank you'.

Michael has got a Christmas present from his sister. 'Just what I really needed,' he thinks to himself, 'I must drop her a card to say thanks.'

Paula has just got a birthday present from her brother. The family watches as she opens it. When she sees what's inside the parcel her face falls. 'Ah', she says, 'I wish you hadn't got me one of these. I really don't like them any longer.'

Sandra's birthday was last week. She was really surprised when a parcel arrived from her brother. However, when she opened it and found what was inside her face fell. It was something she neither needed nor wanted. The card she sent to her brother read, 'Thank you very much for the present. It was just what I needed'.

Discuss

Which of the above responses were most likely to have been made by a child and which by an adult? Give reasons for your answer.

Can you think of other situations where a child's actions or responses are likely to be different from those of an adult?

Who Is The Greatest?

At that time the disciples came to Jesus, asking, 'Who is the greatest in the Kingdom of Heaven?'

So Jesus called a child, made him stand in front of them, and said, 'I assure you that unless you change and become like children, you will never enter the Kingdom of Heaven. The greatest in the Kingdom of Heaven is the one who humbles himself and becomes like this child. And whoever welcomes in my name one such child as this, welcomes me' (*Matthew 18:1-5*).

Jesus Blesses Little Children

Some people brought children to Jesus for him to place his hands on them and to pray for them, but the disciples scolded the people.

102 Jesus said, 'Let the children come to me and do not stop them, because the Kingdom of Heaven belongs to such as these.'
He placed his hands on them and then went away *(Matthew 19:13-15)*.

Discuss

What do you think it is about children which prompted Jesus to point to them as people who are fit to belong to the Kingdom of Heaven?

In Your Religion Journal

Write about someone you know, whom you think fits the description of a person 'to whom the Kingdom of Heaven belongs.'

The Forgiveness of God

Discuss

Think of a time when someone forgave you for something you had done. How did you feel?

Think of a time when someone did something to you which caused you so much anger or hurt that you found it difficult or impossible to forgive that person. How did you feel then?

Jesus and Forgiveness

Then Peter came up to Jesus and asked, 'Lord, if my brother keeps on sinning against me, how many times do I have to forgive him? Seven times?'
'No, not seven times,' answered Jesus, 'but seventy times seven' *(Matthew 18:21-22)*.

Discuss

Imagine a situation where someone has offended you seven times and each time you forgive them. Then they offend you once again. Do you think that you would find it easy to continue to forgive them? Why?

What do you think of the standards which Jesus set for his followers in the area of forgiveness?

Read Matthew 18:12-14.

In Your Religion Journal

Pretend that you are the lost sheep in that story. Write down four words which describe how you feel about what happened in the story.

Read Matthew 18:23-35.

In Your Religion Journal

Having read the story of the 'Unforgiving Servant', how do you feel about the way in which you succeed and fail in forgiving those who offend you?

It is because we often find it difficult to forgive those who offend us that we find it difficult really to believe that, when we are sorry for the wrong that we have done, God always forgives us.

In Your Religion Journal

Write your own parable about the forgiveness of God.

Find Your Group

What do you think is the principal challenge for you in your own life in the extract from chapter 18 of Matthew's Gospel which you have read?

Who is Jesus?

One of the reasons why the evangelists wrote their gospels was to help us to get to know Jesus. Write out, in your religion journal, five different ways in which you would describe Jesus. Now read these words of Mother Teresa of Calcutta. How many new ways of talking about Jesus have you learned?

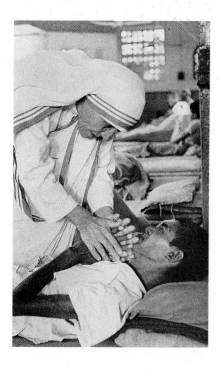

Who is Jesus to me?

Jesus is the Word made flesh.

Jesus is the Bread of Life.

Jesus is the Victim offered for our sins on the cross.

Jesus is the sacrifice offered at holy Mass for the sins of the world and for mine.

Jesus is the word – to be spoken.

Jesus is the truth – to be told.

Jesus is the way – to be walked.

Jesus is the light – to be lit.

Jesus is the life – to be lived.

Jesus is the love – to be loved.

Jesus is the joy – to be shared.

Jesus is the sacrifice – to be offered.

Jesus is the peace – to be given.

Jesus is the Bread of Life – to be fed.

Jesus is the thirsty – to be satiated.

Jesus is the naked – to be clothed.

Jesus is the homeless – to be taken in.

Jesus is the sick – to be healed.

Jesus is the lonely – to be loved.

Jesus is the unwanted – to be wanted.

Jesus is the leper – to wash his wounds.

Jesus is the beggar – to give him a smile.

Jesus is the drunkard – to listen to him.

Jesus is the mentally ill – to protect him.

Jesus is the little one – to embrace him.

Jesus is the blind – to lead him.

Jesus is the dumb – to speak for him.

Jesus is the crippled – to walk with him.

Jesus is the drug addict – to befriend him.

Jesus is the prostitute – to remove from danger and befriend her.

Jesus is the prisoner – to be visited.

Jesus is the old – to be served.

104 Read this story:

The stranger came among them in early June. He was carrying only two items by way of worldly possessions, a staff and a rucksack. However, he had only just set foot on their remote shore when he was struck down by a mysterious illness. Just before he drifted into a coma he said, 'I came to bring you the Good News.' Naturally, the words 'Good News' aroused their curiosity. But they had no way of telling what he meant, for he never recovered consciousness, and died two days later.

Only when they had buried him did they go through the contents of his rucksack. There was nothing in it to fight over – just one change of clothes and a small book. The clothes were somewhat threadbare and ill-suited to the rigours of their climate. As for the book, its edges were frayed and its cover coming apart from age and use. Absent-mindedly, somebody opened it. On the inside cover he read the title, 'The Good News'. 'Ah!' they cried, 'so this is what the stranger was talking about.' Without further ado, they began to read it.

Though the book was old, they soon realised that its message was new. The central character leaped out at them from its musty pages – a man full of vitality and strength, yet possessing great gentleness and compassion. They read accounts of amazing miracles he performed on behalf of the sick and the needy. While they were deeply moved by these, what really went straight to their hearts were the accounts of ordinary incidents, if you could so describe them. Incidents telling how he went out of his way to associate with outcasts; how he not only refused to condemn but actually pardoned a woman who had been caught committing a grave sin; and how on the eve of his death he washed the feet of his friends to show them how much he loved them. Then there was the beauty and authority of his words. For instance, his unforgettable stories, his words to a condemned criminal, and above all the so-called 'Sermon on a Hill'. What a strange and fascinating book!

'What a pity the carrier of the book died,' someone said, 'obviously he was a follower of this Christ.'

'But there must be more where he came from,' another said. 'Could we not send someone there to see how the people live this new teaching? Then he could come back, make a report, and perhaps we could try it ourselves?'

The suggestion met with the approval of all. They chose a man called Francis. Though still in his twenties, Francis was wise beyond his years. He was also keenly intelligent and a man of deep integrity. Before he set out, one of the elders of the tribe gave him the following piece of advice:

'Don't be deceived by words, son. Words are cheap. Look for deeds.'

With these words ringing in his ears Francis set out. He travelled widely and observed keenly. He went out of his way to meet as wide a cross-section of people as possible. He took his time. He didn't jump to conclusions or rush to judgment. He had many encounters.

For instance, there were the preachers he met at street corners, who vociferously claimed to speak in Christ's name. But how come they were preaching not good news but bad news? The placards they carried bore stark messages such as: 'The end of the world is nigh', and 'Judgment is at hand'. Their preaching was laced with warnings about some terrible catastrophe that was soon to fall upon the world.

Then he met others who claimed loudly that they were 'saved'. Did that, he wondered, imply that everyone else was damned? According to them the end had already come. The sheep and the goats had already been separated. But if they were saved, why did they look so gloomy?

He came across some who dismissed the Book outright, saying, 'Ah that! That's only a work of fiction. There never was such a person as Christ. He was invented by the Churches.'

And he came across a few cynics who said to him, 'Looking for the real followers of Christ, are you? You might as well look for the crock of gold at the end of the rainbow.'

He noticed as he went around that lots of people lived in the most appalling poverty, a thing almost unheard of in the country where he came from. There were people who lacked such basics as food, clothes, shelter, education and medical care. Now, according to the Book, Christ had lived a very simple life. It came as a

shock then to Francis to discover that his followers, by and large, were well-off. They lived in comfortable houses. They drove cars. They spent money, not just on necessities, but on luxuries. And while they expressed concern for their poorer brothers and sisters, and occasionally helped them out, they did not take up

The Good News

their cause and demand justice for them.

In his travels he also learned about the so-called arms race. He was puzzled to find adherents of the Book who defended it. Even a cursory glance at the Book would seem to show that Christ preached reconciliation, not confrontation. Yet some twenty centuries later his followers were preparing for a war that could easily mean the end of all life on

earth.

Finally the day came when he felt he had seen enough, so he headed for home. His return was eagerly awaited. No sooner had he arrived back than he was bombarded with questions:

'Do the adherents of the Book love one another?'

'Do they live at peace with one another?'

'Do they live simply?'

'Are they happy?' These and many other questions came at him from all angles. But all the questions could be reduced to one. All, in one way or another, were asking the same question, 'Do the followers of Christ live according to the Book?' Here, in summary, is the account he gave them of his findings.

'Basically, I found five kinds of Christians,' he began.

'Firstly, I found some who clearly are Christian in name only. They were baptised. But they adhere to none of the observances of Christianity, and have no commitment whatsoever to it.

'Secondly, I found some who are Christian by habit only. They are committed to the outward observances, but

106 even where this commitment is strong, it doesn't seem to affect the way they live.

'Thirdly, I found some who are clearly devoted to the Christian faith. They are engaged in a lot of good works. Yet a vital element seemed to be missing. They seemed to possess few if any of those qualities which made their Master so appealing.

'Fourthly, I met some whom you might call practical Christians. It seemed to me that these have grasped the heart of what the Book is about. They are obviously concerned about other people, and they are not ashamed to be seen to be Christians. In some places I saw them being persecuted, imprisoned, and even killed. In other places I saw them meeting, not so much with hostility or opposition, but with something that is probably worse – the deadly indifference of their fellow citizens.

'Lastly, I met some, admittedly not many, whom I would have no hesitation in calling the genuine article. They are people to whom their neighbour is as dear as themselves. In meeting them I felt I was meeting Christ himself. I felt I was touching him and being touched by him. By the way, they have a name for these. They call them "saints".'

'And what then is your overall judgment?' they asked when he had finished his account.

'I need some time to reflect on what I've seen,' he replied.

They gave him time. He took a week to think it over. At the end of the week he called another meeting. His judgment went like this:

'During the past week I read the Book once more, keeping in mind all I'd seen and which I related to you. I had an interesting experience which I would like to share with you.

'When I set out as your envoy, I was like a man looking for a field of golden wheat without a single weed or barren spot. But now I believe I was naïve. I took no account of human nature or of the kind of world we live in. I didn't allow for the fact that wild birds devour some of the seed as soon as it is sown. I didn't allow for the rocks which prevent the seed from sinking roots deep enough to enable it to withstand the drought. Nor did I allow for the weeds which sometimes choke the young shoots.

'Christ was an idealist. But it seems to me that he was also a realist. He knew what lies in the heart of people, and what makes the world a mixture of garden and jungle. As I re-read the Book, certain sayings of his which I had previously glossed over, now hit me for the very first time. Sayings such as, 'I did not come to call good people but bad people to repentance,' and 'I came to seek out the sheep that are lost'.

'And something else dawned on me. As I studied the little band of his chosen friends, what did I find? I found among them one who denied him, and another who betrayed him. Thus, even in the garden which he himself had tended so carefully for three whole years, the weeds persisted. Yet he didn't write the garden off.

'You don't refuse to believe in a famous brand of wine even if someone offers you a glass of it that has obviously been watered down, or that is not of a particularly good vintage. In any case, you have to drink it to tell the difference. It is easy to demand of others that they live the Book, while excusing oneself from even trying.'

'You're asking us to live the Book, then,' they said.

'I'm suggesting that you might give it a try,' he answered.

'And what about you?' they asked.

'Oh, I've already made up my mind,' he replied.

Discuss

Which of the five categories of 'Christian' do you think you belong to?

What do you think you would be doing, at home, at school, in your neighbourhood, if you decided, like Francis, to 'give it a try'?

A Time to Pray

Read quietly and reflectively what St Matthew says about prayer.

When you pray, do not be like the hypocrites! They love to stand up and pray in the houses of worship and on the street corners, so that everyone will see them. I assure you, they have already been paid in full. But when you pray, go to your room, close the door, and pray to your Father, who is unseen. And your Father, who sees what you do in private, will reward you.

When you pray, do not use a lot of meaningless words, as the pagans do, who think that their gods will hear them because their prayers are long. Do not be like them. Your Father already knows what you need before you ask him. This, then, is how you should pray:

> Our Father in heaven:
> may your holy name be honoured;
> may your Kingdom come;
> may your will be done on earth as it is in heaven.
> Give us today the food we need.
> Forgive us the wrongs we have done,
> as we forgive the wrongs that others have done to us.
> Do not bring us to hard testing,
> but keep us safe from the Evil One.

If you forgive others the wrongs they have done to you, your Father in heaven will also forgive you. But if you do not forgive others, then your Father will not forgive the wrongs you have done.

(*Matthew 6:5-15*)

Think quietly about these questions:
When do you pray?
Do you need to make more regular time in your life for prayer?
Do you need to think about the way in which you pray?

LOOKING BACK

Do the Looking Back exercises for Unit Three at the back of this book.

Advent

Prepare for the year 2050!

'D-ring'. That bell signalled the end of the school week for all at Highfield Secondary School. Mr Johnston had given out the script of the play which would be put on next April. Olivia and Carol couldn't contain their excitement. They would be joining up with the nearby boys' secondary school for the event. This play wasn't some stuffy adult play, it was a futuristic drama about school life in the year 2050 AD. Most of the year gathered outside the school gates and it was decided that everyone would get involved.

On the following Friday Mr Johnston and Ms Teeling from the boys' school called the excited chatter to order. Olivia and Carol had been practising their lines all weekend. Olivia was hoping for the leading role where she would play the 'misunderstood teenager', misunderstood by her robot-teacher. On the other hand, Carol was determined to get the part of 'Zodiac' (a futuristic hairstyle was mentioned in the character description).

The auditions were held on the Monday of the next week. They started with try-outs for the part of 'Bronco', the futuristic school idol. Most of the boys who got up on stage were all nerves, you could hear their voices shaking and their red cheeks weren't caused by the temperamental school heating system.

When John Power got up he took everyone's breath away. Olivia and Carol knew him vaguely, he hung around the local basketball courts with a gang of lads, which included Carol's brother. He wasn't exactly good-looking, but boy, could he act. Up on the stage he didn't look like the John Power they knew, cursing with the lads and wolf-whistling at any female passers-by.

Rehearsals began after school on the following Monday. Olivia didn't get the part she had hoped for, which was just as well, as she hadn't read the small print where it said she would have been the school lick as well as being misunderstood. She got a much better part as Bronco's sister. Carol got the part she had hoped for, including the hairstyle. Needless to say, John Power got the part of Bronco.

Their whole year was involved in the play in some way. Some were doing the lighting, some the scenery, others were involved in making the costumes and the stage props. There was a real buzz at rehearsals, everyone knew what they were doing and did it well, well almost everybody.

John Power or, rather, Bronco (that's all he'd answer to lately) was absolutely brilliant, when he knew his lines. Patience was growing thin when, week after week, Bronco was still reading off his script or, when Ms Teeling took that away from him, getting his mate Barry to prompt him. Barry, who didn't know what the word whisper meant, let the whole hall know how he was helping Bronco.

'I'm sick to death of John... sorry, Bronco, not knowing his lines. We've got to play that real serious scene where the 'Zinc-mobile' has malfunctioned and neither of us is going to get to the 'Satellite Zone' (or local picture house). What's the point in me learning my lines when he doesn't know his?', complained Carol to Olivia, at rehearsal one day. 'I agree, someone's got to take him in hand, he'll ruin the show and we'll be the laughing stock of the whole place', replied Olivia.

'Can I have quiet please?' exclaimed Mr Johnston, 'Unfortunately, I have to announce a change with regard to the leading part – Bronco.' There was dead silence now. 'John Power is being replaced by his understudy, Shane O'Rourke.'

John Power (safer to call him that under the circumstances) had gone a whiter shade of pale. All eyes were on him to see his reaction. Colour was coming back to his cheeks, he was shouting and then he was gone. Nobody had the heart to rehearse after that, so everyone went home early.

It was two nights before the play was opening and everything was going smoothly. Shane had all his lines word perfect, but the play really lacked the spark John was able to give it, when he *did* know his lines. He had so much talent. 'What a waste', thought Olivia to herself while she was walking home that night with Shane O'Rourke. They had talked it over and he agreed with her. He hated his part. He wanted to activate the lighting on the night. He knew he would just die on stage in front of the world.

'Mind the kerb there, Shane ', cried Olivia, too late. 'Oh no, are you all right?' 'Yeah, yeah, I'm fine, but I think I've sprained my ankle, it's killing me and I don't think I can walk on it.'

Shane's ankle was strapped up in casualty that night. Mr Johnston decided that a hop-a-long Bronco didn't quite fit the macho image, so John Power got his part back....

The whole cast, and everyone back stage, held their breath after the last line of the show was uttered. Then the applause started, and it wouldn't stop. There were cheers for Bronco, who had known and played his part brilliantly, and more clapping.

John Power (now known as John both on and off stage) went up to the mike. The crowd's clapping died down. 'I'd like you all to give a big hand to our teachers, Ms Teeling and Mr Johnston, for making this night possible, to the lighting crew, the make-up artists, to those who worked on the scenery, costumes and props, and to all who made this show such a success.'

Discuss

Describe the preparations which were involved in the school production.

How do you think the third years were feeling when John didn't know his lines?

Do you think Mr Johnston made the right decision when he replaced John Power as Bronco?

What do you think John learned from his involvement in the play?

List times when you had to prepare for something important. Explain what was involved.

How important do you think preparation is?

The Jewish people spent many years waiting for the coming of the Messiah. They pinned all their hopes on the Messiah. He would set them free, they hoped, from all the things that oppressed them. They looked forward to, hoped for, and dreamed of the time to come when things would be better. The prophets told the people that it was not sufficient simply to wait for the Messiah, that they must actively prepare for his coming.

The prophet Jeremiah said:
> See, the days are coming – it is Yahweh who speaks –
> when I am going to fulfil the promise I made to the
> House of Israel and the House of Judah:
> In those days and at that time,
> I will make a virtuous branch grow for David,
> who shall practise honesty and integrity in the land.
> In those days Judah shall be saved,
> and Israel shall dwell in confidence.
> *(Jeremiah 33:14-16)*

Discuss

Who do you think was being referred to as a virtuous branch for David? When these words were first spoken, in what way do you think they were understood?

The people were told that it would be a time of rejoicing when the Messiah would come:
> Let the wilderness and the dry-land exult,
> let the wasteland rejoice and bloom,
> let it bring forth flowers like the jonquil,
> let it rejoice and sing for joy *(Isaiah 35:1)*.

The prophets, however, also warn the people:
> Trouble is coming to the rebellious, the defiled,
> the tyrannical city!
> She would never listen to the call,
> would never learn the lesson.
> When that day comes
> you need feel no shame for all the misdeeds
> you have committed against me,
> for I will remove your proud boasters from your midst;
> and you will cease to strut
> on my holy mountain.
> *(Zephaniah 3:1; 11)*

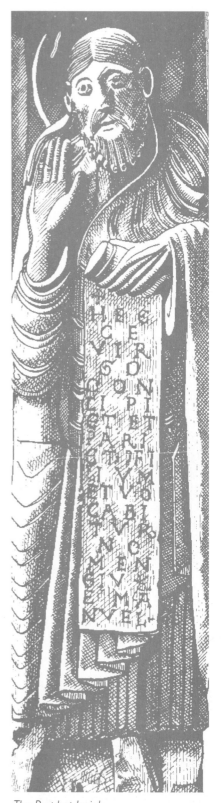

The Prophet Isaiah

Discuss

How do you think people who heard those words might have reacted?

The prophets also spoke of their expectations of the Messiah:

> The eyes of the blind shall be opened,
> the ears of the deaf unsealed,
> then the lame shall leap like a deer
> and the tongues of the dumb sing for joy.
>
> (*Isaiah 35:5-6*)

Discuss

How would you describe all the things that you would hope for for the world?

In Your Religion Journal

Describe in writing what you would most like to see happen.

• •

DRAMA

John the Baptist prepares the way for Jesus

Cantarini, St John in the Wilderness

Cast:

Samuel (Sadducee)	Jesus
Joshua (Sadducee)	God
John the Baptist	Narrator

Scene 1: Outside the temple

Narrator: At this time John the Baptist was preaching and baptising in the River Jordan. This activity angered some, others were excited, all were curious.

Samuel: Why don't we go down to the River Jordan to hear that preacher, John the Baptist?

Joshua: What, go down there and be seen with that lunatic who's turning all the people against us?

Samuel: I just think we should at least go and hear what he's filling people's heads with.

Joshua: I don't know.

Samuel: There's no point in us condemning him until we hear what he's about.

Joshua: Okay, just remember it wasn't my idea.

Scene 2: At the River Jordan

Narrator: The scene at the River Jordan was a sight to behold. There were people crowded around the river in droves. There were people in the water queuing. John the

Baptist was among them up to his waist in water. John was urging the people to turn away from their sins because the Kingdom of God was near. After the people confessed their sins they were totally immersed in water.

Joshua: Would you look at this? It just proves my theory that if you give people an easy option they're all suckers.

Samuel: Maybe there's something to this guy. Let's go and have a closer look.

Narrator: The two Sadducees went to have a closer look. They joined the crowd queuing to be baptised by John the Baptist.

Samuel: This scene reminds me of the way I had pictured Isaiah's prophecy about the Messiah in my head:
'A voice cries out, Prepare in the wilderness a road for the Lord, Clear the way in the desert for our God.'

Joshua: Surely you cannot mention the prophet Isaiah, our God and the Messiah in the same breath as this lunatic?

Samuel: Is he a lunatic?

Joshua: My ears must be deceiving me. What you've imagined is coincidence. All this guy is doing is brain-washing.

Samuel: Brain-washing or not, he has people coming from all corners of the province.

Narrator: It was then that John the Baptist's eyes came to rest on the two Sadducees.

John the Baptist: You snakes – who told you that you could escape from the punishment God is about to send? Do those things that will show you have turned from your sins. And don't think you can escape punishment by saying that Abraham is you ancestor. I tell you that God can take these stones and make descendants for Abraham! The axe is ready to cut down the trees at the roots; every tree that does not bear good fruit will be cut down and thrown in the fire...

Joshua: How dare you insult a Sadducee? Do you know what you're saying? May God strike you down for such blasphemy...

Samuel: Leave it, Joshua, do not sink to the level of heathens. Let's get out of here.

Narrator: However shocked the crowds were at this confrontation, more startling events were to happen.

John the Baptist: I baptise you with water to show that you have repented, but the one who will come after me will baptise you with the Holy Spirit and fire. He is much greater than I am: and I am not good enough even to carry his sandals. He has his winnowing shovel with him to thresh out all the grain. He will gather his wheat into his barn, but he will burn the chaff in a fire that never goes out.

Narrator: These words heightened the anticipation of the people listening. John continued baptising until he came to one man who had come with a group of friends.

John the Baptist: What am I doing? I cannot baptise you. I ought to be baptised by you.

Jesus: Let it be so for now. For in this way we shall do all that God requires.

Narrator: At this point John agreed to baptise this man. It was then that an extraordinary thing happened. As soon as the man came out of the water heaven was opened, and the Spirit of God came down on him like a dove. Then there was a voice which seemed to come from above...

God: This is my own dear Son, with whom I am pleased.

Scene 3: At the prison where John the Baptist was being held

Narrator: Some time after Jesus

was baptised in the River Jordan, John the Baptist was imprisoned. He kept up with the activities of Jesus through his friends. When he heard of all that Jesus was doing he became concerned and wanted to know if Jesus was the one he had spent his life preparing for.

John the Baptist: Listen, David, I want you to go to Jesus of Nazareth and ask him if he is the real thing or is there another to come after him. I've got to know. It has been preying on my mind. I can think about nothing else.

David: Of course, that's no problem, there's a lot like you who'd like to know the truth about this man.

Scene 4: The place where Jesus was preaching

Narrator: David travelled to where Jesus was with his twelve disciples.

David: Tell us, are you the one John said was going to come, or should we expect someone else?

Jesus: Go back and tell John what you are hearing and seeing: the blind can see, the lame can walk, those who suffer from dreaded skin diseases are made clean, the deaf hear, the dead are brought back to life, and the Good News is preached to the poor. How happy are those who have no doubts about me!

Narrator: David seemed satisfied with this and so went back to John in prison. The rest of the crowd still looked at Jesus as if he was from another world!

Jesus: When you went out to John in the desert, what did you expect to see? A blade of grass bending in the wind? What did you go out to see? A man dressed up in fancy clothes? People who dress like that live in palaces! Tell me, what did you go out to see? A prophet? Yes, indeed, but you saw much more than a prophet. For John is the one of whom the scripture says: 'God said, I will send my messenger ahead of you to open the way for you.' I assure you that John the Baptist is greater than any man who has ever lived. But he who is least in the Kingdom of heaven is greater than John. From the time John preached his message until this very day the Kingdom of heaven has suffered violent attacks, and violent men try to seize it. Until the time of John all the prophets spoke about the Kingdom; and if you are willing to believe their message, John is the one called Elijah, whose coming was predicted by the prophets. Listen, then, if you have ears!

Narrator: The crowds were listening now but they still only half-believed what he said.

Jesus: Now, to what can I compare the people of this day? They are like children sitting in the market-place. One group shouts to the other, 'We played wedding music for you, but you wouldn't dance! We sang funeral songs, but you wouldn't cry!' When John came, he fasted and drank no wine, and everyone said, 'He has a demon in him!' When the Son of Man came, he ate and drank, and everyone said, 'Look at this man! He is a glutton and a drinker, a friend of tax collectors and other outcasts!' God's wisdom, however, is shown to be true by its results.

Discuss

Why do you think the Sadducees were sceptical, even angered by John the Baptist?

Since the Jewish people had been hoping for the Messiah for many years, why was it that they failed to accept and believe in Jesus when he came?

The strengthening sun filters into the passage at Newgrange

The Beginning of the Church's Year

The Church has its own calendar, and in the Church's calendar the new year begins with the first Sunday of Advent. Advent is a special time of preparation for Christmas. Christmas itself was not celebrated until four centuries after Christ's birth. However, the time of year was celebrated by pagans before that. It was believed that in the world there was a great cosmic struggle between the powers of darkness and the powers of light. It was as if they were watching two great cosmic wrestlers and every once in a while they would see that the wrestler called darkness would pin down the light and almost defeat it. They noticed this because the days at this time of the year were getting shorter. If they were getting shorter that meant that the light, or the sun, was getting weaker. And they were afraid that some day darkness might even kill the sun and the light.

When 21 December came they noticed that the tables began to turn, and that the sun was regaining its strength (just like wounded heroes in those old cowboy movies we see).

They noticed that the sun suddenly seemed to get a second wind and began to push darkness off. Around 21 December the days started to get longer. It meant that darkness was getting weaker and the sun was getting stronger. When this happened, the pagans celebrated the transition time from darkness to light. It was the sun feast.
Christians took over this pagan celebration.

They said, 'Perhaps we could adapt this celebration of the sun feast and celebrate the fact that Jesus, the light of the world, overcame the darkness of sin and death'. So they called this time Christmas, and they made Advent the time for considering an end to the darkness of sin and evil and looking forward to the coming light of Christ in the world.

That light first shone when Jesus was born in Bethlehem; it still shines in those who receive him into their lives; it will shine in its full brightness when Jesus comes again at the end of time and God's plan for Creation is completed. In Advent we prepare to celebrate the first coming of Jesus at Christmas, so that we may be ready to receive him into our hearts throughout our lives, and so be prepared to welcome him, when he comes again in glory.

Discuss

Do you think the pagan festival of the victory of light over darkness is a good basis for an understanding of Advent and Christmas?
What are the signs of the tide of darkness in the world today?
What are the signs of the coming of the light of Christ in the world today?

In Your Religion Journal

What is the darkness in your life at present?
What do you most need to overcome?
What do you think is the greatest source of darkness in the world?
How do you think this can be overcome?
Can you do anything, even something small, to help this to happen?

This Christmas, if Christ is to come into the world, it will be through his coming into the hearts of those who believe in him.

Are you ready to welcome Christ into your heart this Christmas?

Advent is the time the Church has set aside for preparation.

How can you prepare?

Research

Look up these Bible references about the final coming of Christ into the world at the end of time.

Matthew 24:37-44
Matthew 25:31-46
Mark 13:24-27
John 14:1-7
Thessalonians 4:13-18
Revelation 7:1-17

What is your impression of what the final coming of Christ will be like?

Write about this in your religion journal.

Activity

The Jewish people dreamed of the time when Christ would come into the world and all their hopes would be fulfilled.

Read these accounts given by two people of their dreams for the future:

To dream the impossible dream,
to fight the unbeatable foe,
to bear with unbearable sorrow,
to run where the brave dare not go,
to right the unrightable wrong,
to love, pure and chaste, from afar,
to try when your arms are too weary,
to reach the unreachable star.
This is my quest
to follow that star,
no matter how hopeless,
no matter how far,
to fight for the right,
without question or pause,
to be willing to march into hell
for a heavenly cause.
And I know if I'll only be true
to this glorious quest,
that my heart will lie peaceful and still,
when I'm called to my rest.
And the world will be better for this
that one man, scorned and covered with scars,
still strove, with his last ounce of courage,
to reach the unreachable stars.

– Don Quixote in *The Man of La Mancha*

The following is an extract from a speech made by Martin Luther King on 28 August 1963 about his dream for the future:

I have a dream that one day on the red hills of Georgia the sons of former slaves and the sons of former slaveowners will be able to sit down together at the table of brotherhood.

I have a dream that one day even the state of Mississippi, a desert state sweltering with the heat of injustice and oppression, will be transformed into an oasis of freedom and justice.

I have a dream that my four little children will one day live in a nation where they will not be judged by the color of their skin but by the content of their character.

I have a dream today.
I have a dream that one day the state of Alabama will be transformed into a situation where little black boys and black girls will be able to join hands with little white boys and white girls and walk together as sisters and brothers.

I have a dream today.
I have a dream that one day every valley shall be exalted, every hill and mountain shall be made low, the rough places will be made plain, and the crooked places will be made straight, and the glory of the Lord shall be revealed, and all flesh shall see it together.

And if America is to be a great nation this must become true. So let freedom ring from the prodigious hilltops of New Hampshire. Let freedom ring from the mighty mountains of New York. Let freedom ring from the heightening Alleghenies of Pennsylvania!

When we let freedom ring, when we let it ring from every village and every hamlet, from every state and every city, we will be able to speed up that day when all of God's children, black men and white men, Jews and Gentiles, Protestants and Catholics, will be able to join hands and sing, in the words of that old Negro spiritual,
'Free at last! Free at last!
Thank God Almighty, we are free at last!'

Find Your Group
Discuss

Are there any parts of these dreams which you identify with in a particular way?
What, if anything, have they got in common?
What are the differences between them?
If someone were to put together the dreams of the world today do you think that any of the ideas contained in these dreams would be included?

In Your Religion Journal
Write down your own dreams for yourself, for your family, for your country, for the world.

Find Your Group
Discuss what you can do right now to ensure that your dreams for the future come true.
What can you do during this Advent?

Prayer Service

Opening hymn: O come, o come Emmanuel

Leader:
> We have begun our Advent journey. A journey where we will meet the one who came to live among us. We gather together with hope, love and courage so that we might be prepared for the coming of the light of the world.

Reader 1:
> Isaiah 2:2-4
>
> In the days to come the mountain where the Temple stands will be the highest one of all, towering above all the hills. Many nations will come streaming to it, and their people will say, 'Let us go up the hill of the Lord, to the Temple of Israel's God. He will teach us what he wants us to do; we will walk in the paths he has chosen. For the Lord's teaching comes from Jerusalem; from Zion he speaks to his people.' He will settle disputes among great nations. They will hammer their swords into ploughs and their spears into pruning-knives. Nations will never again go to war, never prepare for battle again.

The first purple candle on the Advent wreath is lit.

Reader 2:
> This candle is a symbol of our preparation for the light of Christ which will come into the world. Are you ready to bring the light of Christ into the world this Christmas?

Reader 3:

Open my eyes!
Walking in the darkness is hard!
We turn the wrong way
and bump into things.
We feel our way and stumble.
Lord, I know that you are there!
So bring your light closer
to guide my steps.
Open my eyes!

Picking someone out
of a crowd is hard
amidst the Christmas bustle.
Lord, I know you are there!
So show me your face
so I can come towards you.
Open my eyes!

Forgiving is hard
when we are angry.
It is as though a deep valley
has come between us.
Lord, I know that you are there!
So build a bridge between us
so we can learn
to love one another.
Open my eyes!

And my eyes will be enlightened
and I will see you
everywhere, every day.

Reader 4:
Matthew 11: 2-12

When John the Baptist heard in
prison about the things that
Christ was doing, he sent some
of his disciples to him. 'Tell us,'
they asked Jesus, 'are you the
one John said was going to
come, or should we expect
someone else?'

Jesus answered, 'Go back and
tell John what you are hearing
and seeing: the blind can see,
the lame can walk, those who
suffer from dreaded skin-diseases
are made clean, the deaf hear,
the dead are brought back to
life, and the Good News is
preached to the poor. How
happy are those who have no
doubts about me!'

While John's disciples were
leaving, Jesus spoke about him
to the crowds: 'When you went
out to John in the desert, what
did you expect to see? A blade
of grass bending in the wind?
What did you go out to see? A
man dressed up in fancy clothes?
People who dress like that live
in palaces! Tell me, what did
you go out to see? A prophet?
Yes, indeed, but you saw much
more than a prophet. For John
is the one of whom the scripture
says: 'God said, I will send my
messenger ahead of you to open
the way for you.' I assure you
that John the Baptist is greater
than any man who has ever
lived. But he who is least in the
Kingdom of heaven is greater
than John. From the time John
preached his message until this
very day the Kingdom of heaven
has suffered violent attacks and
violent men try to seize it.

Option: Act out the drama
John the Baptist prepares the way
for Jesus.

Leader:
Let us go out into the world
and, like John the Baptist, spread
the Good News of the coming of
the light of the world. Let all the
barriers that harden our hearts
melt away and all the differences that divide us disappear.

All: Amen

Final hymn: The Light of Christ

Making Your Own Advent Wreath

What you'll need:

6 to 8 evergreen boughs, all between
6" and 12" long
A wire coat-hanger
Green covered wire to bind the leaves
Three purple candles
One pink or rose-coloured candle
Small candle holders or four lumps of
clay that can be formed into low can-
dle holders
A red ribbon

Directions:

1. Shape the coat-hanger into a circle. Bend the hook towards the
   inside of the circle or clip it
   off.
2. Fasten the evergreen to the coat
   hanger with the green covered
   wire until you have a wreath.
3. Wind the red ribbon around the
   wreath.
4. Put the candles into the holders
   and place the candles in the
   wreath.

Christmas

Christmas Eve in the Simon Community

There was left-over food coming in from all sides. We couldn't get enough transport for all the offers. The shops had closed and wouldn't be open until the 28th December so it was useless merchandise off their hands. There was a huge iced Christmas cake, which had been made especially for the Community and which was given a central place.

It seemed like any other night, although you could sense the festivity in the air, even if it was only because the smell of stale alcohol was stronger than usual. One of the co-workers had brought in a guitar and a sing-a-long session started in the kitchen. Even some of the lads, who usually remained glued to the TV, joined in – who could resist Christmas carols?

Somehow the loneliness that was plain to be seen on the faces of the lads didn't seem so obvious or so sad when mince pies were being passed around and 'Joy to the World' was being sung. The shelter was busier than usual. More people were drawn in than was usual on a mild night. But there were also those who didn't want a part of the makeshift festivities. I didn't blame them either – the tree in the corner, the rich food, all reeked of society's crumbs.

Lily had a present for me – an opened box of chocolates – she wanted the box back, it was much-sought-after paper (that and a pen were her only means of communication). We ate the last of the chocolates between us and I persuaded her to come out to the kitchen; even though she couldn't hear the singing, she could at least see the happy faces.

That night is both one of my happiest memories and my saddest memories of my work with the Simon Community.

(A personal account by a Simon Community night shelter co-worker)

Discuss

What is your reaction to the Christmas Eve scene described by the co-worker in the Simon Community?

Why do you think the co-worker called the festivities 'makeshift'?

What do you think the co-worker meant by 'society's crumbs'?

Why do you think this night was both one of the happiest and the saddest memories the co-worker had of the time she spent working in the Simon Community?

How does this Christmas Eve scene compare to Christmas Eve in your house or in your friends' houses?

Describe what you think it would be like to spend the season of Advent and Christmas on the streets.

QUIZ YOURSELF ON THE FACTS OF THE CHRISTMAS STORY

Who was the Roman Emperor two thousand years ago?

In what province was Jesus born?

Who was the Governor of Syria when Mary and Joseph travelled to Bethlehem?

Why were Mary and Joseph travelling to Bethlehem?

Why did Joseph go to Bethlehem when he was from Nazareth?

What does the word 'Jesus' mean?

Why did the shepherds go to see the infant Jesus?

Why did the Magi travel to Bethlehem?

Can you remember from last year the traditional names of the Magi?

Why did Mary and Joseph go the long way home?

Each number in the grid represents a letter. Solve the clues and then transfer the letters to their numbered places in the grid. When you have completed the puzzle, the letters in the grid will spell a phrase to do with Christmas.

1	2	3	4	5		6	7	8		
9	10	11	12	13	14	15	16		17	18
19	20	21		22	23	24	25	26	27	

— Rational: 21 — 11 — 9 — 14 — 4 — 6 — 15

— Fall, overturn: 17 — 10 — 25 — 1 — 20 — 5

— Early morning dampness: 8 — 27 —13

— Good bargain: 12 — 23 —19 —16

— Frank, uncovered: 18 — 22 — 2 — 7

— An excuse, a claim, a defendant's answer: 22 — 26 — 2 — 3

— Opposite of off: 24 — 7

URGENT WARNING:

BEWARE OF GATE-CRASHERS THIS CHRISTMAS!

Invitation to Christmas Celebrations

Date: The fourth Sunday before 25 December

Place: Your local parish community

Essential requirements: Answer the following questions:

a. What were the Jews' expectations of the Messiah?

b. What difference does the birth of Christ make to the world?

c. What difference does the birth of Christ make to your life?

d. Why do you want to participate in the Christmas celebrations this year? (Give your answer in less than twenty words.)

What do you think this statement might mean?

Sometimes we look forward to Christmas without asking what all the fuss is about. Who is this person who has the whole world celebrating his birthday? These are not just any celebrations; people exchange gifts, they sing songs which most of us know, they go to Mass... it goes on and on right up until January. We've often heard the comments that are made at Christmas time: 'Nineteen shopping days left'; 'What are you getting for Christmas?'; 'A good excuse to eat and drink too much'; 'A load of sentimental rubbish'.

In some ways these comments show us how Christmas can be gate-crashed by people who are not answering the right invitation.

The Incarnation

The Incarnation is the word used to describe how God became man in Jesus. 'The Word was made flesh and lived among us' (*John 1:14*). Jesus is the Word. The Word existed from the beginning of time, the Word became man in Jesus. In John's Gospel we read 'In the beginning was the Word. The Word was with God and the Word was God' (*John 1:1-2*). Jesus was a real person. Those around him could talk to him, could touch him and could love him.

The meaning of the Incarnation for us today is that Jesus Christ is really present in our world. The Incarnation happened two thousand years ago, but it is also a real challenge for us today. When we live as Jesus calls us to, we are the Body of Christ in the world

122

and through us Jesus Christ is present in the world today.

This Christmas Christ's presence in the world can be shown through us.

During the season of Advent and Christmas, we make a renewed effort to make Christ's values our own, to recognise Christ's living presence in the world around us and in all the people we come in contact with.

Discuss

What kind of things would you have to do in order to make Christ's presence real in the world today? In your own family? In your school? In your neighbourhood?

In Your Religion Journal

Write down three things you are going to do this Advent to prepare for the coming of Christ into the world, one at home, one at school, one with your friends.

Activity

Read Matthew 1:1-17. Which of the people mentioned in this genealogy of Jesus have you heard about before?

Granacci, The Holy Family with St John the Baptist

One Solitary Life

He was born in a stable,
in an obscure village,
the child of a peasant woman.
He worked in a carpenter's shop until he
was thirty.
From there he travelled,
less than two hundred miles.

He never wrote a book.
He never held office.
He never had a family or owned a home.
He did none of the things one usually associates
  with greatness.

He became a nomadic preacher.
He was only thirty-three when the tide of
popular opinion turned against him,
he was betrayed by a close friend,
and his other friends ran away.
He was turned over to his enemies
and went through the mockery of a trial.
He was unjustly condemned to death,
crucified on a cross between two thieves,
on a hill overlooking the town dump,
and, when dead, was laid in a borrowed grave,
through the pity of a friend.

Nineteen centuries have come and gone,
all the armies that ever marched,
all the navies that ever sailed,
all the parliaments that ever sat,
and all the kings that ever reigned
have not affected the life of man on this earth
as that One Solitary Life.

He is the central figure of the human race,
He is the Messiah,
the Son of God,
JESUS CHRIST.

Discuss

What do you think is the important message
in this reflection?

The Jews at the time of Jesus had long been expecting
a messiah to come to free them from Roman rule.
Many of them rejected Jesus because he was a
Nazarene, a carpenter's son, and he was born in a
stable. He was not a king, a powerful person in the
worldly sense. Do you think Jesus would be rejected
today for the same reasons?

The following is a song written to show that perhaps
Christ wouldn't be so welcome today if he didn't
match our expectations of what he should look like,
what he should say and do, or where he should be
born, etc.

Standing in the Rain

1. No use knocking on the window.
There is nothing we can do, sir.
All the beds are booked already.
There is nothing left for you, sir.

Chorus   Standing in the rain,
         knocking on the window,
         knocking on the window
         on a Christmas day.
         There he is again,
         knocking on the window,
         knocking on the window
         in the same old way.

2. No use knocking on the window.
Some are lucky, some are not, sir.
We are Christian men and women,
but we're keeping what we've got, sir.

3. No, we haven't got a manger,
No, we haven't got a stable.
We are Christian men and women,
always willing, never able.

4. Jesus Christ has gone to heaven.
One day he'll be coming back, sir.
In this house he will be welcome,
but we hope he won't be black, sir.

5. Wishing you a merry Christmas.
We will now go back to bed, sir!
Till you woke us with your knocking,
we were sleeping like the dead, sir.

Discuss

What is your
reaction to
this song?
Do you
agree/disagree
with what is
being said in
the song? Give
reasons for
your answer.

Christmas as celebrated in other cultures:

Filipino Family

Perhaps no activity brings out the family unity as much as the nine-day novena before Christmas when even the children rise early and attend the 4 a.m. Misa de Gallo. Families pause for socials after the Mass as they buy some choice foods.

After they attend Midnight Mass, the celebration of Christmas is finished, since they have no big meal to look forward to and no gifts to exchange. They share each other's presence.

Discuss

Do you think the Christmas celebrations of a Filipino family are short-lived?
Do you think the Christmas celebrations of a Filipino family bring out the real meaning of 'Christ's Mass'? Explain.

Research

Find out all you can about Christmas celebrations in other cultures. Make a wall chart illustrating what you have discovered.

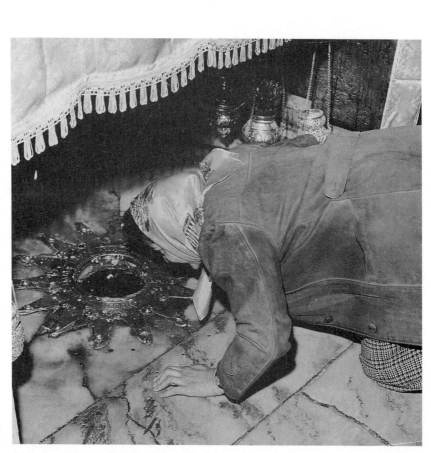

Praying at the site of Jesus' birth in Bethlehem

Where Christ was born

In Hebrew, Bethlehem means 'House of Bread'. Its Arabic name is Beit Lahm or 'House of Meat'. Often mentioned in the Bible, it was the scene of the love story of Ruth and Boaz, as told in the Book of Ruth. It is more famous as the birthplace of King David and, above all, of Christ.

About six miles south of Jerusalem, Bethlehem stands on a 2,500-foot-high ridge of the Judaean highlands. Some 30,000 people, mostly Arabs – of whom ten per cent are Christians – live there today. Many of the streets are narrow and lined with well-built, flat-roofed houses.

The first Church of the Nativity was a basilica built here by Constantine, the first Christian Roman Emperor, in 326. It was badly damaged during the Samaritan revolt in 529 and was rebuilt soon after by the Emperor Justinian. Restored by the Crusaders in the twelfth century, it still stands today. It is now shared by the following Churches: Armenian, Catholic, Coptic, Greek and Syrian Orthodox. Disputes about possession of its sanctuary and about which Church has precedence in worship there have unfortunately often led to disorderly scenes up to recent times.

Every year millions of Christians come to worship there. To attend the Christmas liturgy in the Church of the Nativity is indeed an unforgettable experience. Catholics and other western Christians celebrate Christmas there on 25 December, but the Eastern Orthodox Churches do so on 7 January and the Armenian Church on 18 January.

Those who have attended the Christmas celebrations in Bethlehem say that there is something about the Christmas atmosphere which hovers over all of Bethlehem, something which overshadows all the hubbub and commercialisation, which invites us to reflect on the meaning of the 'peace' and 'joy' that the Son of God brought us here.

Discuss

Why do you think millions of Chirstians come to Bethlehem every year to attend the Christmas liturgy? What do you think the writer means by 'something which overshadows all the hubbub and commercialisation'?

The Three Wise Men from the East

Matthew's Gospel is the only one where we find the story of the visit of the three wise men from the East.

Matthew 2:1-18

Jesus was born in the town of Bethlehem in Judaea, during the time when Herod was king. Soon afterwards, some men who studied the stars came from the east to Jerusalem and asked, 'Where is the baby born to be the king of the Jews? We saw his star when it came up in the east, and we have come to worship him.'

When King Herod heard about this he was very upset, and so was everyone else in Jerusalem. He called together all the chief priests and the teachers of the Law and asked them, 'Where will the Messiah be born?'

'In the town of Bethlehem in Judaea,' they answered. 'For this is what the prophet wrote: "Bethlehem in the land of Judah, you are by no means the least of the leading cities of Judah; for from you will come a leader who will guide my people Israel." '

So Herod called the visitors from the east to a secret meeting and found out from them the exact time the star had appeared. Then he sent them to Bethlehem with these instructions: 'Go and make a careful search for the child, and when you find him, let me know, so that I too may go and worship him.'

And so they left, and on their way they saw the same star they had seen in the east. When they saw it, how happy they were, what joy was theirs! It went ahead of them until it stopped over the place where the child was. They went into the house, and when they saw the child with his mother, Mary, they knelt down and worshipped him. They brought out their gifts of gold, frankincense and myrrh, and presented them to him.

Then they returned to their country by another road, since God had warned them in a dream not to go back to Herod.

After they had left, an angel of the Lord appeared in a dream to Joseph and said, 'Herod will be looking for the child in order to kill him. So get up, take the child and his mother and escape to Egypt, and stay there until I tell you to leave.'

Joseph got up, took the child and his mother, and left during the night for Egypt, where he stayed until Herod died. This was done to make what the Lord had said through the prophet come true, 'I called my Son out of Egypt.'

Discuss

What type of men do you think the men who studied the stars were?
Why do you think Herod was upset when he heard there was a baby born who would become king of the Jews?
Do you think Herod really wanted to worship the child? Why?
Why do you think Matthew was sufficiently convinced of the importance of the story of the three men to have included it in his Gospel?

In Your Religion Journal

Give examples of times when you were convinced that you were doing the right thing but when the end result was not what you expected.

History of the Magi

How did the 'men who studied the stars' and 'came from the east' become the three wise kings?

At first the men from the east were portrayed as astrologers. During the sixth century mosaics of Ravenna gave them the names Balthasar, Melchior and Caspar. At around the same time they were first referred to as 'kings'. Many think this came from a reference to kings in Psalm 72. Up until the twelfth century they were portrayed as identical figures. However, in the twelfth century they were given individual characteristics representing the three stages of life: youth, middle age and old age, and the three known continents of the world: Asia, Africa and Europe. Legend has it that the three men died in Armenia in 54AD while they were there for Christmas Mass. By this time they were all over one hundred years old. Their gifts also came to have different purposes: gold was given as a symbol of kingship; incense was a sign of divinity and myrrh was said to be a prophecy of the Passion. St Bernard interpreted the meaning of the gifts in a different way: gold represented money for the poor; incense was brought to disinfect the stable and myrrh was given as a useful remedy for worms in children.

Activity

Find a partner. Take on two roles, A and B. A is on the way to celebrate Midnight Mass this Christmas. B is one of the wise men, who has arrived back on earth. He meets A and the following conversation starts:

A — Excuse me. I'm a stranger. Could you tell me where everyone is going?

B — We're on the way to Midnight Mass of course!

Finish the conversation.

Activities

Look up Psalm 72 in your bible.
Draw or describe how you picture the three men in your mind.

The Three Wise Men and Christmas Today

What does this story mean for us today?

1. The Magi saw a star. For them this was of great significance. They were compelled to follow this particular star. They saw it as a calling from God. The star was calling them to set out on a journey to find the Messiah – it was a journey of faith. They had no idea where or how this journey would end. We also are called to set out on a journey of faith.

The men from the East had to follow the light of the star. Throughout our journey we too must always seek and be faithful to the light. The light can be seen in many different ways in our world. We see it in the people who are trying to live as Jesus asked us to. When Jesus was on earth he had a special care and concern for all those who were oppressed. If we want to be faithful to the light of Christ in the world today we must also seek to help those who are oppressed to change their situation.

2. The Magi did not travel alone. They travelled together. Throughout our faith journey we

128

travel with others, our family, friends and parish community. Our faith is nourished when we pray together and when we get involved in all sorts of work for the good of others and of the world we live in.

3. King Herod can be seen as the type of ruler who controls and deceives. This type of ruler is more dangerous than a dictator. A dictator is up-front about her/his intentions, whereas Herod pretended to be religious when all he really wanted to do was kill Christ. In today's world Herod can be seen in all those who try to manipulate and put down those people who try to live the message of the Gospel. We need to see through any kind of manipulation that threatens the message of Christ.

4. The Magi entered 'the house' and 'saw the child with his mother, Mary'. Where do we find Christ today? In what situations do we see Christ's presence at work? Where do we try to make Christ's real presence felt in our lives and in the lives of others? Where would you look in today's world to discover what Christ is like?

5. One purpose of the journey which the Magi made was to offer gifts. Everyone has a gift to offer the world for the sake of others. What gift can you offer the world?

6. For all their learning the wise men were totally unaware of how Herod was tricking them until they had their dream. We must take a look at all our thoughts and actions – have we any misconceptions? Do we need to take a closer look to discover the meaning behind the things we do and say?

7. The Magi returned 'another way'. Very often, if we want to be Christians we must search for another way – a way other than that which is presented to us by the world. Can you think of any situation where you need to search for another way?

Activity

Match up the letters with the numbers:

1. Magi see a star	a. What do the things we say and do mean?
2. Magi travel together	b. Where do we find Christ today?
3. King Herod	c. Symbol of calling
4. Magi enter the house	d. Where do we find today's alternative?
5. Magi offer gifts	e. Faith nourished by others
6. Magi unaware of trick	f. Manipulates the gospel message
7. Magi go another way	g. Give for the sake of others

Read Alan's reflections on the Magi as he lies in his hospital bed. Perhaps you could do this at home.

The Magi

My name is Alan – in case you didn't know. I just want to talk with you. In ordinary language if you don't mind. Okay?

I feel happy tonight, Lord. Don't know why, but it's a nice feeling and it's sort of new to me. I want to tell you about something that happened to me the other night. As I lay on my bed I was looking up at the ceiling. I've been doing a lot of that lately. My bed is a hospital bed. But more about that later.

Anyway, that night I closed my eyes and, perhaps because Christmas is coming, I found myself thinking about the Magi. Suddenly I began to envy them. They had everything going for them – not just the camels! How could they possibly go astray with that bright star to guide them, radar-like, to your crib? They could rest up during the heat of the day and travel in the cool of the evening and night. All they had to do was follow that star. Could anything be simpler?

Lord, let me tell you something. If I was relying on the stars I'd never have found you. You see, I grew up in the heart of the city. At night I was blinded by the street lights and driven to distraction by the winking of multi-coloured neon lights. So how could I be interested in the stars when I couldn't even see them? To tell you the truth I scarcely ever looked at the sky, though one of my teachers used to call me a star-gazer because I spent so much time looking out the window day-dreaming.

In any case, I couldn't tell one star from the next. For years I thought the Milky Way was a bar of chocolate. And I'm not into horoscopes either. I feel I've enough misfortune in my life without going looking for more. No, the only stars I knew when I was growing up were the stars on television.

Those three guys were three wise guys. They didn't rush out blindly looking for you. They sat down and planned their journey. They weren't beyond seeking advice. They even picked old Herod's brain when they got to Jerusalem and lost the star for a while.

As for me, I was a complete fool. I thought I knew it all. I was convinced I was a genius. Even though I could hardly be trusted to whitewash the garden wall, I remember once looking at a copy of Leonardo da Vinci's painting of the Last Supper, and thinking that I could spot some flaws in it. And I thought that, all things being equal, I could have done a better job myself.

Another thing about the Magi. They were up and doing. I was as lazy as a well-fed cat. To me all labour was forced labour.

Yet another thing. There were three of them. They were company for one another. When in

doubt they could always put their heads together. But I was nearly always on my own. Of course, it was my own choice. That was the way I wanted it. I called it independence, freedom, doing my own thing. I had perfect communication with my parents – we never talked. That way we never fought either.

At that time lots of young people my age were going on trips. No, not trips to Bethlehem. They were going on drug trips. Like a fool, I had to follow them. I very nearly lost myself.

And yet, when I think about it, I had one great advantage over the Magi. Whereas they were stuck with slow-moving, cumbersome camels, I had a shiny new motorbike. While they were getting their kicks out of the camels, I was getting mine out of a Honda. God bless that Honda! It very nearly cost me my life. Yet without it there's no way I'd be here talking to you tonight. You see, two months ago I had a bad accident. That's why I'm lying here on this hospital bed on the flat of my back.

Today the doctor cheerfully informed me that I can look forward to being here for at least two more months. But, Lord, if you were to say to me at this moment, 'Take up your bed and walk', I would do better. I would take it up and run.

As I was saying at the start of this little conversation, the other night I was looking up at the ceiling. In other words, I was thinking – something I never did in my life before. I thought: 'Here am I, nineteen years of age, and what have I done with my life? Nothing. Where have I gone? Nowhere. I'm still living for thrills and excitement. When this truth dawned on me

I got quite a shock, I can tell you. I felt I had wasted the best years of my life. I had squandered what some poet called 'the splendid years'.

The Magi didn't have you at the start. But they set out to look for you, and they persevered until they found you. For me it was the opposite. I didn't have to go looking for you. I had you from the very start. I was baptised and brought up a Catholic. I went to Mass regularly until the age of fifteen. But then I gave it all up. I lost you. And instead of looking for you, I deliberately turned my back on you. I was in full flight from you. Worse, I was in rebellion against you.

That was a very black night for me when all this came crowding in on me. But it was when the blackness was at its thickest that I somehow caught a glimpse of your light. But then, maybe this wouldn't have surprised me. After all, we can't see the stars in the bright of day, but only in the darkness of night. In fact, they say that the blacker the night, the brighter they shine. You're on to something there, you know. Did I hear you say something, Lord?

You did. It is usually through an experience of darkness that people discover my light. So you can thank the darkness you've been experiencing. Everybody needs a star to follow, Alan, just as ships at sea need a lighthouse beacon to guide them safely to port.

I was certainly at sea, Lord.

Some make it very difficult for themselves.

I certainly made it difficult for myself. Your light, your star, was always there but it was hidden from me by clouds. But from now on I feel I have a star that will not play me false, I have a compass that will not lie to me.

That's true, but don't be surprised if some of those clouds return. Just remember this. The stars continue to shine even when they are hidden from us.

One thing about the Magi puzzles me. It is this. How come they and no one else saw your star?

By the way, you have several misconceptions about those gentlemen. But first of all let me deal with your question. You're wrong, you know. Many people saw that star. But they weren't prepared to make the necessary sacrifices to follow it.

I never thought about it like that before. I always thought the star beckoned to them and to no one else, and that it cast a spell over them so that they had no choice but to follow it.

As I said, you have a lot of misconceptions about those men. You seem to think that the journey to Bethlehem was one long joyride for them. Far from it. They encountered many difficulties. Many people, including their friends, thought they were mad. Then, when they finally reached the goal of their journey, what do you think they found?

Oh, the way I imagine it is this. The star came down over the cave where they were. Its brightness filled the whole countryside. Then they saw you lying there with a bright halo around your tiny head. Joseph and Mary were kneeling by your side, also with halos, though of weaker wattage. Nearby stood the ox and the donkey with a serene look on their faces, as if they were lost in meditation. Then in the background a choir of angels was singing 'Silent Night'.

I must say you've got a splendid imagination. But it wasn't like that at all. All they saw was a child just like any other child, except poorer than most.

Just another child, you say? That I find hard to accept. There must have been something special, something unusual, that they could see at a glance.

I repeat. They saw just another child. But they somehow came to believe that in this child God's light had come into the world.

I'm not sure that I understand. But if I may come back to my own story, my own journey to you. Awful isn't it?

Not at all. It's a very good story. I like it. It's honest. It's accurate, except for one important detail.

What's that, Lord?

Alan, it wasn't you who found me. It was I who found you. All those years I had been looking for you.

Really?

Yes.

I'm bowled over. I don't know what to say. I never thought I mattered to anyone, least of all to you. When the Magi found you they offered you splendid gifts – gold, frankincense and myrrh. But now that I have found you, sorry, now that you have found me, I have nothing to offer you.

Don't worry, Alan. I don't dig gold and that sort of thing. Nor am I big into frankincense or myrrh either. But there is one thing you can give me.

What's that?

Yourself.

(A long pause followed. Alan looked uncertain).

Don't worry. I didn't say I wanted the gift right now. Only when you're ready. You have to find yourself before you can offer yourself as a gift to anyone else.

Christmas came. Alan remained in hospital. But people saw an amazing change in him. Up to this he had been full of bitterness about life in general and about his accident in particular. Now he had a smile and a cheerful word for everyone.

Years later he said, 'That was the first real Christmas in my life. No, I didn't hear angels singing in the sky. But I did experience some of the peace they sang about on that first Christmas night.'

Discuss

Alan says, 'I felt I had wasted the best years of my life'. Alan was nineteen. According to him you are now living through the best years of your life. How can you make sure that you don't waste them?

If you wanted to follow 'the light' that Alan speaks of, where would you find it?

What do you think accounted for the change in Alan's attitude?

Prayerful Reflection

You could read this reflection quietly and reflectively, either by yourself at home, or with the others in class:

When Jesus came on the first Christmas night, he came to fulfil the hopes and dreams of many people. The Jewish people had been hoping for centuries for the coming of the one whom they believed would deliver them from their enemies and bring them peace and prosperity in their land.

The men from the East, the three wise men, had been watching the stars, looking for some indication of the time when the Messiah would come.

His mother Mary was looking forward, like every young mother, to the forthcoming birth of her child.

What are you looking forward to this Christmas?

Take a few moments and gather together all of your hopes for yourself this Christmas.

How many of these do you think are in keeping with the true Christian meaning of Christmas?

How many are not?

Is there anything which you think you ought to add to the list of your hopes for yourself this Christmas?

What can you do between now and Christmas to make these hopes come true?

Think of something concrete which you can decide to do.

When Jesus was born in the stable in Bethlehem he was the Son of God made human. He was the promised Messiah, the one for whom they had been waiting for years. Yet when he came very few people recognised him. they were not looking for a baby born in a manger. They were looking for someone rich, famous and powerful, a great king or a great leader. And so they searched in all the wrong places. So it is often with us also. When we try to find Christ in our world, we too look in all the wrong places:

Where do you look when you want to find Christ in your world?

What will you have to say to him when you find him?

What do you think he will have to say to you?

Do the Looking Back exercises for Unit Four at the back of this book.

The Orthodox Church

FINLAND

Helsinki

• St Petersburg

• Novgorod

• Moscow

POLAND

CHURCH OF RUSSIA

CZECHOSLOVAKIA

• Kiev

BALTIC SEA

ROMANIA

Belgrade •

CHURCH
OF
SERBIA

Bucharest

• Sofia

BULGARIA

CASPIAN
SEA

CHURCH
OF
GEORGIA

BLACK SEA

Constantinople

ALBANIA

•Thessaloniki

• Nicaea

PATRIARCHATE
OF
CONSTANTINOPLE

GREECE

•Athens

Ephesus

Crete

MEDITERRANEAN SEA

Antioch

Cyprus

Damascus •

Jerusalem •

Alexandria •

PATRIARCHATE
OF
ALEXANDRIA

PATRIARCHATE
OF
ANTIOCH

PATRIARCHATE
OF
JERUSALEM

Sinai •

After the fall of the Roman Empire in the west, communications between the Church in the east and the west became more difficult and less regular, and were increasingly affected by political pressures. These pressures became more intense after the formation in the west of the Holy Roman Empire under Charlemagne. In 1054 a dispute over the Pope's addition of a new phrase to the Creed was the occasion for a decisive split. Most of the Churches in the eastern part of the empire rejected the authority of the pope, and the division that occurred then has never been healed.

The Eastern Churches eventually became known as the Orthodox Church, which is nowadays a loose federation of independent national Churches, under the nominal leadership of the Patriarch of Constantinople. Since then there has often been great friction between the Orthodox and Catholic Churches, when they have come into contact. This was not helped by the historical incident in the Middle Ages, when the armies of the Fourth Crusade, which were supposed to be defending Christianity against the Muslims, sacked Constantinople which was then still the capital of the Eastern Roman Empire.

There have been two major attempts at reunion. At the last of these, the Council of

Florence in 1439-45, the representatives from the east reached agreement with Rome on all disputed points, including the authority of the pope, but this agreement was subsequently rejected by the Eastern Churches as a whole.

Today, especially since the Second Vatican Council, relations have improved. In 1965 Pope Paul VI and Patriarch Athenagoras symbolically revoked the excommunications which had been issued in 1054. This symbolic action showed the desire to overcome the hostility of the intervening centuries.

The Fourth Crusade

Activity

There are small groupings of Orthodox Christians all over the world. However, within these boundaries – latitude 35-60 North and longitude 20-40 East you will find more than ninety per cent of all Orthodox Christians. On a map of the world indicate the principal Orthodox countries – Greece, Bulgaria, Romania, Russia, Serbia

The Catholic Church and the Orthodox Church

The beliefs of the Catholic Church and the Orthodox Church are very similar. They both accept the authority of the first seven Ecumenical Councils and, with one small but important variation, they both profess the same Creed (the Nicene Creed). They both have the same seven sacraments, and believe basically the same things about them and about the Mass. They both believe that the bishops are the successors of the Apostles.

The Catholic Church recognises the validity of the Orthodox sacraments; it recognises that Orthodox clergy are validly ordained bishops, priests and deacons. It recognises that the Orthodox Church celebrates a valid Mass, and that when Orthodox Christians receive communion, they truly receive the body and blood of Christ.

Apart from one difference in the Creed (which we will look at later), the main differences in belief are:

(a) Orthodox Christians, like Catholics, greatly honour the Blessed Virgin and call her 'Theotokos', which is equivalent to 'Mother of God', but while they believe that she was granted a very special holiness, they do not accept the Catholic doctrine of the Immaculate Conception.

(b) The Orthodox Church regards the Pope as holding first place in honour among bishops, but they do not accept his authority over them.

Orthodox Christians have their own very ancient liturgical practices and special spiritual traditions, but these are not obstacles to unity. The Catholic Church greatly respects the ancient heritage of the Orthodox Church, which is part of its own heritage, and considers it to be the closest to itself in faith and practice. It believes, however, that it does not fully conform to what Christ wanted for his Church, especially because it does not acknowledge the special unifying authority of the Pope, the successor of Peter.

Sacraments

Like the Catholic Church, the Orthodox Church looks after believers from birth to death through the sacraments. The Orthodox Church gives some of the seven sacraments different names. They are: Baptism, Chrismation (Confirmation), Holy Communion, Confession, Marriage, Ordination and Holy Unction (Anointing of the Sick). Baptism and Holy Communion are considered most important. Babies are usually given the Sacrament of Chrismation (Confirmation) at the time of their Baptism.

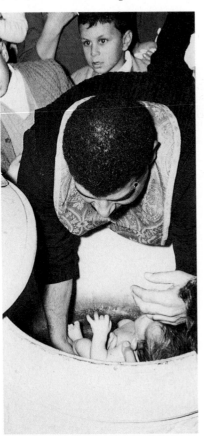

Baptism in an Orthodox Church

The Latin Addition to the Creed

For centuries it had generally been taught in the west that, since the Holy Spirit was the Spirit of the Father and the Spirit of the Son, it would be a fuller expression of the truth to say that the Spirit proceeded 'from the Father and the Son' rather than simply 'from the Father', as was said in the Creed drawn up at the Council of Constantinople (the Nicene Creed). Eastern Church writers sometimes taught something similar, when they talked about the Spirit proceeding from the Father 'through the Son'. This is how Patriarch Tarasius of Constantinople expressed the matter in 787, and the Pope of the time defended this way of putting things when the Emperor Charlemagne protested to him about it.

However, this Pope and his successors, though they believed in the doctrine, were unwilling to interfere with the text of the ancient Creed of Constantinople and for a long time refused to insert the words 'and the Son' (in Latin, *Filioque*) into it. This was probably first done at the court of Charlemagne, but without the approval of Rome. What brought about the quarrel with the east was when, in 1014, the Pope himself finally decided to insert these words into the official text of the Creed at the Mass in Rome for the coronation of the Emperor, Henry II. The Eastern Church objected because this had been done without consultation with them, and this led to the dispute which eventually brought about the split. Today many Orthodox theologians would admit that the Roman doctrine can be understood in a way they agree with, but that it should not have been inserted into the Creed without proper consultation. Many Catholics would agree that the whole matter was dealt with badly and in a high-handed manner.

To this day the Orthodox Church uses the original form of the Creed, which states that the Holy Spirit 'proceeds from the Father', while the Catholic Church uses the expanded form 'proceeds from the Father and the Son'. The Orthodox Church still finds this very objectionable.

An Orthodox Place of Worship

The form of worship which takes place in a church usually accounts for the style of the building. Just as a person will arrange their home to suit the family's needs, so the congregation of a local church will build somewhere suitable for the needs of their acts of worship.

Features of an Orthodox Church

Many features of an Orthodox church help to remind the worshippers of heaven. As one patriarch of Constantinople in the eighth century said: 'The Church is the earthly heaven in which the heavenly God dwells and moves'. Most Orthodox churches have domed roofs that are centred over a cross-shaped interior. As you enter an Orthodox church you will at once notice that there are no pews, only a few chairs around the sides. Standing in the entrance you can see that the far end of the church is divided from the nave, or the main body of the church, by a screen. The area behind this screen is much narrower. There is a wing or transept on each side of the nave which forms the two arms of the cross. The walls and ceiling, as well as the screen, are richly decorated with icons of Christ, of the Virgin Mary and of the saints. The icons are all painted in bright, vivid colours and depict scenes from the life of Jesus. They provide a lively and colourful way of teaching the faith of the Church.

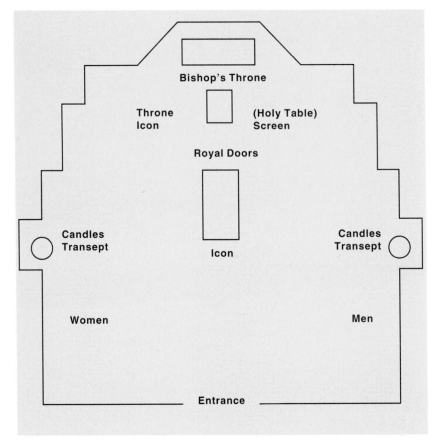

Plan of an Orthodox Church

The most striking feature of an Orthodox church is the icon-screen or **iconostasis**. This is a screen which separates the people from the sanctuary where the priests celebrate **the mysteries**. In the centre of the screen are the **royal doors**. At certain times during the Orthodox service the doors are opened to show that God has opened the way for all people to be reunited with him. Beyond the doors you can see the **holy table,** also called **the throne**. The priest stands there during the communion service. Beyond the holy table is the **bishop's seat**. No one but the clergy may go into this area behind the screen. In the alcove on the left of the holy table the bread and wine are prepared for the service,

and in the one on the right the priest's vestments or special robes are kept. The icons on the screen form a pattern showing how God has rescued all people from sin and reminding worshippers that God makes himself known to his people (through the Gospel writers, evangelists or angels who are God's messengers).

In the transepts of the church there are stands which hold the many candles which are lit by the people and are a most important part of the liturgy. Oil lamps often hang before the icons. There will frequently be a strong smell of incense as

it is regularly used in Orthodox worship.

In Your Religion Journal

Draw a plan of your own local church, indicating the main features and furnishings of the church.
Imagine the parish priest has asked you to give a guided tour around your church for some visiting Orthodox Christians. Prepare a short talk which you would use during your guided tour.

Discuss

What features of an Orthodox church help to remind the worshippers of heaven?

Orthodox Worship

Read this letter from your Greek pen-pal:

Sirov 41
Holargos
Athens
Greece

Dear Jane,

Thanks for your letter. It was great to hear from you again. I enjoyed reading about the Mass. In many respects your form of worship is very similar to the Orthodox Divine Liturgy.

I hope my letter will help you understand more about Orthodox worship when you come to study it in class.

On Sunday, I go with my family to the local church. When I first enter the church, and before the liturgy begins, I buy a candle, light it and place it on the candle-stand in front of an icon. I make the sign of the cross and kiss the icon as a mark of reverence. When Orthodox worshippers make the sign of the cross we touch the right shoulder before the left, using the thumb and next two fingers — a sign of the Trinity.

There are very few pews in the church except for a few chairs around the sides for the elderly. My grandmother, who comes to church with us, takes a seat. I stand with my father on one side of the church, while my mother stands with my sisters on the other side of the nave. With no pews or rows of chairs, the worshippers feel a greater freedom to move to another part of the church, possibly to greet a friend or light a candle during the service, although this freedom of movement does not lead to a lack of reverence.

The choir gathers in one corner of the church beside the iconostasis. No organ or piano is played as we believe singing should be unaccompanied. The normal length of the Sunday service or Divine Liturgy, as it is called, is about an hour and a half, though at festivals it can last up to three or four hours.

The Divine Liturgy commemorates and makes present the events which took place at the Last Supper and the death and resurrection of Jesus. The service falls into two parts. The first part of the service is known as the Liturgy of the Word. It starts with the choir singing psalms from the Bible. Prayers are said for various people and for the needs of the Church. The worshippers respond, 'Lord, have mercy', after each short prayer. Throughout the service we pray silently and often make the sign of the cross. The climax of this part of the service comes with a procession. The priest, carrying the **Book of the Gospels** raised above his head, accompanied by servers with candles and incense, comes out from behind the icon-screen. The priest then reads from one of the letters in the New Testament or from the Acts of the Apostles. This is followed by a reading from one of the gospels. The readings differ each Sunday so that throughout the year the life and teaching of Jesus will have been covered. After a short homily the priest then returns behind the icon screen to prepare for the next and most solemn part of the service. The frescos, the icons, the chants which the choir sing and the burning of incense all help to create an atmosphere of wonder and awe, and a feeling of timelessness and changelessness.

The next part of the service — the Eucharist — begins with another procession. The priest carries the bread and wine in the holy vessels down through the church. Many worshippers bow down to the ground out of reverence. The priest then proceeds back through the church and lays the bread and wine on the holy table. The royal doors of the iconostasis are then closed while the congregation recite the Nicene Creed. Behind the screen the priest offers thanks to God for sending his Son, Jesus Christ, into the world as he promised, ending with the words Jesus himself spoke at the Last Supper: 'This is my blood of the new covenant which is shed for you and for many for the forgiveness of sins' (Mark 14:23-24).

The most sacred moment of the service follows when the priest offers up the bread and wine, saying 'Thine of thine own do we offer thee!' He prays that the gifts of the bread and wine may become the body and blood of Jesus. A moment of silence follows before the choir sings a hymn, the bells are rung and the whole church is filled with praise and thanksgiving. We all say the Lord's Prayer and prepare ourselves to receive the **holy gifts**. The priest comes out from behind the royal doors, and those who have said they wish to receive the holy gifts come forward. The priest offers the body and blood of Christ in the form of **holy bread** dipped in the consecrated wine on a spoon.

The service ends with a short blessing. However, at the end of the Divine Liturgy we all go and kiss the Cross the priest is holding and take a piece of bread or cake. This has been blessed but not laid upon the holy table. It is a sign of fellowship and love, just as in the early Church.

I hope this has been of some interest to you. Write soon.

Your friend,

Panos

1 January
St Basil's Day
Celebrates St Basil, a bishop in the fourth century AD. A special cake containing a silver coin is made and eaten.

6 January
Baptism of Jesus
Water is blessed and bottles of holy water are taken home. Crosses are thrown into the sea and people compete to rescue them. Children baptise oranges.

JANUARY

Lent
Remembers Christ's fast in the desert. Begins on 'Clean Monday' with a special meal and ends at Easter. It is a time of family prayer and fasting. The exact time of Lent is determined by the date of Good Friday which is the Friday following the first full moon after the Spring Equinox.*

FEBRUARY

MARCH

APRIL

Easter
The most important feast of the year which celebrates the resurrection of Christ. A time of great joy with special meals and activities. Also a celebration of the end of winter.

APRIL

MAY

Ascension
Celebrates the return of Christ to heaven and is the end of the Easter festival.

MAY

JUNE

The Orthodox Year

*The Orthodox Church continues to encourage very severe fasts at different times of the year, especially in the Great Fast (Lent) before Easter; no meat is taken, no fish or dairy produce, wine or oil.

Most Orthodox Churches, including the Greek, use the normal calendar.

Some, such as the Russian and Serbian Churches, follow the old calendar which is thirteen days behind. There are festivals during all seasons of the year.

The Church festivals remind us of the birth, life, death and resurrection of Jesus: Christmas, Epiphany, Lent and Easter.

Name Days

The Christian name given to an Orthodox person is celebrated each year on the feast day of the saint of that name. A special ceremony takes place in the church, where everybody is given a candle which is lit during the service.

17 July
St Marina's Day
A name day

JULY

15 August
Assumption
Remembers the reception of Mary, the mother of God, into heaven.

AUGUST

26 October
St Demetrius' Day
A name day

OCTOBER

8 November
The Holy Day of Archangel Michael
A name day

30 November
St Andrew's Day
A name day

NOVEMBER

25 December
Christmas
Celebrates the birth of Jesus Christ

DECEMBER

Icons

Instead of statues, Orthodox Christians use religious paintings called icons to help them pray and come closer to God.

'Icon' is the Greek word for image. The pictures of Jesus, Mary and the saints are painted on wood or executed in mosaic with gold leaf.

The portraits on the icon may strike you as unusual. They are deliberately painted out of perspective and although there is a certain lifelike quality, they have an 'other-worldly' look about them. The icons capture and reflect stillness and perfect peace. Each icon forms part of the pattern of the way in which the Orthodox Church believes God is redeeming the world.

women of Jerusalem gave Jesus a linen cloth to wipe his face on his way to the crucifixion, and the image of his face remained on it. Soon after, Saint Luke is believed to have painted the Virgin Mary. The icon painters regard their task as a sacred one. They live a monastic life, much like the Irish artists who designed the Book of Kells.

Contemporary icon painter

Christ Pantocratur Icon, Moscow School, about 1670

The earliest Christian icon is, by tradition, of Jesus himself. There is a story that one of the

Read the following interview with an icon painter:

Interviewer: Well, Petros, can you tell me how you became an icon painter?

Petros: Icon painting is very skilled work, requiring a lot of patience. It is a skill which I was taught many years ago. I am now teaching other monks the icon tradition. You are recognised as an icon painter only after prayer and meditation or if it is felt that you have a special gift.

Interviewer: What preparations do you need to make before beginning your work?

Petros: Before I begin to paint an icon it is important that my attitude is right, so I pray and meditate in silence. I prepare myself by fasting, by going to confession and by receiving communion. I choose the wood and paint carefully and make sure that they are both blessed.

Interviewer: Can you paint any image you want?

Petros: No, an icon painter is not free to paint what he likes. He must follow certain rules and traditions unless it is revealed through prayer and meditation that the traditional pattern is to be changed.

Interviewer: Can you describe briefly the method and technique you use when painting an icon?

Petros: There is a very special technique used in painting an icon. The icons are usually painted on wood in tempera, that is with colours that have been mixed with natural emulsion, for example, egg yolk, or artificial emulsion such as oil and gum.
When I finish painting an icon, it is blessed with holy water and in this way the icon becomes more than just a painting. It is a sign, a reflection of a transfiguration in heaven.

Interviewer: Can you tell us the purpose of the rich images used in Orthodox worship?

Petros: The purpose of such rich and ornate images in Orthodox worship is to stimulate the imagination and to help people go beyond everyday life and focus their minds on God.

Interviewer: Thanks for the interview, Petros, I'll let you get back to your painting.

The Icon of Vladimir

This icon of the Mother and Child was brought from Constantinople to Russia in 1131. It was painted by a Greek artist, probably just before its transfer to the town of Kiev in southern Russia. In 1155 it was brought from Kiev to Vladimir where it got its permanent name.

The icon has survived fires and wars in a most remarkable way. Indeed, the scars of age and hardship are to be seen on the painting itself. Yet it remains a very beautiful example of the art of making icons.

Look at the lady, Mary, the Mother of God. She is beautiful in a strange and haunting way, as if she no longer lived in our world. She is clearly a woman but her expression is unmoving, fixed for all time. She is beyond change and decay.

Discuss

In what ways do icons differ from western religious art? Why do you think icons are so important for Orthodox Christians?

Orthodox Church Organisation

The Orthodox Church consists of a number of self-governing national Churches.

No one bishop or patriarch is supreme over the others, though the Patriarch of Constantinople has a special position of honour and is called the Ecumenical or Universal Patriarch. He can call conferences and make suggestions, but has no authority to interfere in the internal affairs of another Church.

Like the Catholic Church, there are three major orders of ministers in the Orthodox Church. **These are bishops, priests and deacons**

Bishops: are considered the successors of the Apostles. They must be monks and, therefore, unmarried. They have different titles according to their importance.

Priests: are responsible for both the church services and the Orthodox Christians in their parish. Priests who wish to marry must do so before they are ordained as deacons. Those who do not wish to marry are normally expected to become monks before their ordination. These celibate priests cannot change their minds and decide to get married at a later stage. If a priest's wife dies he cannot marry again.

Deacons: The order of deacons is far more prominent in the Orthodox Church than in the Catholic Church and many deacons have no intention of ever becoming priests. All priests are first ordained deacons.

Patriarch:
means Father – ruler, rules over a
Patriarchate
like the four ancient Churches of Constantinople, Alexandria, Antioch and Jerusalem.

Archbishop or Metropolitan:
head of provinces or groups of dioceses under a patriarch

Bishop:
A bishop is in charge of each diocese as in the Catholic Church.

Monks:
remain unmarried and must live in monasteries.

Priests:
may marry or remain single; responsible for Church services; live in parishes with parishioners.

Deacons:
not yet ordained priests, they may choose to marry before ordination.

In Your Religion Journal
Draw an illustration showing the organisation of the Catholic Church.

Discuss
What are the similarities and differences between the Roman Catholic Church and the Orthodox Churches?

Monks and Monasticism

In the fourth century a movement known as monasticism arose in Egypt and spread quickly throughout the eastern and western communities. It was a movement of ordinary men, who dedicated their lives to Jesus, choosing not to marry and separating themselves from the world.

Particularly in the east, these men were drawn together to live in communities known as monasteries. They lived a strict, austere lifestyle. They had guidelines for prayer and charitable works, and shared in the liturgy. They accepted the grace of God and made it real in their lives.

Mount Athos is still the great symbol and centre of Orthodox monasticism. There are twenty mountainside monasteries. Pilgrims long to visit Orthodox holy places, especially Mount Athos in Greece.

Research

Make a study of the life of St Anthony and the origins of the monastic movement. Do you think there is a place in the modern world for such a way of life?

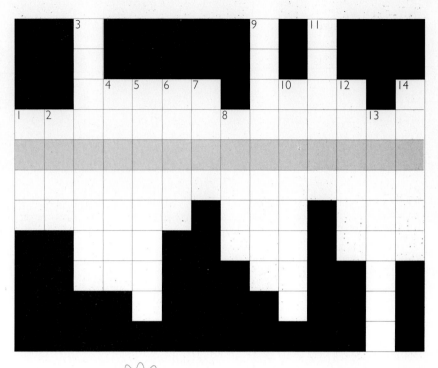

Activity

Using the clues, fill in the mosaic to reveal, in the shaded area, the name given to the Christian capital of the east.

Clues

(1)   Painted on wood or executed in mosaic

(2)   Year of the final break between eastern and western communities

(3)   Formerly Constantinople, now Istanbul

(4)   Opposite of western

(5)   Name given to Churches belonging to this religious tradition — Greek, Russian

(6)   A specific day celebrated in honour of a particular saint

(7)   The Great Fast

(8)   Mountain housing twenty large monasteries

(9)   Derived from two Greek words meaning Father — Ruler

(10)   Solidarity. A way of life for a monk

(11)   One of the three orders of the Orthodox Church

(12)   Papal government/Office of Pope

(13)   Icon of Mother and Child, named after a Russian city

(14)   A country which is mainly Orthodox

Islam

Islam is an Arabic word meaning 'submission or surrender'. A follower of Islam is known as a Muslim, meaning 'one who submits'. Muslims are asked to surrender their lives in obedience and reverence to the one true God, whom they call Allah.

They believe that Allah has spoken to them through the prophet Muhammad and that the sacred book, the Koran (Qur'an), contains the actual words of God which the angel Gabriel revealed to Muhammad. However, according to its tradition, Islam did not begin with the prophet Muhammad. The Word of God, Allah, was revealed from the beginning of time. Great men like Adam, Abraham, Moses and Jesus were his prophets. But it was to Muhammad, the last and final prophet, that the Word of

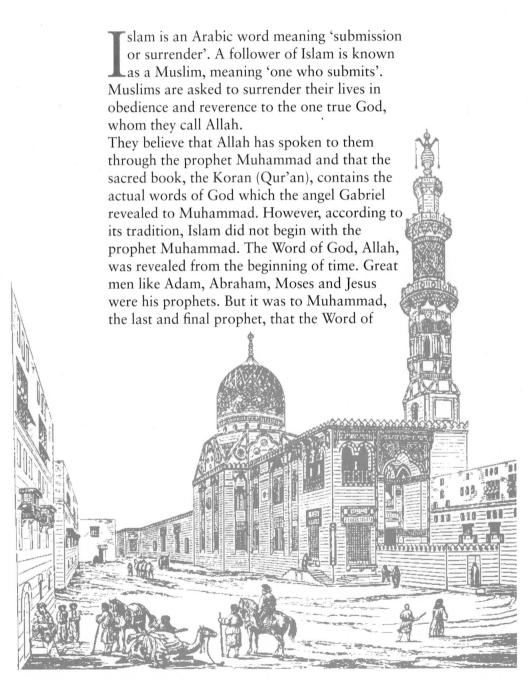

Mosque, Cairo

God was fully revealed and written down. Like the Christian and Jewish religions, Islam is also considered a way of life. Followers of Islam live their lives as the Koran instructs and encourages. The **Five Pillars of Islam** establish some important ritual obligations. The **Shiriah**, which is Islamic law, deals with all aspects of life; from marriage and the family, to social oppression, to lack of equality.

The Beginning of Islam

Muhammad was born about 570AD into a reputable family of the Koreish tribe in Mecca. He showed an early interest in religion and became familiar with Judaism and some of the teachings of Christianity. He would often listen to the preachers who travelled through Mecca giving sermons. They spoke to the crowds about one God, the last judgment and the punishment of idolators in everlasting fire.

By the time he was eighteen his friends called him Al-Amin, meaning 'the faithful'. He was saddened by the life he saw in Mecca, by the people's foolish worship of gods and goddesses, by excesses in drinking and sex and by the terrible injustices suffered by the poor. He realised that the religion of Mecca was corrupt and ineffectual.

At the age of twenty-five, Muhammad met a rich widow called Khadijah who was fifteen years his senior. They married and had six children. Over the years Muhammad began to spend more time on his own. He would often go alone to a cave near Mecca where he could meditate.

In 610AD while he was on one of his retreats to the cave, Muhammad had his first revelation, which would change his future. He heard the voice of God telling him that he was to be a prophet of the one God, Allah. This night is known as the **night of power** and **excellence** (Lailat ul-Qadr). This religious experience was to be the starting point which inspired the spiri-

tuality and values which Muhammad brought to bear on the Islamic religion.

Reassured by his wife, Muhammad gradually accepted that he was to be the mouthpiece of God, that it was a sign that he had been chosen as the prophet of a new era. Muslims believe that over the next ten years Muhammad had more revelations through the angel Gabriel and these were written down in the Koran.

Muhammad began to preach in Mecca. He told the people that there was only one God, Allah, the creator and judge of humanity. He asked people to be kind and merciful and to act justly. He asked them to give away to others what they themselves had received from God. He condemned their immorality and worship of idols. He made enemies of the merchants who sold idols and who lived off the pilgrims coming to Mecca. He was bad for business. Threats on Muhammad's life became frequent.

The Hijra – A Turning Point

Pilgrims from the city of Medina heard Muhammad preach and were impressed. In July 622 they invited him to go and live in Medina, a city located 400 kilometres north of Mecca. With an assassination plot threatening his life, Muhammad left Mecca and made the long journey across the Arabian desert to the city. This journey to Medina is called the **hijra**, meaning the departure or exodus.

It was in Medina that the Muslim community was born, under the leadership of Muhammad. The first mosque was built in the city as a place of prayer and worship for the community. Muhammad was recognised as the **rasul**, or messenger, of Allah and he also assumed political and military leadership.

The hijra is an important event for Muslims as they date the official beginning of Islam from the year of Muhammad's journey to Medina. Their lunar calendar begins from the year of the hijra, 622.

Muhammad began by trying to convert Mecca from its evil ways and to subdue many of the pagan tribes. By 630 he had conquered Mecca and people rapidly began to convert to Islam. It became the centre of Islam. He was accepted by most Arabs as the Prophet-King of Arabia. He died soon after, in 632.

In Your Religion Journal

Copy a map of Saudi Arabia into your religion journal. Indicate the cities of Mecca and Medina on the map and mark out the possible route of Muhammad's hijra through the desert.

The Expansion of Islam

Under Mohammad's successor, Omar, who was a military genius, there began a rapid expansion of the new religion – in the first place through military conquest. Islamic armies from Arabia swept through parts of the east, and by 650 had overwhelmed several provinces of the eastern Roman Empire, with their mainly Christian inhabitants, including Syria, Palestine and Egypt, and also the Persian Empire. Fifty years later the conquest of the North African coast commenced. Roman Africa, in which the great St Augustine had been a bishop, was taken in 695, and in 711 the Muslim armies crossed into Spain and even overran the south of France. They were finally stopped at the Battle of Poitiers, but remained in control of much of Spain for centuries. In the conquered territories new Islamic regimes were set up, and Islam was in the ascendancy. In Egypt and parts of the Middle East, the sites of some of the earliest Christian Churches, Christianity eventually

became a minority religion.

During the Middle Ages there was frequent conflict between Islam and the Christian states of Europe. Crusades were organised by Christian kings to regain conquered territories, particularly Jerusalem, but none had any lasting success, except in Spain. The final great expansion occurred in the fifteenth century when the Muslim Turks overran what was left of the old eastern Roman Empire, took Constantinople itself in 1453, and gained control of Greece and certain neighbouring territories in eastern Europe. That is why, even today, in some parts of eastern Europe, like Albania, which fell for some time under the control of the Turks, there are still large Muslim communities.

Elsewhere Muslim merchants and travellers introduced Islam into parts of Asia, including Malaya and Indonesia. Islam also spread into India, especially the northern part of the subcontinent where Pakistan and Bangladesh are today.

The Koran

The Koran (Qur'an) is the Muslim sacred book. The Koran was an oral tradition prior to being written down. The word Koran means 'that which is to be proclaimed'. Muslims believe that their sacred book is the Word of God, exactly as the angel Gabriel revealed it to Muhammad, over a period of twenty-three years. They believe that the book was revealed to Muhammad in Arabic, a language which most Muslims can still recite. He chose people to write it down on his behalf. Some years after Muhammad's death the bits of parchment were gathered together and compiled into a book. The Koran is divided into 114 chapters, called **suras,** with a total of 6666 verses; slightly shorter than the New Testament.

Faithful Muslims read the Koran every day. It offers guidance and direction for everyone on how to live a good life. It explains how to serve God.

When Muslim infants are born, the first thing they hear are words from the Koran. It is the source of Muslim education – very often a child's first reading lesson at home is from the Koran, and many Muslim parents are eager to arrange for evening and weekend classes where their children can learn to recite it by heart. There are some people who can recite it all. These people are known as **hafiz**.

The Koran mentions twenty-five prophets in all. The five most important prophets are Abraham, Moses, Noah, Jesus and, of course, Muhammad. According to the Koran, God used each of these prophets as messengers, but it is Muhammad who is called the **seal of the prophets** because the revelations given to him are believed to be final and complete.

So while Jesus is respected as a great prophet in Islam he is not treated as divine.

Two pages from a Koran, dated 8th-14th centuries

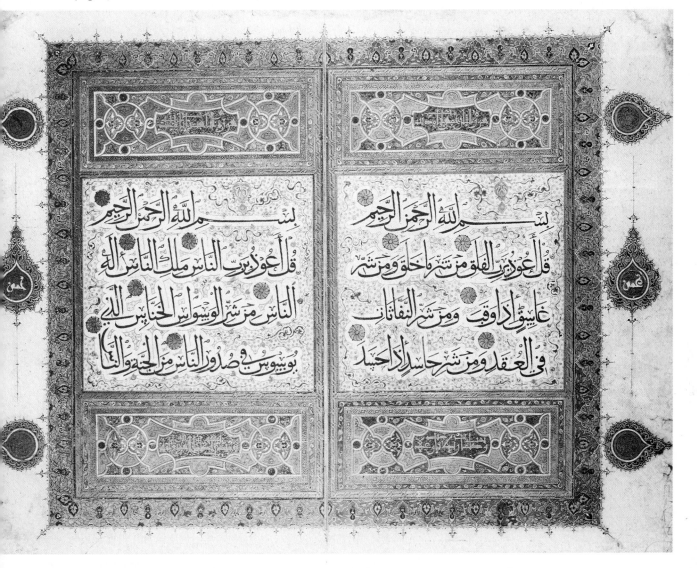

The Five Pillars of Islam

Certain beliefs and practices are essential for every religion. In Islam, these obligatory practices are the **five pillars**. The five pillars are commands contained in the Koran.

1. Creed (Shahadah)

The Islamic profession of faith is short and apparently simple:

There is no god but God, and Muhammad is the messenger of God.

This creed says that God is One and that God rules. It also proclaims that God has spoken in a unique way through the prophet Muhammad. To be considered a Muslim, one must recite and believe this creed. The creed is recited as a prayer many times a day by the devout Muslim. When the muezzin calls the people to pray five times a day, he uses the creed as part of his invitation.

2. Prayer (Salat)

Muslims pray five times a day. They pray not just at the mosque but anywhere — at home, at work etc. The muezzin calls from special tall towers called minarets which are part of every mosque.

At prayer the Muslim turns towards Mecca. Before praying, all Muslims must become 'clean' by washing their head, arms to the shoulder, and feet. The Arabic name given to this washing before prayer is wudu. Each Muslim remains barefooted for the duration of the prayer. The Muslim expresses submission to Allah by an act of prostration. This means crouching in such a way that their knees and head touch the ground. Usually a small rug is spread out to kneel on. Friday is the day of public worship, when Muslims go for midday prayer.

3. Fasting (Sawm)

Muslims also express their submission to Allah by fasting. Such acts of self-discipline are seen as surrender to God's will. The pangs of hunger and thirst are to remind Muslims of the suffering of the poor.

The Muslim is expected to fast from sunrise to sunset, all through the month of Ramadan. During the day devout Muslims carry out only essential business and when they are not working, they meditate on passages from the Koran. Ramadan is the ninth month in the lunar year (354 days).

The month rotates gradually through all the seasons. During the fasting period from dawn to sunset, one may not eat, drink or smoke and married couples may not have sexual intercourse. There are heavy penalties for people who break the fast; for instance, providing a meal for sixty people! At the end of the month, Muslims celebrate, much as Christians do at Christmas. Families gather for a special meal and sometimes gifts are exchanged.

4. Poor-due/Alms-giving (Zakat)

Muslims have a popular saying which, roughly translated, says, 'Pray to overcome pride: fast to conquer the appetites, and give the poor-due to overcome greed.' This obligation rests on men and women who are wealthy enough to give a percentage of their goods to the poor and the needy. It is an act of thanksgiving to God, the Giver of all. Zakat purifies the heart of the believer.

Poor-due (or alms-giving) is compulsory once a year on cash, cattle and crops. The minimum rate on cash is two and a half per cent. There is no upper limit. The poor-due is given only from what is left after reasonable living expenses are met.

5. Pilgrimage (Hajj)

Every true Muslim must try to make a pilgrimage to the sacred city of Mecca at least once in his lifetime. The spirit of pilgrimage is one of total surrender and sacrifice. The pilgrim wears simple dress. No extras or forms of adornment and fashion are permitted. The white, unsewn cloth is a sign of humility, equality and consecration to Allah.

The pilgrim takes part in many acts of devotion. The pilgrim walks around the Ka'bah, a small shrine, seven times, reciting prayers and then walks the thirteen miles to Mount Arafat, the summit of the pilgrimage in many ways. Later the pilgrim sacrifices a sheep, goat or camel in memory of Abraham's act of submission to God.

Around a million Muslims take part in the Hajj during that one week every year. No non-Muslim may enter Mecca or Medina because they are not sacred places for non-Muslims. Jerusalem is also a pilgrimage centre for Muslims.

Pilgrimage to Mecca

The sacred place of Islam is Mecca. Travelling to Mecca on pilgrimage is the fifth pillar of Islam. Every Muslim tries to make the pilgrimage to Mecca, known as the Hajj, at least once in his or her lifetime. During the festival of Ramadan, which is celebrated during the ninth month of the Islamic year, Muslims from all over the world travel to Mecca.

The Hajj lasts for five days. On arrival at Mecca, before entering the city, the male pilgrims change their clothes and put on long white robes, a symbolic gesture which reminds them that they must be prepared to give up everything for God and that everyone is equal in God's sight.

The Hajj begins when the pilgrims walk seven times around the Ka'bah in an anti-clockwise direction. The Ka'bah is a simple rectangular building

which Muslims believe was built by Abraham and his son Ishmael to worship God. A black stone, believed to be a meteorite given to Abraham by the angel Gabriel, is kissed by the pilgrims.

After walking around the Ka'bah the pilgrims then proceed to two nearby hills, each of which they climb seven times. They believe that it was between these two hills that Abraham's wife Hagar desperately searched for water for her suffering child, Ishmael.

Eventually Hagar found a spring and the water saved their lives. After climbing the hills the pilgrims go to take a drink from the well of Zam Zam.

On the following day the pilgrims walk thirteen miles to the Mount of Arafat. Most of the day is spent praying to Allah.

The next day they set out for the small village of Mina where they assemble at about midday around three stone pillars. Animals – probably sheep, goats, cows or camels – are sacrificed. This reminds the pilgrims that Abraham was willing to sacrifice his son at God's command, and that when God spared him, Abraham sacrificed a ram instead.

The stone pillars mark the place where Muslims believe that the devil tried to persuade Ishmael to disobey Abraham. Ishmael drove the devil away by throwing stones at him. The pilgrims throw stones at the pillars to show that they reject evil and want to follow God. The pilgrims finally return to Mecca where they circle the Ka'bah one more time to complete the pilgrimage.

Put these events from the Hajj in the order in which they happen:

1. Stoning the pillars at Mina
2. Putting on pilgrims' clothes
3. Sacrificing an animal
4. Spending the day at Arafat
5. Walking between the two hills
6. Going seven times round the Ka'bah
7. Collecting forty-nine stones

Discuss

How many Christian places of pilgrimage do you know of?
Have you ever been on a pilgrimage? If so, describe the experience.
What do you consider are the similarities or differences between Christian pilgrimages and the Hajj?

Research

Read the story of Abraham and Ishmael. Look up the following references in Genesis 16:1-16; 17:1-27; 21:1-21.

The Mosque – A Place of Worship

Muslims use special buildings called mosques to pray in. The word mosque means 'place of prostration' because Muslims bow low to God when praying. On a Friday, the usual noon prayer is extended to include a sermon. If there is no mosque locally, the prayers can be said anywhere — in a park or on a farm.

Most mosques have one or more tall, slender towers called minarets. The muezzin calls faithful Muslims to prayer from the balcony of the tower.

In some places a loudspeaker may be used instead of the muezzin but the same words are spoken in Arabic:

Allah is the greatest.
Allah is the greatest.
Allah is the greatest.
Allah is the greatest.
I bear witness that there is no God
    but Allah.
I bear witness that there is no God
    but Allah.
I bear witness that Muhammad is
    Allah's messenger.
I bear witness that Muhammad is
    Allah's messenger.
Rush to prayer, rush to prayer,
Rush to success, rush to success,
Allah is the greatest.
Allah is the greatest.
There is no God but Allah.

Every mosque must provide a place where Muslims can wash before going inside to pray . A cloakroom is also provided where shoes must be left before entering the mosque. This is to prevent dust entering the holy building. The floor of the mosque is covered in prayer rugs. Inside, the mosque is very bare. There are no seats, altars, candles, flowers, statues or paintings. Muhammad had stopped people praying to idols. He was afraid that people might go back to worshipping these images if they were in a mosque. Mosque walls may be decorated with brightly coloured tiles or mosaics and, in some cases, words or sentences from the Koran may be written on the walls. Standard to all mosques is a niche in one wall which indicates the direction of Mecca. Muslims always pray facing Mecca.

The congregation stand in rows, shoulder to shoulder. Women may attend the services but they stand apart from the men so they don't distract each other. In some Muslim countries, mosques have special areas for women.

Islam has no priests. Every Muslim must take responsibility for his or her own prayers.

Whenever a group of Muslims gathers for prayer a leader, called an **Imam,** is selected. This is someone who is very religious and is known to be a good Muslim. The Imam stands at the front of the group and leads the worshippers in prayer and movements. Sometimes instruction will be given by an Imam who may also be an Islamic scholar.

Many mosques run schools where Muslim children can learn about their religion. They are taught to read Arabic so that they can learn the Koran.

Other educational and religious programmes may also be organised in the mosque as well as financial and building projects.

Find Your Group

Imagine that a new mosque has opened near where you live. Design an illustrated booklet giving information about the new mosque and the facilities it offers.

Opposite: Friday prayer at the Great Mosque in Paris

Muslim Festivals

154

Islam, like all other world religions, has its festivals. Each is called **Eid,** meaning festival. Throughout the Islamic year these festivals are celebrated to give thanks to God.

Eid-ul-Fitr

This festival is celebrated at the end of Ramadan. Muslims thank God for the Koran and for helping them fast through the month. The festival begins with prayers at the mosque. It is a time when Muslims ask God's forgiveness.

Eid-ul-Fitr is a national holiday. Families get together, presents are exchanged and a special dinner is cooked to mark this occasion.

Eid-ul-Adha

Another major festival is Eid-ul-Adha, meaning festival of sacrifice. It commemorates the time when Abraham was ready to sacrifice his son, Ishmael, because God commanded it. Eid-ul-Adha is celebrated towards the end of the Hajj. Muslims symbolically sacrifice an animal to show God their devotion. The meat from the animal is shared with friends and relatives as well as the poor.

Events in Muhammad's Life

Muslims also celebrate events in Muhammad's life. They are not considered festivals but most

Crowds outside a mosque

Muslims remember them. Lailat ul-Qadr marks the night when Muhammad was first given the words of the Koran.

12 Rabi ul-Awwal is the birthday of Muhammad.

Ashura, on 10 Muharram, reminds Muslims of the day when Noah left his ark and Moses saved the Israelites from the Egyptians. Muslims mark this occasion with two days of fasting.

The Islamic year is only 354 days long. Ramadan is the sacred month, a time of spiritual discipline, a time of strict daily fasting, reading the Koran and paying the poor-due. It is the ninth month of the Islamic calendar. This means that if we use the western calendar, Ramadan falls eleven days earlier each year. So, over a thirty-year period, Ramadan occurs in every possible season in turn.

In Your Religion Journal

Work out in which month Ramadan will fall in the year 2000 AD.

Match up the events in list A with what they celebrate in list B.

A	B
Eid-ul-Fitr	Night of power
Eid-ul-Adha	Muhammad's birthday
Lailat ul-Qadr	Festival of sacrifice
Ashura	The end of fasting
12 Rabi ul-Awwal	Noah leaving the ark

Lent

'The part of the day that I enjoy most is about 10 a.m. every morning. The children are gone to school. I have the house to myself. I can make a cup of coffee, sit down and have a bit of peace and quiet.'

Angela

'I was thoroughly miserable when I was told that it would take at least six months to recover from the back injury which happened when I was playing basketball. I would be unable to go to work. I would, I thought, be bored and fed up. The time, I felt sure, would drag on and on. I had always been involved in many things outside of work — basketball, keep fit, swimming, and I loved going to the pictures. There was scarcely ever a night when I hadn't planned to do something after work. You can imagine how surprised I was to find that I enjoyed having the time to read, something I had done very little of since I left school. I also found that I liked to sketch and paint. It was good too to have time to think. In fact, I decided that I would always leave more time in my life for thought and reflection, rather than trying, as I had been doing, to fill every moment with activity.'

Nuala

'I have to cross the city every morning to get to college. It takes at least an hour because of the traffic. But I don't mind. It gives me time to think.'

Joe

158

Discuss

Talk about times when you have heard someone say that they needed time to think or to reflect.

Talk about times when you felt that you benefited from having time to think or to reflect.

What do you think is missing from your life when you don't take time to think or to reflect?

We need time to think at times of

**MAKING CHOICES
DECISION**

**CHANGE OF DIRECTION
CRISIS**

Sometimes we tend to rush into things, to take life in a hurry. This makes it difficult for us to assess what we are doing and where we are going.

It is also important to remember that while some of the choices that we make in life are of more significance than others, each day brings choices and decisions. All of the choices and decisions that we make, while they may not have a lasting significance in terms of our direction in life, are nevertheless important in themselves.

In Your Religion Journal

List some of the major choices and decisions which you have made so far in your life.

List some of the day-to-day choices and decisions which you have made in the recent past.

What helped you while you were considering the decisions you had to make?

What made it more difficult?

During the year the Church sets aside Lent as a period when we are encouraged to take time to think about the way in which we are living, the choices we are making and how we are responding to the teachings of Jesus. It's a time for reviewing our lives and taking stock. It's also a time for making decisions and choices for the future.

Find Your Group
Discuss

List some situations in your life where you think you would benefit from spending some time reflecting on how you have been living and considering how you might do better in the future.

In Your Religion Workbook
Fill in the following. Then use it to check from time to time how you are doing during Lent.

In my relationship with my parents

Areas where things are going well	Areas where there is need for improvement	Things I could do

At school

Areas where things are going well	Areas where there is need for improvement	Things I could do

In my relationships with my friends

Areas where things are going well	Areas where there is need for improvement	Things I could do

In my relationship with God

Areas where things are going well	Areas where there is need for improvement	Things I could do

160

The Season of Lent

The season of Lent lasts for forty days.
The forty days of Lent recall the forty days
which Jesus spent in the desert, and the forty
years during which the Israelites journeyed
through the desert to the Promised Land.
Read Luke 4:1-13.

Discuss

Why do you think that Jesus spent forty days fasting in the
desert at the beginning of his public ministry?

Fasting

During Lent we are all called to fast. In the past,
for Catholics, every day in Lent was a fast day.
That meant that people only ate one full meal
and two very small snacks, and abstained from
eating meat. Now there are only two fast days
during Lent: Ash Wednesday and Good Friday.
We are, however, still challenged to fast during

Lent by deciding not to eat something that we
are especially fond of or by giving up something
else that we like. We could also decide not to eat
every time we feel like eating. We are encouraged to become aware that the most important
thing in life is not that we satisfy all our desires,
but that we live as Jesus wants us to live. Fasting
is encouraged not only in the Catholic Church
but also in the Islamic and Jewish faiths. Doing
without some things which we want helps us to
develop self-control. If we want to live as followers of Jesus we often need to
be able to use the quality of self-
control.

Find Your Group

Discuss

Think of some advertisements on television which
encourage us to have everything we want.
Which of these do you find influence the decisions you
make about what to eat, what to buy, etc.?
Talk about a time when you tried very hard to get something even though you really did not need it.

Giving to those less well-off than ourselves

During Lent we are called by the Church to give money to those who are poor in our own country and also in the Third World. During Lent there is a 'Family Fast Day' when Catholics are asked to eat less food and give what they save, and probably something more as well, to help the Church's work for the needy in the developing world.

Pope John Paul II has said: 'Going without things does not consist only in giving what we do not need; sometimes it also consists in giving away what we do need.'

In Ireland, Trócaire's annual Lenten campaign urges people to collect money which will be used to fund development projects in the Third World. In Britain, Cafod calls on people to remember those who are less well off in the Third World.

Perhaps you could take some of your money, your pocket money for a week, or money you were given as a birthday present, and say to yourself, 'With this money I could buy X or Y or Z; without this money I would be unable to buy those things. However, I will nevertheless choose to give it so that those who are less well-off may be helped.'

On the other hand, you could also arrange with your classmates to organise some fund-raising event, the proceeds of which would be given either to an agency working for the Third World or to a group which looks after the needs of the poor in your own country. You could have a sponsored fast, a sponsored walk, a bring-and-buy sale, a raffle or any other appropriate event. You have the whole of Lent to organise it. Other groups in the school may be very willing to help.

By doing this we are reminded that God created the earth and everything on it for the sake of all people, and that we are called by God to share what we have so that everybody has enough.

Prayer

During Lent we are also asked to try to spend more time in prayer each day.

In this way we will become more conscious of God as someone who loves and cares for all people. We will be more ready to trust in God and to have confidence that God will always take care of us. You could decide to spend a short time in prayer each night before you go to sleep.

You might find the following suggestions helpful:

1. Make sure that your body is in a comfortable position. You could sit on a chair, or on the floor, or you could lie on your bed, or on the floor.

2. Relax your body, starting with your toes. Make sure that all the parts of your body right up to the top of your head are relaxed. You may find it helpful to play some music quietly in the background.

3. Pay attention to your breathing. Feel the life-giving air move in and out of your lungs.

4. Think back over the day.

(a) Recall an incident which made you feel happy. Perhaps you were able to help somebody out. Perhaps somebody else helped you. Perhaps you did something which you really enjoyed. Thank God for all the good things in your life.

(b) Recall an incident from the day which did not make you feel good. You may have been disappointed about something which happened at school or in your family. You may have felt that you failed. You may have been hurt by someone close to you, one of your friends or someone in your family. Perhaps you did something which hurt somebody else. Ask God to help you to cope with the times in your life which are most difficult.

5. You could conclude with the following prayer or a psalm from the Bible which you would like to use.

Evening Prayer

This evening, Lord, I give you thanks.
    For the good things of today,
    for the people whose friendship I value,
    for the work well done,
    for deadlines met,
    for home and for shelter,
    for the food I ate,
    Thank you, Lord.

May the darkness of tonight
take with it the bitterness of today;
may sunset put to rest my anger,
and the starlight be a reminder that your
    forgiveness never fails.
For my failure in your service this day,
I ask your forgiveness, Lord.

I see now that you were present to me this day;
In the love of those I met,
In the call to sympathise and console,
In the cries of those poorer than I —
Those who have no friends,
No food, no home, no shelter.
I remember them now, Lord, in your presence.

For today, Lord, thanks and sorry.
I put to rest with you the troubles of this day;
I ask the peace of your presence until the new
    day dawns,
May the protection you give at the end of a day
be with me and my loved ones
all the days of our lives.

Donal Neary SJ

In Your Religion Journal

Write about the prayer that is most meaningful for you each night.

Find Your Group

Discuss practical ways in which you could make this Lent a time for reflection and renewal.

What about fasting?

Would you be prepared to stop eating something which you particularly like?

You could then offer the money which you saved to an organisation which will use it to help those less well-off. Perhaps you could organise a family fast day in your home and contribute the money you save to help those less well-off.

Are there other ways in which you will contribute some money which could be used to help lessen the suffering of those who are poor?

Are you prepared to spend some extra time in prayer this Lent?

Will you spend some time thinking about your own life, the choices you make, the way you treat others, the kinds of relationships you have with those in your own family, with your friends in school, and with people in your neighbourhood? Are there some resolutions which you should make about the future?

In Your Religion Journal

Lent is a time when we are asked to examine our consciences about the way in which we try to live as followers of Jesus. Write out some questions which you might ask yourself if you wanted to examine your conscience.

Not only individuals but communities are called to examine their consciences during Lent.

If the people of the country you live in were to examine their conscience this Lent as a community, what questions might they ask themselves?

In the Early Church

In the first centuries of the Church those who wanted to join the followers of Jesus spent some time listening to the life story of Jesus. They heard about the way Jesus lived and the way he treated others. They heard the things Jesus said to his followers while he was on earth. They became aware of the demands that Jesus makes on those who wish to be called his followers. The final weeks of their preparation were the weeks before Easter. They would be baptised during Mass on Easter Saturday night. The Church would celebrate the new life of Christ at his resurrection and the new life those believers would receive at Baptism. The weeks before Easter were for them a time of special preparation for their Baptism. They prayed and fasted and read Scripture. They were trying to understand more clearly what would be required of them as followers of Jesus in the Church. Also, people who had committed serious sin used the period of Lent to be reconciled with the Church. During Lent they did public penance. They sat in a special place in the church. They fasted and spent long periods of time in prayer.

Ash Wednesday

Lent begins on Ash Wednesday. On Ash Wednesday ashes are blessed and are used to mark people's foreheads with the sign of the cross. The ashes remind us that our lives here on earth will not last forever. Ashes are also a sign of repentance. In the Old Testament people showed their wish to repent by putting ashes on their heads and wearing sackcloth. The sign of the cross reminds us that we will often have to suffer if we want to live as true followers of Jesus.

Penitential Prayer Service for Lent

Leader:
In this season of Lent let us ask God to help us to examine our lives so that we will be more aware of the ways in which we fail to live up to our calling as followers of Jesus in the world today.

Opening Hymn:
Only in God

Reader:
A reading from St Matthew's Gospel:
Ask and you shall receive; seek and you will find; knock, and the door will be opened to you. For everyone who asks will receive, and anyone who seeks will find, and the door will be opened to him who knocks. Would any of you who are fathers give your son a stone when he asks for bread? Or would you give him a snake when he asks for a fish? Bad as you are you know how to give good things to your children. How much more, then, will your Father in heaven give good things to those who ask him.
(*Matthew 7:7-11*)

Hymn:
Do not be afraid.

Leader:
Let us ask God to listen to our prayers this Lent.

Response:
Lord, hear us, we pray.

Reader :
We pray that we will have the courage to change the behaviour which keeps us from living as followers of Jesus.

Response:
Lord, hear us, we pray.

Reader:
We pray that we will encourage others who we know are also trying to make changes in their lives.

Response:
Lord, hear us, we pray.

Reader:
We pray that we will be able to make this Lent a time for making new beginnings.

Response:
Lord, hear us, we pray.

Reader:
We pray that we will be more careful about the choices we make.

Response:
Lord, hear us, we pray.

Reader:
We pray that we will be more generous towards those who are less fortunate than ourselves.

Response:
Lord, hear us, we pray.

Leader:
Let us pray together in the words of the Confiteor.

All:
I confess to almighty God,
and to you, my brothers and sisters,
that I have sinned through my own fault
in my thoughts and in my words,
in what I have done,
and in what I have failed to do;
and I ask blessed Mary, ever virgin,
all the angels and saints,
and you, my brothers and sisters,
to pray for me to the Lord our God.

Leader:
Let us now spend some time in silence, reflecting on the different areas of our lives. Once again, we ask God to help us to recognise all that is good in our lives and to change all that should be better.

(Play some background music quietly, while the following is read slowly, leaving lots of time for reflection.)

Leader:
We think about our relationships with God.

Reader:
How often do we spend time in prayer?
Do we speak of God and of Jesus with respect?
Do we go to Mass?
Or
Is there no time at all in our lives for God?

(Pause)

Leader:
We think about our lives at home.

Reader:
Do we play our part at home?
Do we grumble and complain unnecessarily?
Do we treat those who are in charge of us with respect?
Are we aware of the effort it takes to provide us with food, clothes and education?
Do we show appreciation or do we take these for granted?
Are we open and honest at home?

(Pause)

Leader:
Let us think about our relationships with our friends.

Reader:
Do we treat our friends with respect?
Do we respect their freedom to make choices?
Do we try to make sure that no one is left out or lonely?

(Pause)

Leader:
Let us think about our lives in the school community and in the neighbourhood where we live.

Reader:
Are we honest?
Do we respect things that belong to others and public property?
Do we make an effort to look out for the needs of others, especially those who are more vulnerable than we are ourselves?
Do we bully those who are weaker than ourselves, or stand by and watch them being bullied by others?
Are we truthful?
Are we prepared to take a stand if we see something happening which we know to be wrong?

(Pause)

Leader:
For all the times when we left God out of our lives,
Lord, have mercy.

All:
Lord, have mercy.

Leader:
For all the times when we did not show love and respect at home,
Lord, have mercy.

All:
Lord, have mercy.

Leader:
For all the times when we were in any way a bad influence on our friends, Lord, have mercy.

All:
Lord, have mercy.

Leader:
For all the times when we were the cause of suffering or disruption in the communities where we live, Lord, have mercy.

All:
Lord, have mercy.

Leader:
For all the times when we were untruthful or dishonest in any way, Lord, have mercy.

All:
Lord, have mercy.

Leader:
For all the times when we showed disrespect for God or for Jesus, Lord, have mercy.

All:
Lord, have mercy.

Leader:
Let us express our sorrow together.

All:
Act of Sorrow
O my God, I thank you for loving me.
I am sorry for all my sins:
For not loving others and not loving you.
Help me to live like Jesus and not sin again. Amen.
Or
O my God, because you are so good,
I am very sorry that I have sinned against you,
And with your help I will not sin again.

Final Hymn:
My soul is longing for your peace.

Justice

Different people mean different things when they use the word justice, so it is important to have some clear ideas of what justice really is.

In Your Religion Journal

Complete the following:

The words I think of when I hear the word justice are:

_____

_____

_____

When I hear the word justice the scenes that come to mind are:

_____

_____

_____

Describe an incident when you acted justly.

_____

_____

_____

Justice is often thought of as being associated with the law, the courts and prisons. But justice is much more than just complying with the law, it has to do with equality and fairness.

Justice begins with ourselves and our dealings with others. It is concerned with developing right relationships with other people, whether they are our close friends, those we find it difficult to get along with, or even those we know little or nothing about. Justice means that we respect the rights of everyone. In doing so we co-operate with one another and this encourages us to live in peace together. In a practical way, justice demands that we treat others in the same way that we like to be treated ourselves. Justice is about our work, our lifestyle, our business. It is about honesty and truthfulness at home and at school.

I Deserve it

Mike has a part-time job in the local supermarket. He gets paid £2.85 per hour. On Saturday night when he got home he found he had £5.00 too much in his pay packet. 'Well', he thought to himself, 'the manager won't miss it and anyway I deserve it.' That night he went out with his friends and spent it.

The Price You Have to Pay

Sarah hadn't meant to cheat in her exams, but she realised that she hadn't done enough work throughout the year. She didn't want to come last in the class. When the exams were finished Jill, a classmate of Sarah's, called her to one side. 'Sarah, I've seen you cheating in your French and Maths exams and maybe you cheated in others, I don't know, but don't worry, I'm not going to tell anyone.'

Sarah looked puzzled. 'Well, then why are you telling me?'

'It's like this', Jill continued, 'I thought I'd ask you for £3.00 a week to keep me quiet'.

'That's blackmail', shouted Sarah. Jill just shrugged her shoulders and said, 'Well that's the price you have to pay for my silence'.

Loose Change

The third year class were organising a sponsored walk to help raise money to buy a minibus for the old people's home in the town.

After the walk Mark was put in charge of collecting the other students' money. He was supposed to keep a record of the amount of money each person gave him.

Mark didn't mind collecting the money, in fact, he saw it as an opportunity to make a few pounds on the side. Any time one of his classmates gave him loose change, for example, £12.60, sixty pence would go in to his pocket.

'Nobody will notice', he thought, 'and anyway, if I'm caught, I'll just say I miscalculated the amount.' At the end of the week the teacher collected the money. She praised the class for all their hard work and for collecting the grand total of £200, but little did she realise that it should have been £230.

Underpaid

Michelle has started college this year. She has to get a part-time job to help buy her books and clothes and pay her bus fare to college.

She applies for a job at the local newsagent. Mr Jenkins knows that she really needs the job so he decides to employ her. However, he pays her £1.00 less than the standard hourly rate of pay. Michelle realises that she is being paid very little, but because she needs the job she has to keep working.

Life made difficult

'Joe doesn't seem to be enjoying his new school and I can't understand why', said Mrs Power to her husband. 'He's made a lot of new friends since he went to St Pat's and he seems interested in the new subjects he's learning. He's even been asked to be a member of the junior basketball team.'

But there was one reason why Joe wasn't enjoying school, and that's because he was being bullied by a boy in the third year class.

Damien had taken a dislike to Joe from the moment he saw him. He had no reason not to like him but, as he had told his friends, 'I just don't like the look of him, he thinks he's great, I'll soon knock some sense into him.'

And so, every opportunity that Damien had, he tried to make life difficult for Joe. He'd make fun of him in front of his classmates. In the corridor he'd knock him over and empty his school-bag on the floor. Going home on the school bus one day he tied him to his seat and wouldn't let him get off at his stop. Joe didn't know what to do. Damien had warned him not to tell his teachers or he'd make life even more difficult.

Find Your Group

In each of these situations find a solution where the people involved could have acted justly.

In Your Religion Journal

Describe an incident when you were treated unjustly. How did you feel?

In Your Religion Journal Activity

Read the list below. Circle the five actions that you think are the most serious forms of injustice and say why you have made these choices. Listen to the choices made by the others in the class.

Teasing a classmate in front of my friends

Stealing from a friend

Spreading rumours

Duplicating a tape

Throwing away most of my food

Carving my initials on a school desk

Not telling when I've got too much change back

Bullying someone who is weaker than me

Taking off sick, when I'm not

Blaming someone else for something I did

Making fun of a classmate who can't afford good clothes

Stealing from a supermarket

Cheating in an exam

Lying to my parents about where I've been

Not telling my parents where I've been

Yelling at Mum or Dad

Ignoring a classmate whom nobody wants to be with

Refusing to hang around with classmates who are not the same race as me

Covering up for someone who has done something seriously wrong

Some people think that as long as you don't get caught and get away with it, it's all right to pilfer from the supermarket, fiddle the books, evade paying income tax, take home 'what falls off the back of a lorry', do the double on the dole, or receive payment under false pretences.

As long as you don't get caught!

When Willie was a small child he was in the supermarket with his mother one day when she received wrong change as they passed through the check-out. As she put the extra cash in her handbag she said, 'It's okay, Willie, everyone does it.' Willie got a summer job in the fruit department of the same supermarket. One of his jobs was to put the overripe strawberries at the bottom of the cartons and the more presentable ones on top. 'It's good for business, son,' his boss told him. Later on in life Willie got a good job as financial controller in a textile company. He was caught fiddling the books and dismissed. When he returned home in disgrace his parents accused him: 'Look at the shame and disgrace you have brought upon us. If there is anything we cannot stand, it is dishonesty.'

Discuss

In what ways were Willie's mother and boss acting unjustly?
Why did Willie's offence bring shame on the family?
What would you say is the moral of the story?
How do we decide what is just?

How do we decide what is just and unjust? If we say justice is based 'on a sense of fair play', well, maybe my sense of fair play is different from yours.

If we say justice is based on the law, maybe we could imagine a country which has laws which oppress the people and aren't fair. In other words, there has to be a standard by which we judge the law.

We could say justice is based on **human rights** — on the dignity and rights of a person. For someone to have human rights, no other qualification is necessary than to be a human being.

Human rights do not come from laws which were made by human beings or from a sense of fair play. They belong to a person because he or she is a person made in God's image.

Therefore, justice demands, in the first place, that in our own dealings with others we should always treat them fairly and with respect for their rights – not behaving dishonestly towards them, doing them any wilful damage or attacking their dignity. This is the most basic requirement but it is not the only one. We should also be committed to the spread of justice in the world, doing what we can, as individuals or in groups, to ensure that human beings have access to those conditions necessary to live their lives with dignity.

170

In Your Religion Journal

Compile a list of conditions you consider necessary for human beings to live life with dignity. Share your list with the class.

What is a right?

We live in a society where there is talk of many kinds of rights – civil rights, student rights, the rights of the working person and so on. However, many of these rights are based on fundamental human rights. Rights are something people are entitled to. They are necessary for living the dignified and meaningful life that God wants for every human being. There is a difference between rights and privileges. For example, the right to food and clothing is the birthright of every person; whereas driving a car is a privilege that must be earned by passing a test.

As Christians we are called to respect and protect the rights of all people. Justice is the attitude which leads people to respect another person's rights. All rights have their corresponding duties. For example, my right to own property imposes on others the duty to respect this right of mine, and in the same way it is my duty to ensure that I respect another's right to property.

Declaration of Human Rights

On 10 December 1942 the United Nations Organisation published its **Declaration of Human Rights**. It is sometimes referred to as the **Universal Declaration of Human Rights**. The outstanding feature of this declaration is that it is universal, it applies to everyone throughout the world. It recognises the equality of all men and women and their right to live with dignity and freedom as well as establishing the responsibilities of all human beings.

It was signed by the representatives of peoples of very different cultures, religions and political systems, for instance Europeans, Africans, Asians, Buddhists, Muslims, Christians, Communists and capitalists and people of the developed and under-developed world. All these people agreed on thirty basic rights which are a common standard of achievement for all peoples and nations.

In Your Religion Journal

Read through the list, on the following page, of human rights as agreed by the United Nations.
Choose what you consider to be the five most precious rights in your life at the present time and say why you have chosen them.

UNIVERSAL DECLARATION of HUMAN RIGHTS

On DECEMBER 10, 1948, the General Assembly of the United Nations adopted and proclaimed the Universal Declaration of Human Rights, the full text of which appears in the following pages. Following this historic act the Assembly called upon all Member countries to publicize the text of the Declaration and "to cause it to be disseminated, displayed, read and expounded principally in schools and other educational institutions, without distinction based on the political status of countries or territories."

Final Authorized Text

UNITED NATIONS

OFFICE OF PUBLIC INFORMATION

Human Rights

Everyone is entitled to all the rights and free-doms without distinct-ion of any kind such as:

race
colour
sex
language
religion
political opinion
national origin
social origin
property
birth

The right:
to life;
to liberty and security of person;
not to be a slave;
not to be tortured;
to protection of the law;
to a fair and public hearing in the courts;
to be presumed innocent until proven guilty;
to freedom of movement and residence;
to a nationality;
to marry and found a family;
to own property;
to freedom of thought, conscience and religion;
to freedom of peaceful assembly and of association;
to freedom of opinion and expression;
to seek and receive information and ideas;
to take part in politics;
to social security;
to work;
to fair wages and equal pay for equal work;
to join a trade union;
to rest and leisure;
to adequate health care;
to education.

Draw the following diagram on a sheet of newsprint. With your group fill in the boxes by compiling a list of the ways you can carry out your duty in showing respect for the rights of other people in each area of your life.

Class Activity
Find Your Group

Design and illustrate a wall chart which will advertise each of the human rights.

Discuss

What are the rights of students in a school?
What are the rights of teachers in a school?
In what ways could teachers be treated unfairly?
In what ways could students be treated unfairly?

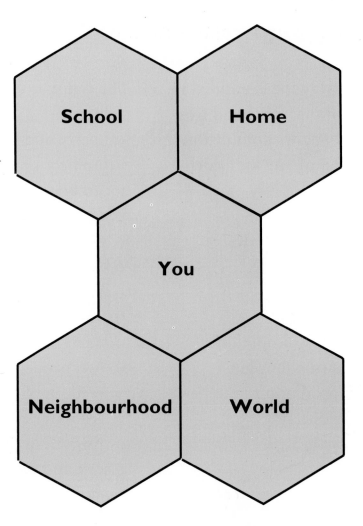

The Ten Commandments and Human Rights

The ten commandments and the United Nations Declaration of Human Rights both, in their own way, state the guidelines which establish the rights and responsibilities of all human beings. The ten commandments were given by God to help people understand how they are to treat one another. They guide people towards right relationships with one another and with God.

The ideals listed in the Declaration of Human Rights are the guidelines for the world community in safeguarding the rights of all people. They aim to protect the dignity and freedom of all people who are made in God's image. They help people to discover how to respect and protect the rights of all other people.

The Ten Commandments

1. I am the Lord your God, you shall not have strange gods before me.

2. You shall not take the name of the Lord your God in vain.

3. Remember that you keep holy the Sabbath day.

4. Honour your father and your mother.

5. You shall not kill.

6. You shall not commit adultery.

7. You shall not steal.

8. You shall not bear false witness against your neighbour.

9. You shall not covet your neighbour's husband or wife.

10. You shall not covet your neighbour's goods.

Respect for God.

Respect for parents and authority

Respect for life

Respect for marriage

Respect for property

Respect for another person's reputation

Respect for loving relationships

Respect for what another person owns

Match up

Which of the commandments can you match up with the rights enshrined in Declaration of Human Rights?

More than one match is possible.

Give your reasons for each match you make.

Activity

Choose a human rights issue that you feel strongly about. Compose a speech on that issue and deliver your speech to the class.

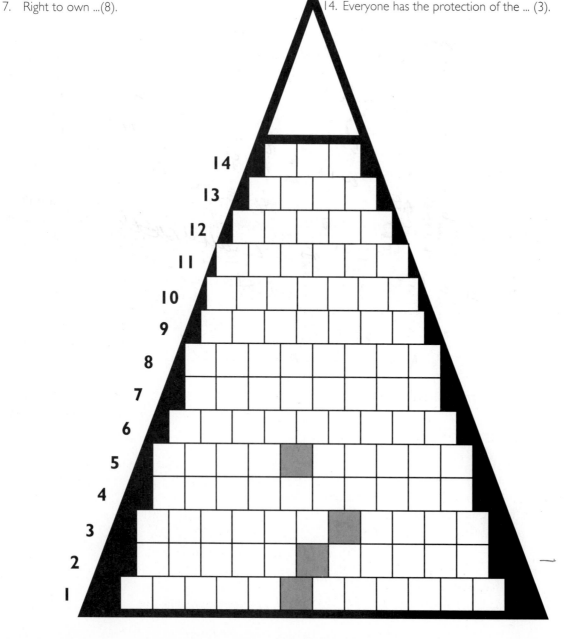

174   **Activity**

Fill in the clues to the human rights pyramid.

1. In 1942 the UN published its Declaration of ...(5,6)
2. You may join one of these organisations if you are working to protect your interests (5,5).
3. Everyone has the right to assistance with their physical well-being (6,4).
4. Another name given to the right to 'work'(10).
5. Equal pay for equal work (4,5).
6. You acquire this by going to school, and it will help you in getting a job when you leave (9).
7. Right to own ...(8).

8. Human rights ensure the ....of all women and men to live with dignity and freedom (8).
9. Another name for liberty (7).
10. Free, unoccupied time (7).
11. Group of parents and children who are related and live together as a unit (6).
12. When a woman and man take part in the Sacrament of Matrimony they...(5).
13. We should have respect for all forms of ... (4).
14. Everyone has the protection of the ... (3).

Prophets who seek Justice

A prophet is a person who is called by God to speak out against the injustices and corruption in society. They speak not only on behalf of God but also on behalf of those who have no voice and cannot be heard. It takes courage and honesty to act and speak out as a prophet.

The message of the Old Testament prophets is a powerful message of justice. It demands that people work for justice in their everyday lives, in their relationships with others and with those people in society who are mistreated and neglected, such as the poor, the deprived and those who are oppressed or exploited. They call for justice to be carried out in all areas of life: in religion, in business, in politics and in the social conditions in which people live. They condemn any religious hypocrisy or any practice of religion that is not linked to working for justice. In today's world, their message is still relevant.

Amos – A Prophet of Social Justice

About eight hundred years before Jesus, there was a farmer called Amos who looked after a few sheep and goats on his plot of land near Bethlehem. The thing which made him special and different from the farmers and shepherds around him was that he was a prophet. Now a more unlikely prophet than Amos it would be hard to find. He had never wanted the job but still God called him to deliver an important message to the people of his time. They were a people much like ourselves, outwardly religious, regular church-goers and great for going on pilgrimages. Four times a year they would head for Jerusalem on pilgrimage and on the way they would pass Amos' little plot chanting their hymns and psalms to God. In Jerusalem they would offer their sacrifices of thanksgiving and praise to the Lord. But despite this outward show of religion there was widespread dishonesty. Farmers were fiddling, shopkeepers were giving short measures and the poor were exploited and were unable to get justice in the courts. Judges were corrupt and took bribes, people who couldn't repay their debts were thrown out on the streets and everyone was after a quick buck. Their religion was a gigantic fraud. And so God sent Amos to them as his mouthpiece to demand that they change their attitude and behaviour and this was his message:

I hate...I reject your pilgrimages;
I am not pleased with your sacred ceremonies.
When you present your sacrifices and offerings
I will not accept them;
I don't want to hear your hymns
I can't endure your music.
Though you offer countless prayers
I will not listen.
Let justice roll like a river!

Dom Helder Camara

Dom Helder was born in 1909 in Fortaleza, the capital of the state of Ceara, north-east Brazil. As one of thirteen children, five of whom died of dysentery when young, his experience of suffering and injustice was at first hand. He became a priest in 1931 and devoted much of his time to helping the poor in the slums of his native state of Ceara.

In 1952 he was appointed auxiliary Bishop of Rio. During this time he began to speak out, through his preaching, against the policies of the government of his country which he said did nothing but 'enrich thousands and bring poverty to millions'. He never ceased to preach the gospel in a country torn by the extremes of wealth and poverty. He challenged the governments of his own country and other countries around the world when he said: 'Should not our very first step be to seek the cause of injustice, to see clearly what is happening with the unjust structures that are crushing over two-thirds of the human race?'

He identified with the poor by living in squalid conditions in the shanty towns around Rio.

In 1964 Dom Helder was made Archbishop of Olinda and Recife, in north-east Brazil, far from Rio. Many saw it as an attempt to remove him from public attention and controversy and to silence his criticism of the government. In the same year a dictatorship was set up in Brazil and many thousands of people who protested on behalf of the poor were put in prison. Hundreds of priests were imprisoned, many tortured, for seeking to work with the poor.

On many occasions, the Archbishop's own life was threatened. He was not allowed to broadcast on radio or TV. He was banned from writing articles for Brazil's newspapers. The media could only mention him to denounce him.

He is one of the world's great Christian prophets who has crusaded on behalf of the poor and oppressed and who hopes that one day there will be a world free from poverty and injustice.

In an interview to mark his seventy-fifth birthday, Dom Helder Camara reflected on his priesthood: 'For me being a priest is to have the joy of spending my life living with others....for me it is to spend life loving God with all our heart, with all our soul, and loving our neighbour.'

The Just Person

In many ways it is easier to build up a picture or 'identikit' of the just person, indicating the qualities and values which characterise such a person, rather than trying to define what justice is.

In Your Religion Journal

The Justice and Peace Department have opened a file on the just person and have asked you to help them with their investigation. You are to help them identify such a person by giving an outline of the characteristics, qualities and values of this person.

Fill in the details on the file. The more details you provide the easier will be the identification.

FILE

Going Beyond Justice

Justice is about giving people what is their due, and observing their rights. But the teaching of Jesus is about more than justice. It is also about mercy and compassion. These will cause us to seek justice but also to go beyond it.

If someone owes you money you are not unjust if you ask for it back from that person when the time for repayment comes. But what if you know that paying it all back at once will cause him or her serious hardship? How should you act then and why?

If someone repeatedly injures you in some way, and then says she is sorry and asks you to forgive her, it is not strictly unjust for you to refuse. She has no right to your forgiveness. She cannot demand it. But because it is not unjust does not mean that it is right. Injustice is not the only sin.

Jesus tells us: 'Be merciful as your Heavenly Father is merciful.'

Read the story of the unmerciful servant in Matthew 18:23-35.
What message do you think it has for us?

Personal Reflection

Think of a time when someone forgave you when you did not deserve to be forgiven. What words would you use to describe how you felt? Are there times when you could forgive someone else, even if they do not deserve it?

Prayerful Reflection

The Prophet Micah says:
The Lord has told you what is good.
What the Lord requires of you is this:
to do justice,
and to love kindly,
and to walk humbly with your God.
(Micah 6:8)

Think quietly of one thing which you could do at home, at school or in your neighbourhood if you wanted to live up to the demands listed in this extract from the Prophet Micah. Ask God to help you, through Jesus, to do the things you have decided upon.

Lord Jesus, I give you my hands to do your work.
I give you my feet to go your way.
I give you my eyes to see as you do.
I give you my tongue to speak your words.
I give you my mind that you may think in me.
I give you my spirit that you may pray in me.
Above all I give you my heart that you may love in me your Father and all humankind.
I give you my whole self that you may grow in me,
so that it is you, Lord Jesus,
who live and work and pray in me.

In the name of the Father, and of the Son and of the Holy Spirit.
Amen.

Lesson Sixteen

Justice in Action

Prejudice

To be prejudiced means that we prejudge, that is we make a decision about someone or something before the basic facts are known or before we have even experienced the situation.

If prejudice is strong enough, it can blind us to all evidence that points the other way. We will seize on anything that confirms the judgement we have already made, and simply dismiss or pass over the rest. Prejudice causes us to see what we want to see and to overlook what we don't want to know.

Stereotyping

When our prejudices are directed towards an individual or a group of people we call this stereotyping. When we stereotype we make judgements about an individual or an entire group of people based on limited, untested, unjust assumptions. We put people into categories based on our first impressions and preconceived notions. We tend to have a fixed image of people.
Stereotyping deprives an individual or a group of the respect

180

and dignity that is owing to people made in God's own image. It fails to recognise the individuality, uniqueness and equality of people. It prevents us from reaching out and learning from and about others. By stereotyping an individual or a group of people we overlook the fact that each person has skills and interests and abilities that we cannot be aware of until we take time and trouble to meet one another and to learn more about the value and dignity of each human being.

In Your Religion Journal

Read the following accounts and answer the questions in your religion journal.

Does she take milk?

In many ways Michelle is like the others in her class. She studies the same subjects, laughs at the same jokes and looks forward to the disco on a Saturday night. But in one respect Michelle is different from her classmates. She cannot run or jump or take part in sport. Michelle is confined to a wheelchair. Her thin, twisted legs cannot support her. Sometimes on a Saturday morning her mother takes her into town. While out shopping they usually go for a cup of coffee. The people who serve behind the counter ask her mother, 'Does the young girl take milk in her coffee?'

Discuss

In what way has Michelle been stereotyped?
What kind of person do you think Michelle is?
Have you ever treated someone like Michelle in the same way as the people who served in the coffee shop?
Do you think the people in the coffee shop intended to act unjustly?
What mistake have they made?

Trouble in the bowling alley

It was Friday night and Fintan and his friends decided they would play a few games of ten-pin bowling in the local bowling alley.
They arranged to meet each other at 8.00 p.m. outside the complex. They all paid their money when they went in and then went over to the cloakroom to change into the special bowling shoes which they had to wear.
Immediately the manager of the bowling alley came up to the group, called Fintan to one side and, pointing at Peter, he said, 'I don't want the likes of him in here, this is a respectable place. It wouldn't go down too well with the rest of the people who come here if they knew a Traveller had been wearing a pair of bowling shoes.' Fintan began to protest, but the manager interrupted him. 'Anyway, I don't want any trouble in here, it's okay if you want to stay but I'll have to ask your friend to leave.'

Discuss

What was the first sign that the manager was discriminating against Peter?
Why did the manager want Peter to leave?
How has the manager stereotyped Peter?
Can you give any reasons why he might have stereotyped Peter in this way?
How do you think Peter feels?
In what way is the manager acting unjustly?

My Son! My Son!

The rain was heavy that night. The lorry was travelling too fast when it turned the corner and tried to brake before ploughing into a father and his son who were out walking. The father was killed outright. The boy was taken to hospital. The surgeon who was on casualty duty at the hospital recognised him. 'My son! My son!' cried the surgeon, horrified, 'That's my son'.

Discuss

Why did the surgeon shout 'My son! My son!'?
Did your immediate reaction stereotype the surgeon?

Seventy and past it

Mrs Bell lives on her own. Her family live abroad and so she doesn't get to see them very often. A few years ago she fell and broke her leg and since the accident she has been using a walking stick. But she keeps herself busy. Each week she attends a couple of evening

classes in the local college. She is learning conversational French and has planned a holiday in France with some of her friends.

Last week at her evening class, she overheard two young girls talking about her. 'What do you think she wants to learn French for? I'm sure she's well over seventy and past it.'

Georgie's sister

Sarah has recently started post-primary school. She enjoys school and is conscientious about doing her homework. Her older sister Georgie always got into trouble at school. In fifth year she dropped out of school after she became pregnant. As soon as she learned who Sarah was, one of the teachers said 'Well, I hope you understand that we won't have any nonsense in my classes,' and Sarah heard some of the older students saying 'I bet there's going to be some fun in the first year. One of the new girls is Georgie's sister'. Sarah feels that people who hardly know her are already comparing her with Georgie.

Looking Scruffy

Patsy dresses all wrong. He wears clothes that everyone finished with years ago. Very often he would forget to comb his hair before coming to school and generally he looks scruffy. Most of his friends dress the same way as each other. Nancy is a classmate and lives next door to Patsy but she avoids walking to school with him and doesn't talk to him in class.

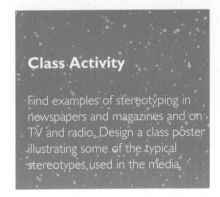

Class Activity

Find examples of stereotyping in newspapers and magazines and on TV and radio. Design a class poster illustrating some of the typical stereotypes used in the media.

Prejudice in Action Happens

— when we generalise or stereotype people;

— when we make irrational or illogical judgements about people;

— when we are narrow-minded and refuse to change our opinions even though we have information which contradicts them;

— when we react to others with resentment or hatred or even suspicion and fear.

Then we are acting unjustly.

Discrimination

When our prejudices cause us to speak unjustly about others or encourage us to act unjustly towards others, we call this discrimination.

Discrimination happens when we put our prejudices into action. It is when we make pre-judgements about people and act accordingly in an unfair and unjust way towards them.

When we treat people unjustly and when we make unfavourable distinctions between people because of such characteristics as colour, sex, religion, culture, intelligence, status and age, then we discriminate.

Discrimination can occur between individuals or groups of people. It can happen anywhere, in school, at the youth club, at the leisure centre or at work.

Discrimination can take many forms. In many ways it is easy to look to other parts of the world and see situations where people are discriminated against and exploited, while at the same time we tend to overlook that there are many victims of prejudice and discrimination in our own country.

Activity

Choose from the following statements, identifying which are examples of prejudice, stereotyping or discrimination. Group them together.

All hippies have rich parents.

No admittance to Travellers

I don't like punk rockers.

Men only in the clubhouse

Over 40s need not apply for the job.

I wouldn't listen to jazz music, it's awful.

Unemployed people are all wasters.

Poor people are usually scruffy.

I don't want to go to university, higher education is a waste of time.

In Your Religion Journal

Do you know of any incident in your neighbourhood where an individual or a group of people were discriminated against?
Write about a time when you were discriminated against. How did you feel?
Write about a time when you discriminated against someone. What reasons can you give for acting in that way?

Are you aware of racial prejudice in your everyday life?

1. Can you say that you are not racially prejudiced?

2. Do you believe that all people should be treated equally, regardless of their colour, culture or background?

3. If a group of your friends made cutting remarks about someone because of his or her nationality, what would you do?

4. Can you think of any individuals or groups of people who are called racist names?

5. What sort of racist names or racially prejudiced statements have you heard being used?

6. Have you ever seen any other person or group being treated unfairly?

7. Can you think of jokes made about particular groups of people according to where they come from, the colour of their skin, their sex and so on?

8. Is there something more serious behind these jokes?

9. If you went to the following places would you prefer to see someone like yourself in terms of culture, colour, background, etc. or would it matter to you?
Hospital/Doctor
Dental surgery/Dentist
Shop/Assistant
Restaurant/Waiter
Bank/Clerk
Swimming pool/Lifeguard

10. Do you consider any of your answers to this questionnaire to be racist answers? Give your reasons.

11. Can you name three notable persons of a race other than your own whom you admire and who are of a different nationality, colour or background from yourself?

Racial Prejudice

People came to believe that the population of the world was divided into different races. They also believed that some races were superior to others. This way of thinking was shaped by white people. It is not surprising, therefore, that it has worked to their advantage while, at the same time, it has been the cause of the oppression of others, for instance black people.

Racial prejudice occurs when people make unfair and untested judgements about others because of the colour of their skin, their values or beliefs, their lifestyle, their ancestry, etc.

People who practise racial prejudice see particular people as 'inferior' to themselves. They tend to stereotype certain characteristics of a race and it is on that basis that they hold their prejudices.

Activity

Answer the following questionnaire in your religion journal.

Discuss

Do you think there are areas in your life where it is necessary for you to change your attitude towards other people?

Racism

Racial prejudice becomes systematic racism when it is a fairly consistent feature of a society in which a group or groups are dominated by one or more other groups. Racism actively discriminates against an individual or a group because of colour, nationality, or cultural background. It is usually directed towards less-powerful groups — in other words, racism combines prejudice with the abuse of power. Racism can occur at all levels of society and is reflected in the attitudes and actions both of the institutions of a country and of individuals.

In a racist society one may find systematic discrimination against others in many areas of life including jobs, housing, access to education or adequate health care; and in some cases people of certain races may be refused entry to places of entertainment.

Until recently in South Africa, black people were kept separate, by law, from the white people who controlled the country. This form of racism is called institutional racism because the various institutions of society openly and legally discriminate against a particular group of people. Thankfully, though this kind of racism has by no means disappeared, and though there is still much political, social and economic inequality between

the races in South Africa, the extent of institutional racism has declined considerably in recent years both in South Africa and other countries. However, there is still a long way to go.

Members of the Ku Klux Klan in their white robes and eye-holed cowls

Discuss

Do you know of any situations throughout the world where the government of a country operates, through law, some kinds of racial discrimination?

The View of the Church

This is what the Second Vatican Council said:
All people are endowed with a rational soul and are created in God's image; they have the same nature and origin and, being redeemed by Christ, they enjoy the same divine calling and destiny; there is here a basic equality between all people and it must be given ever greater recognition...Forms of cultural or social discrimination in basic personal rights on the grounds of sex, race, colour, social condition, language or religion, must be curbed and eradicated as incompatible with God's design.
Gaudium et spes 29

In Your Religion Journal

In what ways can you say that racism is unjust? Give your reasons.
Make a list of the human rights which should protect people against racism.
Give your reasons for saying that all people are basically equal.

Ethnic Groups

One way in which racial prejudice is expressed is through prejudice against a minority ethnic group. People belong to an ethnic group because they are born into it. They cannot join it.

A minority ethnic group of people has a separate culture, language and history which distinguishes it from the majority population of a country. Because they are different from the majority population they are sometimes treated with suspicion and fear. They are looked upon as being inferior and their way of life is not respected. Very often ethnic groups are treated unjustly in that their right to have a distinct identity and culture is not recognised.

However, when we think about it, everyone in the world belongs to an ethnic group with a particular culture, language and history. These differences are part of the richness of the human family.

Discuss

How many ethnic groups do you know of throughout the world? Which ethnic group do you belong to?

Name some of your customs, traditions and values.

Travellers

Travellers are the largest ethnic minority group in Ireland. They are a nomadic people. That means that their way of life is based on moving from place to place. Some of the Travellers may travel throughout the year or some may settle in halting sites temporarily, while others have been known to settle in one place for a number of years before moving on. Their customs, traditions and values are related to their nomadic lifestyle. They have a unique history and ancestry which can be traced back to before the twelfth century.

186 Travellers have a rich oral tradition whereby they pass on their language, history, stories and traditions by word of mouth from one generation to the next. They use their own language, known as Cant, Gammon or Shelta.

However, Travellers are still subjected to the prejudice and discrimination of the settled community. Many Travellers live in deplorable conditions where they lack proper washing, cooking and toilet facilities. In many cases they do not have access to refuse collections or electricity. They also have to face continuous evictions from the roadside. Travellers do not live in these deplorable conditions of their own choice. The local authorities very often do not provide enough halting sites with adequate facilities for them. Travellers' basic rights are often neglected in the areas of employment, health care, education and other social services. In many cases Travellers have been forced into living as settled people in order to receive these basic rights.

Some people from the settled community have a policy of restricting access to Travellers in shops, bars, restaurants and places of entertainment. They treat them with suspicion and open hostility. The prejudice and unjust discrimination of the settled community against the Travellers is a major factor in ensuring the continuation of these conditions.

In Your Religion Journal

Describe a situation where you have seen:
(a) Travellers being treated badly;
(b) Travellers being treated like everyone else.
Imagine you were rejected or continually being turned away from places, how would you feel?
How might you behave towards the settled community in the future?

Find Your Group

Make a list of the human rights which you consider are not respected with regard to the Travellers.
Draw up a declaration of Travellers' Human Rights.

Give Us a Chance

You're different,
Who? Me?
I've the same colour skin,
Don't you see?

But because I was born
On the side of the road,
You say
I don't belong.

You're not wanted here,
Move over,
Shift,
Get out!
The country over
We've heard
The same old shout.

Of our country we are proud,
and can't you see
The hurt you cause
When your voices ring out loud
telling us
We are no good
To society.

But give us half a chance
And you'll see
How good
We really could be.

Mary McDonnell

In Your Religion Journal

In what ways do you think Travellers are treated unjustly?
What needs to be done so that Travellers will be free to live their lives without being troubled by others?
What can you do to improve life for Travellers?

Through the eyes of a Traveller

Activity

Imagine there is a Traveller exchange programme. For one day you swap places with a Traveller. Write a report.

— You live with a Travelling family on the roadside.

— What is your accommodation like?

— How difficult is life for you?

— How does your Travelling family treat you?

— What way does the settled community treat you?

— How do you feel?

— What do you say to the settled community?

— You apply for work, what happens?

— When you have to take one of the family to hospital, how are you treated?

— When you visit the local town, what happens when you go shopping or go to a restaurant or a bar?

People can argue about where the fault lies with regard to the treatment of Travellers. The fact remains that once again we allow our brothers and sisters to remain on the roadside and in open ditches, cold, wet and hungry because there is no room for them in our hearts or our communities. Fear and prejudice can stand in the way of real Christian concern and compassion. I appreciate the fears, both founded and unfounded, of many people in the settled community. Nevertheless, a solution to this problem lies in dialogue and co-operation, not in confrontation and rejection.

Letter from the Archbishop of Dublin 29 January 1989

Research

Choose one example of racial discrimination from your own country and one from another country . Compile a scrapbook and report back to the class.

In Your Religion Journal

Look up James 2:8 in your bible. Copy it into your religion journal and decorate it.

Jesus and Justice

When the book of the prophet Isaiah was handed to Jesus he unrolled the scroll and found the passage where it is written:
> The spirit of the Lord is upon me
> because he has chosen me to
> bring good news to the poor.
> He has sent me to proclaim
> liberty to the captives
> and recovery of sight to the blind,
> to set free the oppressed (*Luke 4:18*).

Jesus began his work by identifying himself with the poor and the deprived in society. He reminded the people of both their dignity and responsibility to love and care for others. Through his words and actions he taught the people how to act justly towards everyone.

Throughout his ministry he constantly sought out those people who were considered outcasts — lepers, tax-collectors or prostitutes — with whom to share a meal or to spend some time.

Jesus insisted that we must act justly. He left no one in doubt that religion without justice was a lie, a fraud. We cannot claim that we have a good relationship with God and then treat some people as if they did not exist or did not matter.

Who is my neighbour?

But Jesus asks more of his followers than simply a concern for justice, important though that is. When Jesus was asked to say which was the most important rule to follow in the Old Testament he quoted the Shema in Deuteronomy 6:5.

'Love the Lord your God with all your heart, with all your soul and with all your strength.' But he followed it up with with a second quotation from *Leviticus 19:18* which says 'Love your neighbour as you love yourself.'

When Jesus was asked the question, 'But who is my neighbour?' he went on to tell them a story.

The Good Samaritan

There was once a man who was on his way from Jerusalem to Jericho. Suddenly, robbers attacked him, stripped him and beat him up, leaving him half dead. It so happened that a priest was going down the same road. When he saw the man lying there, he crossed over to the other side of the road and hurried past. A Levite (someone who helped the priests in the Temple) came by next. He went over and looked at the man. But then he also crossed over and continued his journey.

But a Samaritan (a man from Samaria, considered a foreigner by the Jews) was going that way. When he saw the man, he was instantly sorry for him. He went over to him, attended to his wounds and bandaged them up. Then he put the man on his own donkey and took him to an inn. The next day he had to leave, so he gave the innkeeper two silver coins and said, 'Take care of him and when I come back this way, I will pay you whatever else you spend on him.'
Luke 10:30-35

Discuss

Jesus wanted to teach his listeners that love knows no
boundaries. It reaches out to
everyone. It does not walk on
by. It stops to help, regardless
of who the person is. Jesus
wanted people to rethink their
attitude towards others.

This makes a Christian's task
both easier and more difficult.
Easier because it means that if
someone is in need, we don't
have to work out if he or she is
good or bad, deserving or
undeserving, whether they
have a strict right to the help
they need, or whether or not it
is particularly our responsibility. Some people get into difficulties by accident or misfortune despite all their best
efforts; others bring misfortune
upon themselves by their own
foolishness or even wickedness.
Some are good, kind people;
others are not. For a Christian
none of that matters. All that
matters is that they are our
neighbours, they are in need
and we should treat them with
care and concern.

In that sense it is easier, but it
is also more demanding.

Jesus tells us just how demanding it is:

'Love your enemies, do good
to those who hate you, bless
those who curse you, pray for
those who abuse you.'
Luke 6:27-28

'Love your enemies and pray
for those who persecute you so
that you may be sons of your
father in heaven. For he makes
his sun to shine on bad and
good people alike, and gives
rain to those who do good and
those who do evil'.
Matthew 5:44-45

Love requires us to be just but
it also requires us to be merciful and compassionate even to
those who harm us, to those
who are evil, to those who
don't seem to deserve much
concern. In other words, we
are required to be like God,
who is not merely just, but
merciful and loving. We must be
like him if we want to live with
him.

Discuss

Activity

Understanding the Beatitudes

Presenter: Hello, and welcome to our religious affairs programme. Today we have pleasure in welcoming Jesus to our studio to discuss the Beatitudes. We have also invited a third-year student to join in the discussion.

Student: I hope you don't mind me saying this, Jesus, but I find that the Beatitudes are far too idealistic. Well, I mean no one could live up to them – except yourself, of course, and maybe the saints.

Jesus: I don't agree. In fact, they are extremely practical and are well within the reach of ordinary people – with a little help from God, of course. Let's take a look at them and you'll see that they make great sense.

Blessed are the poor in spirit. Theirs is the Kingdom of Heaven.

Student: Blessed are the poor! Is that some kind of joke? In our world, the person who has nothing is nothing. Surely, then, it's more like: Blessed are the rich, because they can have whatever they want?

Jesus: But rich people are never satisfied. So how can they be happy?

Student: Well, what do you mean by 'the poor in spirit'?

Jesus: Don't you remember the advice I gave to the rich young man who asked me how to gain eternal life? I told him if you want to follow me, sell all you have and give the money to the poor. I value non-material things like kindness, goodness and love.

Student: So what you are saying is that in many ways it is easier for someone who is materially poor to find God in their lives than those people who are materialistic. And that the pursuit of material wealth can often stand in the way of finding God.

Jesus: That's right. But people do need a certain amount of material things in order to live with dignity and freedom. I would prefer to see people put their trust in me rather than in their possessions.

Student: In other words, it's not what you have but who you are that matters.

Jesus: Exactly. To be poor in spirit means that you realise that you need God, that you are dependent on him and that you put your trust in him. So many people forget God in their lives and many others can't find him because they are too busy making a fortune!

Blessed are the gentle. They shall receive all that God has promised.

Student: Blessed are the gentle! You must be kidding. If you're gentle, people will walk all over you.

Jesus: You mean, if you want to get on, you've got to be tough and hard.

Student: Exactly. In this world gentle people get left behind. Aggressive people get on. You know the proverb: the strongest monkey gets to the top of the tree. People respect toughness. They see gentleness as a form of weakness.

Jesus: Gentleness is not a form of weakness. It is a form of strength, and is one of the most necessary qualities in life. Think of the gentleness required in the hands of a mother or a surgeon.

Student: Are you saying that we should never stand up for ourselves?

Jesus: No.

Student: By gentle, then, you don't mean a timid little person who wouldn't say boo to a goose?

Jesus: Of course not. It takes a strong, self-confident person to be gentle. Those who are gentle are in control of their anger, their impatience, their greed, their tongues and their thoughts. They are gentle and strong. By strong I don't mean physical strength, much less brute force, but strength of character.

Student: So as Christians we are called to be gentle and caring with others, especially those whose needs are greatest.

Jesus: Now you're getting the hang of it!

Blessed are those who mourn. They shall be comforted.

Student: Blessed are those who mourn! Who's going to buy that one, Lord?

| Jesus: | There are many people who reach out to God in their sorrow, disappointments, bereavements or loneliness. If they put their trust in God he will bring them comfort. |

Student: I suppose you include people who are sorrowful for their sins.

Jesus: Yes, if anyone reaches out to God in trust and hope, he will comfort them.

Student: And do you also mean those people who suffer a lot because of things over which they have no control, for example, those who are made unemployed and find it hard to make ends meet, those who are discriminated against or those who are deprived in society, and so on?

Jesus: Anyone who is suffering will be comforted if they put their trust in God. But I also want people to be compassionate to others who are suffering and to do their best to help them.

Student: Yes you're right, it's not good enough just to feel sorry for those who are suffering and sit back and do nothing, as Christians we have to get out there and put our concern into action.

Blessed are those who hunger and thirst for what is right. They shall be satisfied.

Student: Let's face it, the only hunger most people know is bodily hunger.

Jesus: People hunger for a lot of things besides food.

Student: Give me an example.

Jesus: They hunger for faith. Without faith one is no better than a sailor on the high seas without a chart or compass or port of destination. They hunger for hope. Without hope one has no future. And of course they hunger for love. One cannot live without love. A human being is made of a body and a soul. The soul too needs nourishment, but in many cases it is neglected.

Student: How do we nourish the soul?

Jesus: The human spirit hungers and thirsts for truth, freedom, justice and goodness. In a word, for what is right.

Student: The only things I see people hunger and

thirst for are power, status, fame and fortune. As for hungering and thirsting for what is right, if people stop to consider something, it's not to see if it's right, but only to see if it benefits them.

Jesus: Now you're making sweeping statements. Not everybody is like that. There are plenty of people who do what is right, who struggle for justice and freedom on behalf of others. Many others in their everyday lives do what is right in their relationships with others, in their work at home and at school.

Blessed are the merciful. They shall have mercy shown them.

Student: Mercy! This makes even less sense than gentleness.

Jesus: Oh, so we're back to hardness and toughness again.

Student: If you're merciful, people will take advantage of you.

Jesus: Are you saying that the world doesn't need mercy?

Student: I'm not saying it doesn't need it, but that it's got no room for it.

Jesus: Well, it's got to make room for it. Without mercy the world would be a jungle.

Student: But that's more or less how it is. People are ruthless, you know. What place is there in such a world for mercy?

Jesus: Yet mercy is the one thing the world is crying out for. How many barriers would fall down, how many broken relationships would be mended, if people were prepared to show mercy and forgiveness to one another?

Student: But let's be practical, Lord. It's just not on to go around forgiving everyone. You'll be regarded as a softie.

Jesus: To be merciful means to be tolerant, patient, sympathetic and understanding towards others. I can't see how this is too much to ask of people. You've heard of the Simon Community? Well, they are a group of people who try to help the poor of the inner cities and towns. They provide shelter for the homeless, they give out food and soup at night and they listen to people telling them about their problems and worries. They are living out the values of God's Kingdom.

Student: I suppose we could all take a leaf out of their book.

Jesus: Now you see, blessed are those who are able to make allowances for the mistakes and sins of others and whose greatness lies in their ability to show mercy.

Blessed are the pure in heart. They shall see God.

Student: Well, what do you mean by pure of heart, Lord?

Jesus: I want people to be more concerned about the evil in the world. I want them to be aware of the dangers of pride, anger, hatred, lust, greed and envy.

Student: So what must we do?

Jesus: To be pure of heart you must be good and honest and kind, not just for the sake of praise or reward or out of fear but because you love God and want to do what he asks of you. You have to be committed to doing all you can to avoid evil in your life.

Student: It's difficult to be good and honest and kind all the time, there are so many temptations and distractions.

Jesus: Take one day at a time, and ask yourself if you are jealous, if you forgive others or if you hold grudges, if you get angry, if you are greedy and so on. As long as you are trying your best and keep trying that's all I ask.

Blessed are the peacemakers, they shall be called children of God.

Student: It's more like happy the troublemakers.

Jesus: Why do you say that?

Student: Because the troublemakers get all the headlines.

Jesus: But troublemakers are very unhappy people. Besides, they are not acting like children of God. I have found that to be a peacemaker you have to have courage, dedication and patience.

Peacemaking is a tough business. There are plenty of peacelovers but only a few peacemakers.

Student: But what can one person do to bring about peace?

Jesus: Peacemaking is a very practical thing. First of all, you have to be at peace with yourself. Peace is also needed between individuals and groups as well as countries. The first step you take is to forgive those who offend you. Welcome the stranger. Do not provoke others to anger. Show tolerance and patience when you are dealing with others. Above all, practise justice. Justice is the foundation of peace.

Student: I suppose you have heard of Brother Roger who founded a community of monks in Taizé in France. The community works for peace and reconciliation between all people, between different religions, between different races and between different nations. They invite people from all over the world, particularly young people, to join them in their work.

Jesus: Yes, the Taizé community is a great example of peacemaking in action.

Blessed are those who are persecuted in the cause of right: theirs is the Kingdom of Heaven.

Student: A lot of people would say: 'Happy are those who lie, steal, cheat and who manage to get off scot-free.' It would seem that people like these are the ones to prosper and go places in the world. Their only commandment is the eleventh commandment.

Jesus: The eleventh commandment?

Student: Thou shalt not get caught!

Jesus: I see. But are they happy? Don't you remember me saying what good will it do you if you gain the whole world but lose your soul?

Wouldn't it be a better world if everybody stood up for what is right?

Student: But it's not easy to stand up for what is

right. You'll bring a lot of trouble on yourself. Far easier never to take a stand on anything. Just mind your own business and you'll have a nice quiet life.

Jesus: Sure, if you take a stand you're letting yourself in for a buffeting. But to suffer in the cause of right is a privilege. It marks you out as a true disciple of mine.

Student: You mean like Oscar Romero who was Archbishop of San Salvador?

Jesus: Yes, the life of Oscar Romero is a good example to take. He saw that his country was full of injustice and the poor suffered greatly at the hands of the rich. He saw all the violence that came about as a result of the unjust situation in the country.

Student: I suppose it would have been easier for him to sit back and do nothing.

Jesus: But instead he worked to rid the country of oppression and violence so that all people could live in equality and peace. He was prepared to continue his work even when he became aware that it would lead to his death. As you know he was shot dead on 24 March 1980 while celebrating Mass.

Student: I know what you're going to say next. That each person should stand up for what is right in their own life, in their place of work, at school, in their relationships with others, even if they get a hard time.

Jesus: You're starting to think like me now. What do you think is the most important thing that you have learnt from our discussion on the Beatitudes?

Student: I think it is that we have to relate the Beatitudes to our daily lives. It's okay to give examples of Mother Teresa or Oscar Romero but if we don't put them into practice then they've lost all meaning.

In Your Religion Journal

As followers of Jesus we are asked to care for others in a practical way.
For each of the Beatitudes, can you give an example of people you know who have dedicated their lives to fulfilling the message of the Beatitudes?

The Christian Law of Love

For followers of Jesus, justice and love for others are inseparable. In fact, concern and love for others leads the way to even greater justice. St Paul takes up this theme of justice and love in his Letter to the Romans when he points out how the Christian life should be lived.

Dear Friends,

Love must be completely sincere. Hate what is evil, hold on to what is good. Love one another warmly as Christian people and be eager to show respect for one another. Work hard and do not be lazy. Serve the Lord with a heart full of devotion. Let your hope keep you joyful, be patient in your troubles, and pray at all times. Share your belongings with your needy fellow-Christians and open your homes to strangers. Have the same concern for everyone.

The obligation you have is to love one another. Whoever does this has obeyed the Law. The commandments, 'Do not commit adultery, do not commit murder, do not steal, do not desire what belongs to someone else', all these, and many others besides are summed up in the one command, 'Love your neighbour as you love yourself'. If you love someone, you will never do them any wrong: to love them is to obey the whole Law.

Paul

Activity

The values in the Beatitudes are not the most popular ideas in the world today. They need a little advertising! Each group is responsible for advertising their particular Beatitude. Think up a slogan for each Beatitude and design a poster.

Amnesty International

Amnesty International is a worldwide movement which works to protect human rights.

It seeks the release of prisoners of conscience. These are people who are in prison because of their beliefs, colour, sex, ethnic origin, language or religion, who have not used or advocated violence.

Amnesty looks for fair and prompt trials for all political prisoners and all people detained without charge or trial.

It opposes the death penalty and torture and any cruel, inhuman or degrading treatment or punishment.

Amnesty International was set up when a British lawyer, Peter Bonorson, wrote an article to a newspaper urging people everywhere to start working peacefully for the release of prisoners of conscience. Within a month more than 1,000 people had sent in offers of help and soon an international organisation was taking shape.

Amnesty International now has more than 750,000 members in over 150 countries. Its members come from all walks of life and have a wide variety of viewpoints.

Safia's Story is an example of the work of Amnesty

Safia's Story

When Safia Hashi Madar was nine months pregnant, the police came to her home in the middle of the night and dragged her away to prison.

This happened in Somalia in 1985. Safia, a biochemist, was separated from her husband, her elderly mother, and her two-year-old son, Ahmed.

Just three days after being arrested, Safia gave birth to another son. She named him Abdi. The security forces took the baby from her at once, and they sent Safia back to her cell.

Safia had not committed any crime. In fact, it is still not clear why she was arrested. Apparently, she was jailed because she had criticised the authorities, and also because she belonged to the Isaaq clan, many of whose members opposed the government. The Somali military had murdered large numbers of unarmed civilians from this ethnic group.

In the early days of her imprisonment, Safia was tortured regularly. She was kicked and choked, beaten with sticks, and burned with cigarettes.

After being held for ten months, she was brought to trial at last. By any legal standard, however, her trial was unfair.

Army and security officers, not civilians, conducted the hearing. They denied Safia access to a lawyer. When she pleaded not guilty to the charge – of belonging to a 'subversive organisation' – the court dismissed her plea outright. The conviction was swift and the sentence severe: life imprisonment. Safia was not allowed to make an appeal.

Amnesty International alerted

By this time, Amnesty International had learned of Safia's plight. After confirming the facts, the organisation decided that she was a prisoner of conscience, that is, that she was confined solely because of her beliefs or her identity, and not for any violent act she might have committed.

The organisation asked members of three Amnesty International groups, each one based in a different country, to launch public campaigns for Safia's release. These groups 'adopted' her and promised to put relentless pressure on the Somali authorities until she was set free.

These volunteers wrote hundreds of letters and postcards to the Somali government. They asked their friends and neighbours to write letters too. They sent telegrams. They publicised the story in their local newspapers and on radio and television. They raised money to help pay for more appeals on Safia's behalf. Meanwhile, the torture had stopped, but the prison conditions remained harsh. Safia's health grew very bad and she suffered a number of painful illnesses. Despite her misery, she received no medical care.

In response, Amnesty International alerted the three local groups that had been working on the case. It also increased the pressure by asking asked large numbers of its members around the world to send emergency appeals.

One of these people was Shelagh Macdonald, a Canadian living in the United States, and herself a young mother. Shelagh and the other members of her Amnesty International group approached medical professionals, students and politicians, and asked them to send urgent pleas to Somalia.

Before long, the Somali Minister of Health had received countless messages of concern from all parts of the world. The pressure worked, and within a month Safia had received medical treatment.

Another year passed, however, and Safia was still in prison. Shelagh and many Amnesty International members worldwide continued to protest at Safia's detention.

Free!

On International Women's Day 1989 Amnesty International again asked its members to demand Safia's freedom. And again, volunteers in many places sent scores of letters and telegrams to the authorities in Somalia.

It was soon after this campaign that, at long last, Safia was set free. She had spent four years as a prisoner of conscience.

Her release from prison was only the first step in putting her life back together. Her safety was still under threat in Somalia. After a dangerous escape from the country and a period during which she was a refugee, Safia was finally reunited with her husband, her mother, and her two sons.

The family settled near London, England, and began to look forward to the day when they would be able to return to their own country and to resume their lives there in peace and security.

'Each of us knows what it is like to read an Amnesty account that fails to move us; perhaps we are too busy, perhaps we can't bear any more just then, perhaps we feel too remote.

Then there are other times when we read about a person in prison, and her or his story reaches inside our soul.

As a mother of young children, I felt a strong and instinctive connection with this woman...'

— *Shelagh Macdonald*

Research

Write to Amnesty International,
International Secretariat, 1 Easten St,
London WC1X 8DJ, England, and request
some further information about the work
of Amnesty International
or to
Amnesty International, Irish Section,
8 Shaw Street, Dublin 2

A Time to Pray

Read the following reflection slowly and
meditatively.

God our Creator, it is often difficult to act
justly in our relationships with others and
with the world we live in.
Help us to live according to the values
which Jesus put before us in the Beatitudes:

Blessed are the poor in Spirit

Help us to recognise those things which are
truly valuable. Give us the courage not to
seek money and material possessions as if
they were the things that matter most. Help
us to share what we have so that everyone
might have enough. Open our minds to
learn from those who do not have material
possessions.

Blessed are the gentle

Help us to develop in ourselves the quality
of gentleness. Make us gentle in all our relationships with other people, with the environment, with animals, birds, fish and
insects. May we never act in a way which
would be cruel to any living thing.

Blessed are those who mourn

When we are sad, help us to realise that you
are always with us. Give us the courage we
need to face the difficult times in our lives
and to cope with all those things which
cause us to experience a sense of loss. Show
us how to comfort and console others who
are mourning so that, through us, they will
experience your love and care.

Blessed are those who hunger and thirst for what is right

Give us the courage to work for a world where all people of every class, every nation, every religious belief, will be able to live in conditions of justice and peace, without discrimination of any kind. Help us to do this even if we ourselves suffer in doing it. Show us how to start in our own homes and in our schools, with the people we meet in games and recreation.

Blessed are the merciful

Help us to be big enough to show mercy to others. May we be quick to forgive those who hurt us. And may we always be ready to reach out to those who are weaker than ourselves.

Blessed are the pure in heart

May we be single-minded in our efforts to develop in ourselves a way of living that is based on the values of truth, justice, peace and love among people. Help us to become more and more the kind of people your Son challenged us to be.

Blessed are the peacemakers

Help us always to work towards peace. May we never deliberately cause disharmony or lack of trust among others at home, at school or among our friends.

Blessed are those who are persecuted in the cause of right

Help us to develop our sense of right and wrong so that our judgements will be based on the values we find in the Gospels. Then give us the courage always to act according to what we know to be right, even if we must suffer in order to do that. Help us also to support those who, in their lives, are making an attempt to do what is right. May we never try to humiliate or make fun of those who are trying to live as followers of Jesus.

Prayer of St Francis of Assisi

Lord, make me an instrument of your peace.

Where there is hatred, let me sow love;

Where there is injury, pardon;

Where there is despair, hope;

Where there is doubt, faith;

Where there is darkness, light;

And where there is sadness, joy.

O divine Master, grant that I may not so much seek

To be consoled as to console;

To be understood as to understand;

To be loved as to love;

For it is in giving that we receive;

It is in pardoning that we are pardoned;

And it is in dying that we are born to eternal life.

Poverty

One of the most obvious signs of injustice and inequality in society is poverty. There are many people in our own country and worldwide who are suffering from the effects of poverty. There may be people in our own school, even in our class, who are suffering because of poverty, people who are denied their basic human rights and who find themselves struggling to live from day to day. It is our responsibility as Christians to show a special concern for people in our community who are poor, to become involved, not only in supporting them to improve their standard of living, but also to work for justice and equality in society.

Activity

Read each item listed below and place a tick in the first column labelled H, if you possess such an item. Leave the space blank if you do not have that item.

Read the list again and decide whether you view that item as a need, a want, or a luxury. Place a tick in the appropriate column under N, W or L.

N = This is a need. It is a necessity for me to live.

W = This is a want. It is not a necessity, but it is desirable and is possessed by most people I know.

L = This is a luxury. It is more than just a want and is way beyond what is needed.

A checklist of possessions

	H	N	W	L
1. A family car	❑	❑	❑	❑
2. An adequate, nutritionally balanced diet	❑	❑	❑	❑
3. The opportunity to travel to another part of the world	❑	❑	❑	❑
4. The opportunity for a second-level education	❑	❑	❑	❑
5. A family television	❑	❑	❑	❑
6. At least two changes of clothes and shoes	❑	❑	❑	❑
7. A holiday away from home for two weeks a year	❑	❑	❑	❑
8. My own personal computer	❑	❑	❑	❑
9. A bedroom of my own where I can have privacy	❑	❑	❑	❑
10. Bath and toilet facilities at home	❑	❑	❑	❑
11. Access to adequate health care	❑	❑	❑	❑
12. A family video cassette recorder	❑	❑	❑	❑
13. Pocket money given to me by my parents	❑	❑	❑	❑
14. Access to a washing machine	❑	❑	❑	❑
15. The opportunity to take part in a hobby/leisure activity of my own choice	❑	❑	❑	❑
16. A compact disc player	❑	❑	❑	❑
17. Enough beds for each member of the family	❑	❑	❑	❑
18. A pet	❑	❑	❑	❑
19. The opportunity to earn pocket money from a part-time job	❑	❑	❑	❑
20. Heating in the home	❑	❑	❑	❑

Relative Poverty

We are often slow to recognise poverty in our own community. Relative poverty occurs when people are suffering the hardships of bad housing, unemployment and dependency on government assistance or social welfare. Low income from low-paid jobs, malnutrition and poor health, inadequate access to health care, education and public transport are also signs of people living below the average standard of living. In order to decide who is suffering from relative poverty in a particular society, it is first of all necessary to discover what the average income is. A point below that average is chosen; those below that point are said to be affected by relative poverty. There is some discussion as to whether that point should be 40%, 50% or 60%. Let's take it that the point below the average is 50%, and let's pretend that the average weekly income of people in a particular country is £100 per week. Then anyone trying to live on £50 per week or less is said to suffer from relative poverty. Relative poverty occurs when some people in society have fewer choices than others. Usually people living on low incomes have very limited choices, particularly in relation to the food they eat, the style of clothes they wear, the standard of housing they live in and the type of work available to them. Very often people on a low income lack the option of participating in a social life that many others in the community take for granted. We can recognise poverty in our own community when we see people facing a constant struggle just to live with dignity.

In Your Religion Journal

What does the word poverty mean to you? Complete the caption: Poverty means...
Choose three captions from the illustration and outline what you think it is like to be poor.

What groups are particularly affected by poverty?

Those with disabilities

Eddie was in a car accident three years ago. Since then he has been paralysed down one side of his body. He would like to work and has applied for a few jobs. But he has found that many employers are reluctant to offer him work. Until he finds a job he will continue to do voluntary work in his neighbourhood. Each week Eddie finds it a struggle to pay his bills. He is living on social welfare payments.

Single parents on a low income

Jacqueline is rearing her three-year-old daughter on her own. She is working in a supermarket in the next town but it isn't a very well-paid job. Each week she has to pay the baby-minder about half of what she gets paid. As well as paying her rent, electricity and food bills, she also has to pay her bus fare to and from work. Jacqueline would like to get a TV but she can't afford to rent one. She doesn't have any extra money to spend on herself or the baby.

People who are long-term unemployed

Mr Jenkins was made redundant five years ago. He used to live in a modern, semi-detached house with his wife and three children. However, he recently fell behind with his mortgage repayments and his house was repossessed by the building society. He now lives with his family in a council house. He had no savings put by and before too long he found himself badly in debt. Mr Jenkins is struggling to pay back the money. He doesn't know what the future holds, and he knows that the longer he is unemployed the less chance there is that someone will offer him work.

Elderly people on a low income

Annie Johnston's husband died last year. He had always meant to take out a life assurance policy which would be paid to Annie if he died before her. This would have given Annie enough money to live on. But he never got around to it. Annie now lives in a run-down, terraced house and struggles to live on a small pension that she receives from the government.

Homeless people

Pat was frequently beaten by his father. He had been running away from home for a night or two since he was about fourteen years old. Eventually he ran away for good when he was sixteen and since then has been sleeping rough, dossing with acquaintances and squatting. He is finding it difficult to get money because he has no fixed address and is not entitled to social welfare payments until he is eighteen years old. He has tried a few places for work but because his clothes are so dirty and he looks so untidy he hasn't had much luck. He would like to get his own bedsit and a job but he isn't too optimistic.

Discuss

For what reasons are each of these people at a greater risk of being affected by poverty?
Can you identify any other groups of people in society who are affected by poverty?

Poverty is likely to affect some people more than others. Unemployed people and their families, those in low-paid jobs, single parents rearing children on their own, those who are self-employed, or small farming households may also be at risk. The sick and disabled or the elderly may also be deprived, yet they often go unnoticed. Travelling people and homeless people are also at risk of suffering the hardships of poverty. In all of those situations women are generally most affected by poverty, since it is they who have to bear the burden of maintaining the family. Women are also often victims of 'hidden poverty' in situations where there is an adequate family income but where this is not distributed.

Class Activity

Using pictures and articles from newspapers, magazines or journals identify the poor in our society. Make a wall display of the information you have gathered.

Things people say about those who are poor

It's their own fault they're so poor; they have too many children.

People who are poor have no way of influencing those who make decisions.

They don't work but just expect charity and depend on hand-outs.

There is a lack of well-paid jobs.

Poor people are lazy!

Poor people are not well-educated.

The wealth of the country is distributed unevenly. The poor get very little.

Their health is so poor they can't do much for themselves.

There have always been poor people.

God created the world that way and it will always be that way. It's God's will.

If people saved money instead of wasting it on drinking and gambling then they wouldn't be poor!

A few people have all the power, that's why others are poor.

Discuss

Choose one statement with which you agree and one with which you disagree. Share your choice and the reasons for it with the rest of the class.

Which of these statements do you consider to be unjust?

In what ways are any of these statements prejudiced against the poor?

Which of these statements stereotype the poor?

Where do your attitudes and opinions as to why people are poor come from?

What, in your opinion, is the main cause of poverty?

In Your Religion Journal

Identify the reasons given in each of the three comic strips as to why people are poor. For each of the comic strips state which side of the argument you agree with and give your reasons.

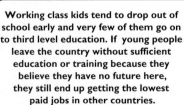

The causes of poverty in a developed industrial society are many and complex. On the one hand, it is caused by a short supply of reasonably well-paid jobs and, in its turn, this shortage may be brought about by a whole host of economic reasons. World trade may be depressed, so that industry suffers; there may not be enough investment, not enough skilled people; there may be bad management, lack of enterprise, harmful government policies and poor labour relations. All these and many other factors affect the general prosperity of society.

Unemployed people are often accused of being lazy and not wanting work. This may be true of a few, but not of the majority. The fact is, that if there are not enough jobs, some people are bound to be unemployed, however much they want to work.

From the point of view of the individual, education and training are the most important factors. It is these which enable people to gain well-paid employment in skilled and responsible jobs. In times of high unemployment they may still have some difficulties at first, but their chances are always much greater. Many more choices and opportunities are open to them. But good education and training are not just good for the individual. The existence of a well-educated and highly trained population greatly increases prospects for general prosperity. It helps industry and commerce to flourish and develop and provides the conditions which will encourage investment and enterprise. One thing, therefore, which is always desirable in the fight against poverty is the provision of sufficient accessible opportunities for education and training.

The trouble is, however, that for those who are already poor it is much more difficult to take advantage of such opportunities. They may live in areas where the provision of education and training is below average, but in any case their ability to take advantage of what is on offer is often very limited. Expenses involved in education, which a prosperous family hardly notices, can be a great burden on them. People who have to struggle just to provide the bare necessities from day to day can find it very difficult to take a long-term view. It can be very hard both for a young person and his/her family to put off the time when he or she begins to earn money for the sake of education. It is very tempting to take a low-paid, unskilled job, rather than continue in education when money is very scarce, and continuing at school or going on to further education and training appears as a waste of time or 'not for the likes of us'.

For these and similar reasons many of those who are unemployed or in low-paid work come from low income backgrounds. On the surface it may look as though they have the same opportunities as anyone else, but in fact it is much harder for them to take advantage of such opportunities.

Activity

Make up a comic strip of your own to challenge the statements below.

(a)   Unemployed people are just lazy. They could all get jobs if they put their minds to it.

(b)   I'm very wealthy and I've worked hard to make my money. If I can do it why can't they?

(c)   What's the point in everyone having a good education? After all, someone has to do those low-paid jobs.

What might make it difficult for poor people to have access to a good education?
What could be done to help them?

Hello, I'm Tom. I'm three years old. This is my flat. We have a lovely little balcony we can go out on to play, but only if Mammy is with us because she's afraid we'd fall off and get killed. Mammy doesn't let us go out and play, she says it's too far down and she wouldn't be able to keep an eye on us. This is my bedroom. Here is my bed. I sleep on this side and my brother sleeps on that side of the bed. We're always fighting over who's taking up too much of the bed. This is my big brother's bed. He got married last month, but they'd no place of their own, so Mammy said they could stay here until the corporation gave them a place. And that's my two sisters' bed there. My Mammy keeps saying she'd like a bigger flat from the corporation, but they said she hasn't enough points. My Daddy is out looking for work at the moment. He was laid off last year and hasn't got a job yet. This is my own book. I got it for Christmas. I don't know what it says because my Daddy can't read and Mammy hasn't time to read to me. I'll be going to school in another two years, and I'll be meeting loads of other kids then, and I hear they have toys in school that you can play with—it'll be great.

Hello, I'm Mary. I'm three years old. This is my house and here is my garden where I play. I like the sandpit over there the best and the swings. This is my bedroom. My sister's bedroom is next door to mine. These are my books on the shelf. Mum buys me a new book with lots of pictures every week; they say it's good for me. This is the book Dad is reading to me at night. It's got lots of fairy stories in it, they're great. I'm going to the nursery school down the road. There are ten of us in the school. We have lots of fun together and there's plenty of things to play with and the teacher is always telling us stories. I love school.

I'm eight now. I've been at school for four years. It's great. My teacher's new in the school. My other teacher was great but she didn't stay too long, I think she got a better job somewhere else. At least that's what my new teacher said. I play out in the yard after school, but often the big boys come and say they've nowhere to play football and so they make us leave. Then I have to go home, and I hate that because there's nothing to do in the flat.

I'm eight now. I've been at school for about four years. It's great. I helped to paint it this year and we chose the colour ourselves. Teacher says you learn better if the room is nice and bright. This is the cupboard where we keep all the paints and things. We have a TV there in the corner and teacher is always showing us things on the video. There was a sale of work last Sunday, they're raising money to buy computers for each class so we'll be having lessons in that soon. Teacher says you'll never get anywhere nowadays if you don't know how to use a computer. I play hockey after school— nearly everyone plays. The playing fields are over there. I'm going to Paris with the school in a few weeks. My parents have paid it all for me. I save some of my pocket money each week so that I'll have spending money when I go away.

I'm fourteen now. I'm going to the local school. My Daddy wanted me to go to a better school down the road but I failed the test and anyway he couldn't pay the voluntary contribution they ask for. I sell papers after school to help them out at home. It's only a few pounds a week but it helps to buy the books for school and pay the bus fare. I'm too tired to do homework by the time I get home. Anyway, with the TV blaring and the kids fighting and my Mammy shouting at my Daddy you couldn't do any work in the house. I'm doing some exams next year and then I'm going to leave. My Mammy says I'm better off leaving because she knows someone who knows someone who works in a supermarket and they'll get me a job there stacking shelves. £60 a week. My Mammy says that's nearly what my Daddy gets on the dole. She says that if I do well in my exams, when I'm working she'll save some of the money every week and take us to a seaside resort next year for a week.

I'm fourteen now. I'm at secondary school. My parents were very pleased I got in because they say that nearly all the boys and girls here go on to university and they want me to become a doctor, like my Dad. It costs them a lot to send me there, but they say it's a good way to spend money. We've got a lovely big gym and squash court. I play hockey for the school team — we're going to Edinburgh next week to play another school. Then at Easter, we're going to Stratford to see two of Shakespeare's plays. I'm doing my exams next year — Dad says I've to study during the summer holidays, so as to be sure I get good results in my exams. The spare bedroom was made into a study room for me and I spend three hours there every night doing my homework. I know I have to, if I'm to get the points to get into medical school. My parents help me with my work if I get stuck. They say they'll take me to America for a holiday so I'm already studying hard.

I'm twenty now. I left the supermarket after a few months as I had a row with the supervisor. I got a job in a pub but I didn't like the hours I had to work. I have a new job now. This is my girlfriend. We're getting married soon. My Mammy says we can move in with them like my other brother did, until the corporation give us a place of our own. We'll probably have to wait a couple of years, but it'll be great when we get it.

I'm twenty now. I'm in medical school, in second year. My parents say they're very proud of me. I passed my driving test last year and now I'm saving up to buy a car. Dad says I should study haemotology when I'm finished, because you can get a consultancy post much quicker in haemotology than in any other branch of medicine. I have a boyfriend, but we've decided not to get married until I've qualified and we've saved enough money to put down a deposit on a house.

In Your Religion Journal

What do you see as the main cause of the difference in opportunities available to Tom and Mary?

In what way has Tom's standard of living been below that of Mary's?

How might their lives out of school affect how well they do in school?

Does Tom have any other options?

What choices can Mary make that Tom can't?

What do you think of the quality of life that each of them has?

What do you think is the outlook for both Tom's children and Mary's children?

208 Escaping poverty enables us to have more choices, but in itself it doesn't make us better people. It all depends on what we do with the choices we have. In the above accounts Mary and her family are materially better off. They might also be very nice, caring people. On the other hand, they might be selfish, smug and snobbish. Who knows?

Tom's material prospects don't look very good, but he might be loving and compassionate, ready to give people a hand, a good friend. Again, we don't know.

People have a right to a decent life and the opportunity to develop their abilities. Material poverty hinders this, and so should be attacked, but there is also another kind of poverty and that is even more damaging. We can live good, valuable lives, if we are poor, and we can live bad, worthless lives if we are rich, even if we seem to be 'successful'.

Activity

Read Luke 12:15-21.
What does being rich in God's eyes mean?

Terri O'Brien has just cleared the rent and paid for the coal. Now this!

With all the children's clothes to wash, Terri needs the machine. She decides to use the money she has saved for the ESB bill to pay for the repair.
Soon, a double ESB bill arrives. The children all need new shoes.

Terri manages to pay the ESB. The kids still need new shoes and clothes for school and the rent is way overdue.

The shoes are bought but the rent is 6 weeks in arrears and the ESB is due again. Terri's husband is unemployed and the bank refuses them a loan

A neighbour suggests a moneylender who offers a loan of £100 to be paid back at £5 a week. Terri is delighted. With the £100 she paid the rent and bought one child a coat..
10 weeks later, Terri is finding it harder to manage. She has £5 less each week, the rent is overdue and the other children need winter coats.

With £30 still to be repaid, the moneylender offers a second loan to clear her.

Terri is cracking up. She keeps screaming at her kids, and is going to the doctor for her nerves. The debts mount up. She is tied in a vicious circle to the moneylender. Is this all the future holds for her?

Find Your Group
Discuss

— What do you think is the underlying reason for Terri being in her present situation?
— What effects do you think being caught in a situation like this has on Terri and her family?
— What alternatives did she have?
— Can you suggest ways of ensuring that Terri and many people like her do not end up in the same position?

In Your Religion Journal

Imagine a family of four has arrived in your country with nothing. Make a list of things you consider necessary for the family to live adequately in your community.

Discuss

Having completed this exercise, in what way have you altered your view towards what is a need, a want and a luxury?

The Cycle of Poverty

In most cases, people who are living below the average standard of living conditions lack the resources and the opportunity to break the cycle of poverty.

The Jones Family

Mrs Jones has a family of five children. Her husband is unemployed, so the family have to live on social welfare payments.

She sends her children to the local school. They miss a lot of school because of poor health. Most of the young people in the area usually leave school when they're sixteen with very few qualifications, so Mrs Jones realises that her children will probably do the same. She would like to see them going to college to get a good education but she just couldn't afford the college fees.

She would like to move from the third-floor flat, it's damp and isn't good for the children's health. But because they are living on social welfare payments the family can't afford to buy better accommodation.

Mrs Jones would like to buy meat, fruit and vegetables for the family. She knows this type of food would keep the family healthy. But they're too expensive, so most evenings she gives the family burgers and chips for their dinner.

Mrs Jones' eldest son Eric left school three years ago. He has been unemployed since leaving school. There is no sign of him getting work. Next month Eric is getting married.

Three years have passed. Eric and his wife are living in a rented flat not far from his mother. He is still unemployed so they can't afford to move to better accommodation. Eric's wife would like to buy meat and vegetables for the evening meal but she can't afford to. They make do with sausages and chips. Next year Eric's oldest child is starting school!

Discuss

What are the key aspects in the cycle of poverty for the Jones family? Identify the reasons which cause this cycle of poverty to repeat itself.

In Your Religion Journal

Complete Eric's cycle of poverty. What would Eric have to do to break this cycle? What needs to happen to allow Eric to break the cycle of poverty?

Sultan the Beggar

Every day Sultan sat with the other beggars by the side of the road near the gates of a prosperous city.

'Give me your money,' he cried. 'Listen to the jingle of your coins. Don't they trouble you? Empty your pockets. Lighten your burden. Set yourself free.' Most passers-by quickened their pace and pretended that Sultan was not even there. Some glared at him as if to say, 'How dare you disturb my day with your begging!' Sometimes a poor street peddler stopped and chatted and occasionally someone tossed a coin to him, and Sultan exclaimed, 'Praise to Allah for lightening your burden!'

One day a merchant observed Sultan and was struck by his unusual style of begging. He was so curious that he asked him, 'When you beg, why do you say, "Set yourself free", and "Lighten your burden"?'

'Let me explain it to you,' Sultan replied, 'since you obviously do not understand the ways of the world. I beg so that I can be of service to people with money. When they walk around with money in their pockets, their minds become preoccupied: "What can I buy with my money? How can I get more money so that I can buy even more things?" They also walk around thinking. "Look at the poor person. I'm glad I am not like him – I have money."

But at the same time they are thinking, "Why can't I be like this other person – he has much more money than I do!"'

Sultan continued to instruct the stranger. 'When people with money meet another person, they ask themselves: "Is this person someone who wants to take my money? I'd better keep my distance for fear that he will steal from me. And I had better buy locks for my doors and perhaps a weapon to protect my money."'

'But how do you fit in, beggar?' asked the merchant.

Sultan replied, 'When some people with money see me, they feel guilty. Some feel angry or sad or perhaps moved to compassion. In any case, I invite them to think about the way that their money causes them so much worry and anxiety and they may begin to see a way out of their trap.'

The merchant thanked Sultan for informing him about 'the ways of the world'.

He stepped aside, and Sultan resumed his peculiar cry: 'Give me your money! Empty your pockets! Set yourself free!'

That night the merchant followed Sultan. As he walked over a bridge, Sultan stopped to examine the fruits of his day's begging. He kept a coin or two – enough for a modest meal – and tossed the rest into the river.

In order to have a fairer society we must change our values and priorities. Our Christian call to justice challenges us to question the injustice of some people having so much while others have so little. It challenges us to take on our responsibility and actively work for justice in society. It calls for a conversion to working for justice both in our own country and throughout the world.

In Your Religion Journal

What do you think is the message of this story?

Why do you think some passers-by pretended not to notice Sultan while others glared at him for disturbing their day?

Why do you think Sultan chose to be poor?

In what way can Sultan's begging cry help us to reconsider our priorities and values?

According to Sultan, what are the dangers of accumulating money and material possessions?

Activity

On the map shade in the areas of the world where you think the majority of the world's poor people live. This map is known as the Peters Projection and, unlike traditional maps, it shows all areas according to their actual size.

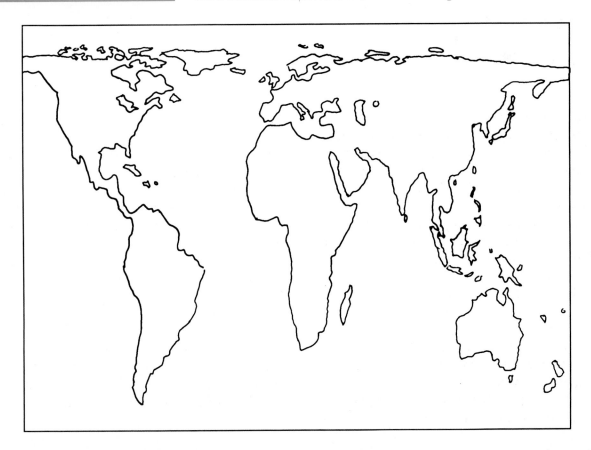

Absolute Poverty

Poverty that is so extreme that people cannot even meet their basic needs — food, clothing and shelter — is known as absolute poverty. The obvious signs of extreme poverty are recognisable when people are suffering from hunger, malnutrition and disease. Absolute poverty is characterised by a lack of food, inadequate shelter and, in some cases, no shelter, lack of any health care or medical services, education or transport system.

Note

The name commonly used to refer to that part of the world where people are suffering from such extreme poverty is the **Third World***. However, this term is misleading. For a start, it divides the world into three parts rather than stressing its unity and interdependence. There is also the danger that by using the term* **Third World** *it somehow implies that the people who inhabit the* **Third World** *are not quite as good, important or civilised as ourselves.*

Read the following story and try to imagine what it is like to live in absolute poverty.

Stripped of all dignity

We begin by invading the house of our imaginary European family to strip it of its furniture. Everything goes: beds, chairs, tables, television sets, lamps. We will leave the family with a few old blankets, a kitchen table, a wooden chair. Along with the wardrobes go the clothes. Each member of the family may keep their oldest suit or dress, a shirt or blouse. We will allow a pair of shoes to the head of the family, but none for the wife or children. We move into the kitchen. The appliances have already been taken out, so we turn to the cupboards and larder. The box of matches may stay, a small bag of flour, some sugar and salt. A few mouldy potatoes, already in the dust-bin, must be hastily rescued, for they will provide much of tonight's meal. We will leave a handful of onions, and a dish of dried beans. All the rest we take away: the meat, the fresh vegetables, the canned goods, the bread and biscuits, the chocolates and sweets. Now we have stripped the house: the bathroom has been dismantled, the running water shut off, the electric wires taken out. Next we take away the house. The family can move to the toolshed. It is crowded, but much better than the situation in Hong Kong, where (a United Nations report tells us) *...it is not uncommon for a family of four or more to live in a bedspace, that is, on a bunk bed and the space it occupies — sometimes in two or three tiers — their only privacy provided by curtains.*

But we have only begun. All the other houses in the neighbourhood have also been removed; our suburb has become a shanty town. Still, our family is fortunate to have a shelter; 250,000 people in Calcutta have none at all and simply live in the streets. Our family is now about on a par with those who live in the city of Cali in Columbia, where, an official of the World Bank writes:

...on one hillside alone, the slum population is estimated at 40,000 — without water, sanitation or electric light. And not all the poor of Cali are as fortunate as that. Others have built their shacks near the city on land which lies beneath the flood mark. To these people the immediate environment is the open sewer of the city, a sewer which flows through their huts when the river rises.

And still we have not reduced our European family to the level at which life is lived in the greatest part of the globe. Communication must go next. No more newspapers, magazines, books — not that they are missed, since we must take

at least 2,000 calories to replenish the energy consumed by its living cells. Our displaced European will average a replenishment of no more than 1,700-1,900 calories.

The human body, like any insufficiently fuelled machine, will run down. This is one reason why life expectancy in India today averages less than forty years. But the children may help. If they are fortunate, they may find work and thus earn some cash to supplement the family's income. For example, they may be employed, as are children in Hyderabad, Pakistan, sealing the ends of bangles over a small kerosene flame, a simple task which can be done at home. To be sure, the pay is small: that is, eight annas – about 5 pence – for sealing 144 bangles. This money is then taxed. And if they cannot find work? Well, they can scavenge, as do the children in Iran who, in times of hunger, search for the undigested oats in the droppings of horses.

And so we have brought our typical European family down to the very bottom of the human scale...

Discuss

What were your feelings as you read through this article?

Absolute poverty exists for a large part of the world's population. What words would you use to describe what it is like to live in conditions like these?

away our family's literacy as well. Instead, in our shanty town we will allow one radio. In India the national average of radio ownership is one per 250 people, but since the majority of radios are owned by city dwellers, our allowance is fairly generous.

Now government services must go. No more postal deliveries, no more fire services. There is a school, but it is three miles away and consists of two classrooms. They are not overcrowded since only half the children in the neighbourhood go to school. There are, of course,

no hospitals or doctors nearby.

The nearest clinic is ten miles away and is tended by a midwife. It can be reached by bicycle, provided that the family has a bicycle, which is unlikely. Or one can go by bus – not always inside, but there is usually room on top. The family income for a year might be the equivalent of £50 to £150 worth of crops; a third of this will go to the landlord and probably another ten per cent to the local money lender. But there will be enough to eat, or almost enough. The human body requires a daily input of

To Change the World

We live in a world which is unjust in many ways. Our world is divided into a rich part in which the majority of people have enough to eat, in which there is work and an opportunity to earn a reasonable living, in which the rights of the individual person and their dignity are respected. However, as we have seen, increasing numbers are affected by poverty.

In the Third World hundreds of millions of people do not have enough to eat. They do not have the opportunity to work so that they could feed themselves. Too often we in the rich world become aware of the Third World only when there is a catastrophe, as happened in Ethiopia, Cambodia and Eastern Africa. Famine brings help. The rich world responds, but not before thousands die of hunger and disease.

There are unjust structures in the world which govern trade and the production of commodities, such as tea, coffee, sugar and fruit . These structures are loaded against the underdeveloped countries and are working against the best interests of the people of these countries. The rich world dictates the price paid for goods and thereby helps maintain millions of people in poverty. There can be no meaningful change for the better in the Third World until these unjust structures are changed. To change them will require a great readjustment of attitude on the part of the rich world.

We can't expect a change of attitude on the part of the rich countries until we change our personal attitudes, our lifestyles, our relations with our immediate neighbours and with the community.

In Your Religion Journal

Why do you think the rich world so often and so regularly is deaf to the appeals of the Third World?
What has your own lifestyle, personally and nationally, got to do with it?
How can you change your lifestyle in a way that would help the poor people of the Third World to change their situation?
How can the governments of the rich world change their policies in a way that would create a fairer society in both their own countries and in the Third World?

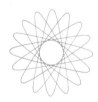

Activity

Make a sentence from the following words:
so, that, live, simply, others, live, can, simply.
What do you think this sentence means?

Research

Your class has been assigned a project called *Operation Awareness*. Each group is to choose an area of the world where people are suffering from absolute poverty. Investigate the causes and consequences of such dire poverty. Mount a display in your classroom or in your school to help make other students aware of the situation.

Find Your Group

Investigate the various groups and organisations which campaign on justice issues. Report back to the class.

Responding to Poverty

Throughout the world Church leaders have called on us as Christians to work actively for justice and to respond to the plight of the poor. They have applied to the situation of the poor, Jesus' message of Good News to poor people. But Jesus did not simply preach the 'good news to the poor', he also shared the life of the poor. He was born homeless, into a poor family, he had no possessions of his own and nowhere to lay his head. Throughout his life Jesus was associated with the poor and powerless — those at the bottom of the pile. In his teaching Jesus constantly takes the side of the poor, as many of his parables show. In the parable of the Good Samaritan, he asks again the question that runs through the scriptures: 'Who is my neighbour?' He did not turn his back on the rich and powerful but rather criticised those who do not share with the poor.

Read Matthew 19:16-24: The Rich Young Man

From the beginning the Christian community understood that faith in Jesus meant a conversion that was social as well as individual and involved a voluntary sharing of material goods. Their way of life is described in Acts 4:32-35.

The group of believers was one in mind and heart. No one said that any of his belongings was his own, but they all shared with one another everything they had. With great power the apostles gave witness to the resurrection of the Lord Jesus and God poured rich blessings on them all. There was no one in the group who was in need. Those who owned fields or houses would sell them, bring the money received from the sale, and hand it over to the apostles; and the money was distributed to each one according to his or her need.

The Irish Bishops, in their pastoral letter *The Work of Justice* have challenged us to change our values and priorities. They say it is not good enough just to stop discriminating against the poor, but that, as a Christian society, we must actively work for justice on their behalf.

If we are to assure basic human rights to everyone it is not enough to cease discriminating against the poor. It is necessary to begin, quite deliberately, to discriminate in favour of the poor. A real transfer of money and of opportunity must be made by the better-off sections of society to the poorer groups, if they are to be raised to minimum standards of human dignity and if we are to lay claim to being a just and Christian society....Surely nothing could be more true to the Bible or more close to the spirit of our Lord or more in line with the tradition of the saints than to show preference for the poor.

The Bishops of north-east Brazil issued a statement, *The Marginalization of a People*, calling for a radically different economy to benefit poor people in their region. Their statement is universal, it applies not only to the situation in Brazil but throughout the world.

We want to see a world in which the fruits of work will belong to all. We want to see a world in which people will work, not in order to get rich, but in order that all should possess the necessities of life: enough to eat for their health, a house, education, clothes, shoes, water and light. We want to see a world in which money is placed at the service of human beings and not human beings at the service of money. We want to see a world in which all will be able to work for all, not a divided world in which all persons work only for themselves. Therefore, we want to see a world in which there will be only one people with no division between rich and poor.

It's hard to know where to begin to work for justice in our own country and throughout the world. Justice, like charity, must begin at home, but must it end there? As St James said, it is not enough just to feel sorry for the poor and needy, if you only wish them well and do nothing for them. What's the point? A concern for justice for the poor and oppressed is central to the Christian message.

Suppose there are brothers and sisters who need clothes and don't have enough to eat.

What good is there in you saying to them, 'God bless you! Keep warm and eat well', if you don't give them the necessities of life?
James 2:15-16

Discuss

What is St James suggesting that we do?

Find Your Group

Put a tick beside the suggested activities which you think you and your class could participate in.

— Discuss poverty issues with your friends/family. ❑
— Write an article for your school magazine or local newspaper. ❑
— Read newspapers and write letters in response to articles. ❑
— Set up an awareness group on poverty in your school to keep one another informed about poverty issues and to organise events. ❑
— Challenge information when you know it is not correct. ❑
— Do a school project on poverty and mount a display in your school, youth club or town centre. ❑
— Use youth programmes on radio and television to voice your views on issues like poverty, unemployment, and so on. Write to the radio/tv station telling them about your interest in doing this. ❑
— Remember how important it is to vote when you are eligible and to inform yourself about the different political parties/candidates. ❑
— Invite someone to your school to speak on poverty. ❑

What can the rich nations do?

Giving food to the hungry is necessary when people are starving, but it is not enough. In any case, poor countries do not want to remain dependent on the rich.
Rich countries can also:
— provide the technology and resources to ensure that poor countries can feed themselves and advance economically;
— provide the training to ensure that people in poor countries acquire the skills needed to make progress on their own;
— reform the system of trade and tariffs which at present works in their favour but against the interests of developing countries.
The last, especially, requires sacrifices, not by governments, but by the people of richer nations. It is they whose lifestyles might be affected. That means you and me. Is it a sacrifice we are prepared to make?

A Time to Pray

A reflection which you could use either with your classmates in school or by yourself at home.

Jesus said:
> The spirit of the Lord is upon me,
> because he has chosen me to bring good
> news to the poor. (*Luke 4:18*)

We are the followers of Jesus in the world today. Today we are being sent to bring good news to the poor.

Let us consider different ways in which we could do this:

There may be someone in class who would be glad to be assured that you are a friend on whom they can truly rely.

Is there, perhaps, someone who would be glad to know that they could borrow a book or a tape if they needed to, someone who is less able to afford these things than you are?

Is there any way in which you can become involved in helping people in the area where you live who are less well off than you are?

Is there, perhaps, an organisation or group which you might join — a group whose members actively work to make life easier for people who are poor, old or lonely, or a group which works at raising funds to help those who are poor at national or international level? Can you, with some of your friends, raise money for one of the international organisations which works to alleviate world poverty?

Let us pray.

Help us, Lord, to become more and more aware of the suffering of those who are experiencing poverty in our own neighbourhood, in our school, in our country and throughout the world. Help us to become more aware of the fact that our own lifestyle can be the cause of poverty in other people's lives. Give us the generosity and the courage to do everything in our power to ensure that fewer people are poor in the world of the future. And forgive us for those times in the past when we have taken what we have for granted and have been unaware of and unconcerned for those who have less than we have.

Closing Prayer
Lord Jesus, I give you my hands to do your work.
I give you my feet to go your way.
I give you my eyes to see as you do.
I give you my tongue to speak your words.
I give you my mind that you may think in me.
I give you my spirit that you may pray in me.
Above all, I give you my heart that you may love in me
your Father and all humankind.
I give you my whole self that you may grow in me,
so that it is you, Lord Jesus,
who lives and works and prays in me.

In the name of the Father, and of the Son and of the Holy Spirit.
Amen.

Do the Looking Back exercises for Unit Six at the back of this book.

LOOKING BACK

The Passion, Death and Resurrection of Jesus

Each year during Holy Week we remember and celebrate the passion, death and resurrection of Jesus.

Holy Week begins on Palm Sunday or Passion Sunday and ends on Holy Thursday. The Easter Triduum begins with the evening Mass of the Lord's Supper on Holy Thursday, reaches its high point in the Easter Vigil and closes with evening prayer on Easter Sunday.

Remembering and Celebrating

All sorts of groups of people remember and celebrate the things that have happened in their past which are important.

These celebrations take place in family groups, in past-student groups, in teams, in groups who come from the same country, etc. The celebrations take many different forms but they have similar aims.

Find Your Group
Discuss

Can you think of three reasons why people might gather to remember and celebrate past events in the life of a family or group?

In Your Religion Journal

Think of times when your own family have gathered to remember and celebrate people and events which have been important to the family.

Write about one of these, saying what form it took and why you think it was important for your family.

Remembering and Celebrating in

A Family	A Nation	A Group	A School	A Team

Births   Victories   Achievements

Visits   Independence   New members

Add to the above.

In Your Group

Talk about the different situations which have been mentioned, saying what you think the significance of each one is.

At most celebrations three things are happening:

1. The past is recalled, e.g. the day you were born or the time when a country gained independence, etc.

2. The past event is linked with the present, e.g. it is a number of years since you were born but each year on that same day not only is your birth remembered but the way in which you have grown and the person you have become are also celebrated.

3. Celebrations also focus on the future, e.g. when the people of a particular nation gather to remember the great things which happened in their country in the past, they look forward with hope to building together a great future for themselves and their friends.

The Christian Church has always remembered and celebrated the chief events from the story of the life, death and resurrection of Jesus.

Look at this diagram which illustrates the seasons in the Church's liturgical year.

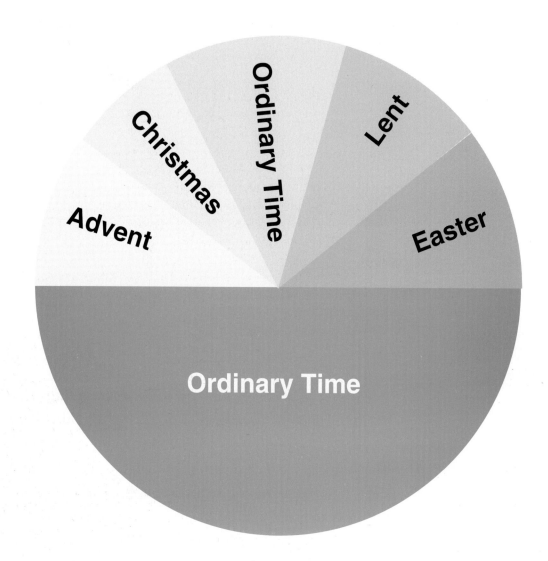

Discuss

Why do you think the Church remembers the life, death and resurrection of Jesus?

Choose one of the seasons from the Church's liturgical year and talk about the way in which you think it focuses on the past, on the present, and on the future.

What events in the life of Jesus do you think are remembered at this time?
What happens in the Church to celebrate and recall these?
How are we challenged to live our lives in the future?

Passion Sunday (The Sunday before Easter)

Today we come together to begin this solemn celebration in union with the whole Church throughout the world. Christ entered in triumph into his own city, to complete his work as our Messiah: to suffer, to die and to rise again.

Passion Sunday Liturgy: The entry into Jerusalem

This is an event from the life of Jesus which we remember on this day.

As they approached Jerusalem, near the towns of Bethphage and Bethany, they came to the Mount of Olives. Jesus sent two of his disciples on ahead with these instructions: 'Go to the village there ahead of you. As soon as you get there, you will find a colt tied up that has never been ridden. Untie it and bring it here. And if someone asks you why you are doing that, tell him that the Master needs it and will send it back at once.'

So they went and found a colt out in the street, tied to the door of a house. As they were untying it, some of the bystanders asked them, 'What are you doing, untying that colt?'

They answered just as Jesus had told them, and the men let them go. They brought the colt to Jesus, threw their cloaks over the animal, and Jesus got on. Many people spread their cloaks on the road, while others cut branches in the fields and spread them on the road. The people who were in front and those who followed behind began to shout, 'Praise God! God bless him who comes in the name of the Lord! God bless the coming kingdom of King David, our father! Praise God!'

Jesus entered Jerusalem, went into the Temple, and looked round at everything. But since it was already late in the day, he went out to Bethany with the twelve disciples.

Mark 11:1-10

Palms are blessed in the church on Passion Sunday and carried in procession to recall Christ's entry into Jerusalem.

Holy Thursday

It was near the feast of Passover.
The Passover is a time when the Jews remember and celebrate the great things that God did for them in the past.
When they eat their Passover meal they remember the night when the angel of the Lord passed over the houses of the Israelites and killed the first-born in each Egyptian household. It was this that finally convinced the Pharaoh to let the Israelites go free. On Passover night the Jews eat the same food as their ancestors ate that night in Egypt.

They read the story which tells of their liberation from slavery and they renew their commitment to live as God's chosen people.

Read Exodus 12

This chapter describes the meal that Jesus prepared to eat with his apostles on the night before he died, the meal that we usually call the Last Supper.

A short time before this an argument had arisen among the apostles as to who among them was the greatest.

Read Matthew 18: 1-5.

Jesus probably had this incident in mind when, during the meal, he proceeded to wash the feet of the apostles.

In that country, at the time of Jesus, people travelled many miles on foot over dusty roads. Then, when they reached their destination, it was a sign of welcome when the host saw to it that their feet were washed so that they would be more comfortable before they sat at table. The washing of the feet was a task that was always reserved for the person who had the role of a servant.

In John's Gospel we read the story of what happened when Jesus washed the apostles' feet.

Read John 13: 1-17.

Discuss

What do you think would have been the first thoughts to enter the minds of the apostles when they became aware of what Jesus was about to do?
Had you been there, how do you think you might have reacted?
What message did Jesus want to give to the apostles?

When the meal was over

The scene is the garden outside the room where Jesus had eaten the Last Supper meal with his disciples. Present are Andrew and James. Imagine a conversation starting in this way:

Andrew: When Jesus stood up from the table my first thought was that he must have been going to look for more wine.

James: I didn't know what he was going to do but I certainly didn't expect what actually happened.

Activity

Find a partner and continue this conversation.

During the Mass of the Lord's Supper on Holy Thursday evening, the priest washes the feet of some of those present.

This is a symbolic action. It helps us to remember the challenge of being followers of Jesus.

I have set an example for you so that you will do just what I have done for you.

Find Your Group
Discuss
Name three things which you think you would actually be doing if you were to follow the example set by Jesus.

Activity

Make a poster to illustrate the caption: 'You should wash one another's feet'.

The poster should show what this command challenges us to do in our everyday lives.

The kind of leadership which Jesus wanted his followers to exercise is a leadership based on service.

Read the following:

All around us
in this world
people are continuously
trying to get elected,
trying to get on, promoted,
trying to get on top,
the very top.
It is a pushing
and a pulling
that is going on
every week,
every day,
every hour,
all the time
> who will be first,
> who will be second,
> who will be third,
> who will be the boss.

This is not bad.
Someone should be at the top.
It is even good,
under one condition,
and that is the condition
Jesus talks about
when confronted
with James and John
in their drive
to the top.

> James and John
> came to Jesus;
> they had a favour
> to ask.
> Jesus asked them
> in his turn:
> 'What favour?'
> And they said:
> 'Would you please allow
> to sit in your kingdom
> one at your right side,
> and one on your left?'

Jesus does not even
answer their question
really. He only said:
'It is not up to me
to make a decision
like that.'
But then he added:
'But why do you want
those places?
What for?'
> And not only the two of
> you, he suggested,
> but even those other ten
> who were so indignant
> that James and John
> had been asking
> for those places
> that they themselves
> had been hoping for.

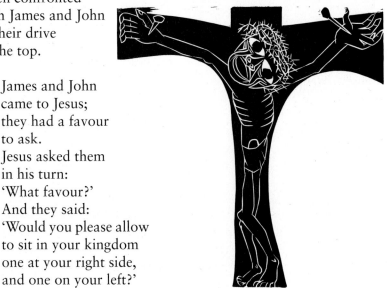

He answered his own question
saying:
'I know why.
I will tell you.
You want to have power.
Power
in the old way.
You want to make
your authority to be felt;
you want to profit
by your position.
You belong
to the old pagan world,
a world not yet
influenced by me.
In my kingdom,
in my community
it is NOT like that.
There, those with power serve;
they make the others grow;
the frail ones they protect;
they are thinking more about
the others
than about themselves.
Look at me,
look at what I do.
Politicians fighting for power
do this in order to serve,
they say,
in order to profit,
they hope.
But let us not blame them.
That kind of power dynamics
does not play only
at that level.
It plays everywhere
where power is involved.
It plays also
where our power is involved.'
> Are we living a pagan life,
> or are we with Christ?

(Based on Mark 10:35-45)

Discuss
In what way is the type of leadership which we find in the world often different from the type of leadership which Jesus spoke of? Give examples.

Jesus Eats the Passover Meal with his Disciples

On the first day of the Festival of Unleavened Bread the disciples came to Jesus and asked him, 'Where do you want us to get the Passover meal ready for you?'

'Go to a certain man in the city,' he said to them, 'and tell him: "The Teacher says, 'My hour has come; my disciples and I will celebrate the Passover at your house'."' '

The disciples did as Jesus had told them and prepared the Passover meal.

When it was evening, Jesus and the twelve disciples sat down to eat. During the meal Jesus said, 'I tell you, one of you will betray me.'

The disciples were very upset and began to ask him, one after the other, 'Surely, Lord, you don't mean me?'

Jesus answered, 'One who dips his bread in the dish with me will betray me. The Son of Man will die as the Scriptures say he will, but how terrible for that man who betrays the Son of Man! It would have been better for that man if he had never been born!'

Judas, the traitor, spoke up. 'Surely, Teacher, you don't mean me?' he asked.

Jesus answered, 'So you say'.

When Jesus stood up to perform the duty of the host by saying the blessing over the cup and over the bread, he startled the disciples by adding the words

'This is my body and this is my blood, which seals God's covenant, my blood poured out for many for the forgiveness of sins. I tell you, I will never again drink this wine until the day I drink the new wine with you in my Father's Kingdom.'

Then they sang a hymn and went out to the Mount of Olives (*Matthew 26:17-30*).

Jesus was anticipating his death on the cross when he said those words.

He would give himself, body and blood, for all humanity. At the Exodus, the covenant set up a new relationship between God and the Chosen People – the Israelites. God said, 'I shall be your God and you will be my people'. When Jesus gave his life for us, a new covenant was established and a new relationship was set up between God and all humanity. Through the death of Jesus we have been reconciled with God through the forgiveness of our sins.

Whenever we come together to celebrate Mass we do again what Jesus did at the Last Supper. We are fulfilling the command of Jesus, when he said, 'Do this in memory of me'.

We remember what Jesus did at the Last Supper.

We remember his death on the cross. And we know that the risen Jesus is really and truly present with us, offering himself to God for us, as he did on the cross on Good Friday.

He was pierced through for our faults,
crushed for our sins.
On him lies a punishment that brings us peace,
and through his wounds we are healed
Isaiah 53:5

Holy Thursday is the day when the Church remembers and celebrates the Institution of the Eucharist. The Last Supper is remembered as the first Eucharist. After Mass on Holy Thursday night the altar is stripped bare in preparation for Good Friday.

Good Friday

The liturgy on Good Friday has three parts:

1. the Liturgy of the Word
2. the Veneration of the Cross
3. Holy Communion

On Good Friday we remember the death of Jesus. At the centre of the liturgy on Good Friday is the reading of the story of the passion and death of Jesus.

Activity

Arrange to have a reading of the story of the Passion in class. Use Matthew's Gospel. Read from Matthew 26:36-27:66. The story-line could be read by a narrator, while the lines said by Jesus and the other characters in the story could be read by various individuals. If you can borrow some missalettes from the local church they will be very useful in this exercise. To create a meditative atmosphere you could arrange to place a crucifix in a prominent position with, perhaps, candles on either side.

Reflect on the following:

1. Have you ever experienced real loneliness?
What words would you use to describe the experience?
Find ten words in the following wordsearch which might describe the experience.

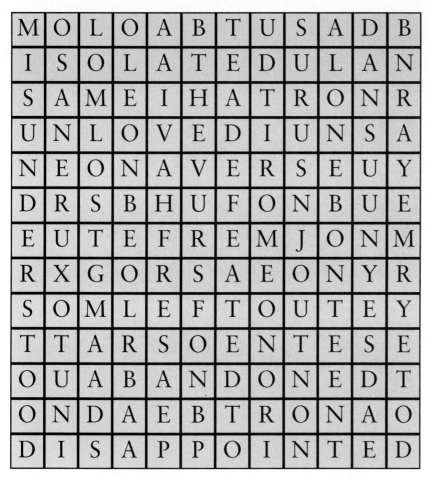

M	O	L	O	A	B	T	U	S	A	D	B
I	S	O	L	A	T	E	D	U	L	A	N
S	A	M	E	I	H	A	T	R	O	N	R
U	N	L	O	V	E	D	I	U	N	S	A
N	E	O	N	A	V	E	R	S	E	U	Y
D	R	S	B	H	U	F	O	N	B	U	E
E	U	T	E	F	R	E	M	J	O	N	M
R	X	G	O	R	S	A	E	O	N	Y	R
S	O	M	L	E	F	T	O	U	T	E	Y
T	T	A	R	S	O	E	N	T	E	S	E
O	U	A	B	A	N	D	O	N	E	D	T
O	N	D	A	E	B	T	R	O	N	A	O
D	I	S	A	P	P	O	I	N	T	E	D

It is clear from the story of the passion that Jesus experienced loneliness in Gethsemane. He knew things were coming to a head. He was aware of all the opposition that had risen up against him. His disciples were unable to stay awake and watch with him.
Can you find the Bible passage which expresses the fear and loneliness which Jesus felt? This shows us that Jesus was truly human. He was not simply going through an act.

It was only because he was able to put his trust completely in God, and because he wanted to do the will of the Father, that he had the courage to carry on.

2. Try to imagine yourself in Peter's shoes. He is puzzled. He doesn't understand what has gone wrong. He thought that Jesus was coming up to Jerusalem to be crowned king, and here he is about to be put to death as a criminal. He is also afraid – afraid that the hostility against Jesus could be extended to the followers of Jesus.

Again, Peter appears in the story as someone who is human, who does wrong but who is ready to acknowledge this and is sorry.

Find the Bible passage which shows that this is the case.

3. Think of Pilate. He washed his hands of the whole affair. He recognised that Jesus was innocent of the crimes that he was being accused of. He didn't want to condemn an innocent man. Neither did he want to go against the wishes of the angry mob. He was probably scared.

Find the passage which shows how Pilate acted.

Have you ever seen anything like this happen?

Have you ever been in this kind of situation yourself?

Radio Zion

You are a reporter for the morning news on Radio Zion. You interview Pilate about the events on the night that Jesus was crucified. Find a partner and present the interview to the rest of the class.

The Veneration of the Cross

The veneration of the cross is an important part of the ceremony on Good Friday. When we kiss the cross we remember the suffering and pain endured by Jesus for us. We think too of all the suffering and pain which exists in the world today, particularly that which is suffered by those who are innocent. Through his death Jesus brought joy to the world. We, who are his followers, are challenged to work to change the pain and suffering which are the lot of many people in today's world.

As the priest unveils the cross, **he says,**
'This is the wood of the cross on which hung the saviour of the world.'
We respond,
'Come, let us worship.'
The custom of the veneration of the cross began when Helena, the mother of Constantine, discovered what was believed to have been the cross on which Jesus was crucified.

In time little pieces of this cross were sent to dioceses throughout the world and the custom of the veneration of the cross spread.

Mass is not celebrated on Good Friday. We can receive Holy Communion, because at Mass on Holy Thursday care is taken that enough bread is consecrated for use both on Holy Thursday and on Good Friday.

Find Your Group

If you had to create a ceremony for Good Friday, which would help people to remember the suffering and death of Jesus and to reflect on their meaning for our lives today, what format do you think you would suggest?

Easter Day: The Easter Vigil

On Easter Saturday night we celebrate the resurrection of Jesus from the dead. This is the greatest feast day of the Church. If Jesus had not been raised from the dead all of his life would have been in vain. He would have been defeated by the power of evil in the world and in the hearts of those who condemned him to death.

But God raised Jesus to new life and so the power of evil had no control over him. As followers of Jesus we can have confidence in our ability to overcome evil when we live our lives as Jesus calls us to.

Find Your Group

Discuss

Can you recall what it was like when you and the people close to you missed someone who was not there any more?

What was it like for your family after a funeral?

What was it like for your friends when one of the group had moved away, etc.?

What words would you use to describe the feeling?

Imagine what it was like for the followers of Jesus on the day after he had been crucified.

What words would you use to describe how you think they might have felt?

The movement from the evening of Good Friday to the resurrection is a movement from:

DARKNESS	to	LIGHT
DEATH	to	LIFE
SADNESS	to	GLADNESS
MOURNING	to	REJOICING

Activity

Can you name some of the symbols used by the commercial world to represent Easter?

Why do you think these were chosen?

Make an Easter poster using some of these symbols.

The Easter Vigil

There are four parts in the ceremony for the Easter Vigil:
The Service of Light
The Liturgy of the Word
The Baptismal Liturgy
The Eucharistic Liturgy

The Service of Light

Jesus died, crucified on the cross as a criminal. The future looked dark and bleak for his followers. But with the resurrection of Jesus from the dead they were given new hope and new light.

At the beginning of the Easter Vigil the church is in darkness. Then, in a suitable place outside the church, a fire is lit. The priest blesses the fire and then the Paschal candle is lit from the fire. This candle is the symbol of the risen Christ and for the rest of the year will be lit in the church at times when the people gather for prayer and worship to show that we believe that the risen Christ is present with us.

Five grains of incense, representing the five wounds of Christ, are inserted into the candle in the shape of the cross. The candle is also marked with the first and last letters of the Greek alphabet, alpha and omega. The priest says:

'Christ yesterday and today. The beginning and the end, alpha and omega; all time belongs to him, and all the ages; to him be glory and power through every age forever. Amen.'

As the priest enters the church he holds the candle on high and says:
'Christ our light'
to which we reply
'Thanks be to God'.

Everyone in the church has a candle which is then lit from the Paschal candle and the church is now full of new light. A hymn of praise to God is sung.

Discuss

Do you think that the service of light is a good way to start the celebration on Easter Saturday night? Why?
Mention places and situations where the light of Christ can be seen shining in the world today.

Activity

Make a poster to illustrate the caption 'The Light of Christ'.

Discuss

In what way do you think that the lighted candle is a good symbol for Easter Saturday night?

The Liturgy of the Word

In the Liturgy of the Word we listen to a number of readings: readings about the many ways in which God worked for the good of the people in freeing them from their enemies; readings from the prophets which urged the people to live as God has called them to do. The readings end with the story of the empty tomb from one of the gospels.

Find Your Group

Using a missalette choose one of the Old Testament readings which has been included in the Liturgy of the Word. Read it and say why you think this reading has been included in the Easter Vigil.

Baptismal Liturgy

In the early Church it was at this ceremony that those who had been preparing to become members of the Church, the catechumens, were baptised. Today when a new baby or a person coming into the Church is baptised during the Easter Vigil, the baptism takes place at this point.

The priest blesses the baptismal water.
Water is an important symbol of new life and hope. In the prayer over the water the following events from the history of God's people are mentioned. In each case water is important:
— The Great Flood;
— The Crossing of the Red Sea;
— The Baptism of Jesus in the Jordan;
— Water and Blood flowed from the side of Jesus during the crucifixion;
— Jesus commanded his disciples to go and baptise all nations.

Find Your Group

Find the biblical stories in which each of the above originates.
Draw your own symbols for the particular aspect of water which is shown in each case.

Renewal of Baptismal Promises

All the people in the church renew their baptismal promises.

Activity

Find the text of the baptismal promises.
Write your version of the promises which you think people should be asked to make at their Baptism.

The Liturgy of the Eucharist

The Mass then continues in the usual way from the preparation of the gifts.

If They Could Speak

One of the women of Jerusalem on the first Good Friday night:

I was there on that Sunday when he rode in triumph into the city. Many of us were influenced by the stories we had heard of the things he had been doing. We had been waiting for the day when he would come to our city. Some people even said that he would be crowned king when he came. We also knew, of course, that he

had his enemies, the Pharisees and Sadducees. They were challenged by the things he said and did. On that Sunday, however, there was very little of that opposition in evidence. There was a feeling of wild excitement in the city, the streets rang with the sound of people's voices singing 'Blessed is he who comes in the name of the Lord. Hosanna to the Son of David'. People spread their cloaks on the ground as Jesus rode by on the colt. Others waved palm branches in the air. When people asked what was happening they were answered with shouts of, 'This is the prophet Jesus, from Nazareth in Galilee'.

Now, as I stand at the foot of the cross it all seems like a dream, no, like a nightmare! I just know in my heart that what this man stood for is right. I can't understand how people could have been so blind. He was betrayed by one of his closest followers and handed over to the authorities. It was obvious that Pilate knew he was innocent but hadn't the courage to release him.

Once again I stood in the crowd and watched as he carried his cross. He was in great pain. The perspiration could clearly be seen on his forehead. The cross dug into the flesh on his shoulders. I felt really sad as I watched. He had given us so much hope for the future. Now it was all destroyed.

He's dead now. Even in his last moments he was ready to think about other people before himself, though he must have been in great pain. He turned to one of the thieves who was crucified beside him and said 'This day you will be with me in Paradise'. He held no grudge, not even against those who had crucified him. 'Father, forgive them, they know not what they do', he said.

I feel very helpless. I'm convinced that he was someone who could have taught us how we should really live. But it's too late now.

In Your Religion Journal

Write this woman's reflections a week later.

Find Your Group

Choose one of the characters in the events surrounding the passion and death of Jesus: the crossmaker, the thief, the mocking soldiers, Simon of Cyrene, Jesus' mother, etc. Write that person's reflections (a) on the night after the crucifixion (b) a week later.
OR
Assign one of the above roles to each one in your group. Pretend that it is the night after Jesus had been crucified. Discuss together the events of the day.

Prayer Reflection

Introduction
Dayenu is a Hebrew word which means 'It would have been enough'. It is the response used in a Jewish hymn recounting the marvellous deeds which God has performed on behalf of his people. This is an adaptation of the hymn.
You could read it yourself, slowly and reflectively, adding your own verses acknowledging some of the things which come to your mind.
Alternatively, you could use it as a class prayer, with individual readers reading the verses and the entire class responding.

It Would Have Been Enough!

Leader: To each line we shall respond by saying: 'It would have been enough!'
If God had created us and not revealed himself in all his marvellous works...

All: It would have been enough!

Leader: If God had revealed himself and not made a covenant with his people...

All: It would have been enough!

Leader: If God had made a covenant with his people and not breathed his Spirit into us...

All: It would have been enough!

Leader: If God had breathed his Spirit into us and not shared with us his heart...

All: It would have been enough!

Leader: If God had shared his heart with us and not watched over us when we strayed from his love...

All: It would have been enough!

Leader: If God had watched over us when we strayed from his love and not delivered us from the bonds of slavery...

All: It would have been enough!

Leader: If God had delivered us from the bonds of slavery and not led us into a land of freedom...

All: It would have been enough!

Leader: If God had led us into a land of freedom and not sent us holy men and women to speak to us of his love....

All: It would have been enough!

Leader: If God had sent us holy men and women to speak to us of his love and not promised us a Saviour...

All: It would have been enough!

Leader: If God had promised us a Saviour and not sent us his own beloved Son...

All: It would have been enough!

Leader: If God had sent us Jesus, his own beloved Son, and he had not become our very brother...

All: It would have been enough!

Leader: If Jesus had become our very brother, and not shared our joy and sorrows, our laughter and tears...

All: It would have been enough!

Leader: If Jesus had shared our life and not taught us how to forgive each other...

All: It would have been enough!

Leader: If Jesus had taught us how to forgive each other and not shown us how to love...

All: It would have been enough!

Leader: If Jesus had taught us how to love and not taught us how to serve each other...

All: It would have been enough!

Leader: If Jesus had shown us how to serve each other and not left us this meal as a reminder of his love...

All: It would have been enough!

Leader: If Jesus had left us this meal as a reminder of his love and not revealed to us the Father's love for us...

All: It would have been enough!

Leader: If Jesus had revealed the Father's love for us, and not called us to carry on his work in the world...

All: It would have been enough!

Leader: But as it is, Father, your Son, Jesus, has revealed your love for us. His whole life, his death and his resurrection from the dead testify to your deep mercy and compassion. Therefore, Father, we bless and thank you. We praise and worship you with all creation, for you are worthy of our worship, and beyond all the praises of our hearts. To you and to your Son, Jesus, and to the Holy Spirit belong all glory, now and forever.

All: Amen

Do the Looking Back exercises for
Unit Seven at the back of this book.

Human Life is Sacred

Unit Eight
Lesson Nineteen

Spend some time quietly reflecting on the wonder of human life, as you experience it in your own body.

Become aware of your breathing.

You breathe in. You breathe out.

This is the breath of life. The moment it ceases you are no longer alive.

Sometimes, when you're excited, or after you have taken physical exercise, you breathe faster. When you are relaxed or asleep you breathe slowly and quietly.

Become aware of your heartbeat and your pulse. You can almost feel your blood circulating and taking with it the oxygen which keeps each part of your body alive. The human body is more mysterious and more wonderful than the most advanced invention of our times. Yet sometimes we take our bodies for granted.

Look around at your classmates.

Note how each one is so unique and different, even in appearance.

We come in different shapes, different sizes, with different skin, eye and hair colours.

Look at your hand. Consider the fact that your fingerprints are yours, and yours only, among all the millions who live or who have ever lived on this planet.

Think of all the hidden gifts and talents of each individual, some that we never even discover we have, some that we know we have and don't value.

Through various individuals' use of their gifts and talents we have all the extraordinary developments which have shaped and moulded the world through the ages.

Consider the human brain, more intricate and marvellous than the greatest computer ever invented.

Created by God, human life is the high point of God's creation. We have been entrusted by God with stewardship for the rest of creation.

Most awesome among the tasks that God entrusted to human beings is the procreation of human life. And so, the miracle of creation continues today every time a baby is born.

Read the following psalm slowly and reflectively. You might like to play some quiet, reflective, music in the background.

Before I was born,
you made each little part of me in secret.

While I was hidden in my mother's
    womb,
you watched me grow.
You saw my bones begin to form
and join together.

From the first moment of my life
you knew me!

I praise you, Lord,
and I am filled with wonder.
For everything you do
is strange and marvellous.

You know me, Lord, so very well,
you know when I get up.
You know when I go back to sleep,
you know each thing I do.

You know what I am going to say
    before I even speak!
You are *always* close to me.
You're wonderful, O Lord.

So if I climb the highest hill,
you would be there with me.
And if I swam beneath the waves,
you'd still be there with me.

Even in the dark at night
you would be next to me.
Yes, even I could not hide,
you would be there with me.

Valuing human life

It is because of our sense of the wonder of human life that the most dearly held of all our values is the sacredness of human life. After a traffic accident or a bad fire the first question on everybody's lips is often 'Was anyone killed?' We usually do everything in our power to protect our own life from sickness and from disease. We dread the thought of going to hospital or facing surgery. The death of someone we love brings pain, suffering and sadness.

However often it happens we are always amazed at the wonder of new life. The miracle which began in the mother's womb nine months earlier leads to the birth of a new human life.
The birth of a baby is a time of joy and celebra-

tion for the parents and for the whole family. For the parents the baby is a living expression of their love. There are very few people who would fail to be moved to wonder at the beauty of a tiny, new-born infant. And we continue to be fascinated as we watch the tiny, fragile life of the baby grow and develop. The first smile, the first word, the first step, are all moments to be remembered.

Parents are always amazed at the way in which each one of their children grows and develops differently. Each child is a unique and special individual, full of promise for the future and full of surprises.

Activity

Using pictures and clippings from magazines, or your own paintings and drawings, make posters to illustrate the following: *The Wonder of Human Life;*
Each Person is full of Surprises

Find Your Group

Find examples in newspaper reports, magazine articles or stories you know of people who have struggled to achieve standards of excellence in sport, in music, in art, in the work of human development. Make a presentation to the class on the topic of 'The Potential of Human Life'.

At Home

You were once the tiny baby who was greeted with wonder and joy in your family. Talk to your parents about your early years. Were you a cross baby? At what age did you say your first word? At what age did you take your first step, etc.?
Search through photo albums for the earliest pictures of yourself.

Activity

You could take some of these early photographs into class. Paste a collection of the photographs on to a large sheet of paper or card.
Have a competition to see who can identify the babies.

Human Potential

There are many people who go to huge lengths to preserve the beauty and dignity of human life. Some spend their whole lives trying to make it possible for others to achieve their full potential as human beings, particularly those who have to face difficulties of one kind or another:
— People who work with those who are affected by poverty;
— People who work with those who are victims of violence;
— People who work with those who suffer from handicap;
— People who work with those who are sick;
— People who work with those who live in areas of the world affected by famine.

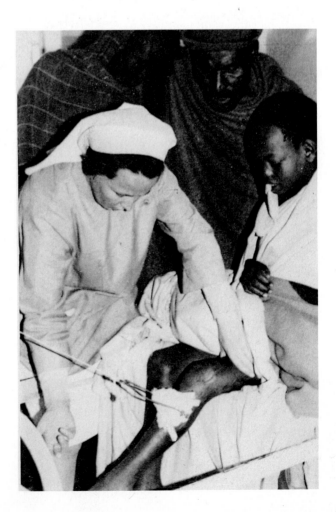

There are many people in your country, perhaps even in your locality, who do these types of work.
If possible, invite one of them to speak to the class about what they do and why they do it.

Alternatively, you could write to a number of such people requesting information about their work.
Read these letters in class.

We Forget

When we look around us and see how human beings treat one another it is obvious that we sometimes seem to forget our sense of the wonder of human life. We forget the amazement we feel when we look at the achievements of those people who have worked to develop their gifts and talents and who use them for the benefit of others. We forget too the amazement we feel when we look at the miracle of life in a new-born baby.

Find Your Group
Discuss

What are the signs which you see in your own locality, in your country, in the wider world, which show that human beings do not always treat human life as if it were sacred?

Life in your own body

How do you rate the way in which you treat life in your own body?	Yes	No	Don't know
Do you smoke?	☐	☐	☐
Do you brush your teeth regularly?	☐	☐	☐
Do you drink alcohol?	☐	☐	☐
Do you think you will smoke in the future?	☐	☐	☐
Do you think you will drink in the future?	☐	☐	☐
Do you shower or bathe regularly?	☐	☐	☐
Do you take exercise?	☐	☐	☐
Do you think that you will use drugs in the future?	☐	☐	☐
Do you get at least nine hours sleep every night?	☐	☐	☐
Do you indulge in stodgy food – chips, chocolates, etc.?	☐	☐	☐

Find a Partner

Exchange the answers you have given to the questionnaire.
Give your partner a mark out of ten.

Find Your Group

You have been asked by your local health board to design a brochure for young people of your own age on the theme of 'Taking care of your body'.
What advice would you give?
Think of a good title for the brochure and find an attractive way to present it.

When Human Life is threatened

Violence

Find Your Group
Discuss

Look at the list on the right. How is each of the items mentioned in the list a sign of the violence which happens in society today?
How many of them are relevant in your own neighbourhood?
Are there other signs of violence in your neighbourhood which are not mentioned in this list?
Say how each one shows a lack of respect for human life.

Telephone vandalised
Neighbourhood Watch signs
Security guards
Security gates and barriers
Posters vandalised
Guard dogs/Dog notices
Barbed wire
Army helicopters
Windows boarded up
Graffiti
Bars and locks on windows
Alarm systems
Hostels for the homeless
Bank security
Security vans
Police stations
Casualty wards
Remedial/Rehabilitation centres
Flower beds, trees, etc. vandalised
Police stations
Litter and unofficial rubbish dump
Security forces' bases or patrols
Security barriers
Sensational newspaper headings and layout
Lack of facilities for Travellers
Posters displaying confidential telephone numbers
Bicycle locks
Security alarms
Protective mesh around trees
Smoke damage to property
Cinema posters
Rape Crisis Centre
Grids on shop fronts

Read these accounts of situations which threaten human life in various ways:

Find Your Group
Discuss

Are there underlying causes for the situations described in these extracts? If so, list what you think the main ones are.
How could these situations have been prevented?

Rose walked slowly towards her house after collecting the Family Allowance for her mother. 'Would they be waiting again this morning?' she wondered. For three days these girls from the other school in the town had shouted insults at her, and yesterday they had thrown stones at her.

The Columbian town of Itagui, although it is an industrial town, with textile, leather, wood furniture and brewing industries, doesn't have a proper water system. When water is scarce the people in the poor neighbourhoods of the south of the town suffer the worst as the water pressure is often too low to reach them and so contaminated that children have died from drinking it. One of the main reasons for this is that money from its industry, which should go to benefit the inhabitants, goes into the pockets of the politicians who control the town.

Chico Mendes was a Brazilian trade union activist committed to the defence of the Amazonian eco-system. Chico led a movement which used peaceful forms of resistance. In response to deforestation he proposed moderation; to end the semi-slavery of the rubber estate workers he fought for the right to work individually and collectively. He had hoped for a better world for the people of the forests and for people everywhere. He received several international awards for his work. On Thursday, 22 December 1988, he was assassinated in the doorway of his home by the hired guns of the area's landowners.

Johnny lit the firework and stuffed it through the letter-box of the house. 'That'll teach the miserable old devil,' he thought. 'Funny how he didn't come out after the first banger had gone off.' Inside the house old Mr Moran lay stretched out on the floor. One banger had been enough.

She was at the kitchen table, studying an English poem.
 'Say it out loud again, dear, so we can hear you one last time before the news.' Her father was always making her learn the poetry well. 'The world is charged with the grandeur of God', she began, and then the doorbell rang. 'I'll go, Dad, it's all right. Sit on and watch the news.'
 'No, daughter, I'll go myself. Stay there and do your poetry.'
 She smiled up at him. He was the best in the world, even if he was a bit of a taskmaster. She began the poem again, this time saying it very quietly to the silence of the room.
 'The world is charged with...'
 Suddenly there was a loud blast. 'The door, O my God, the door and Dad.' She raced into the hallway. He lay there crumpled, with half his face blown off. The hall door wide open. The sound of a motorbike. Her Dad lying there like a sack of spuds, with half his face blown off.

When does life begin?

Life is a gift from God that is given at the moment of conception. The miracle of conception is part of God's plan for the universe. In their ability to conceive a new human life, human beings have been given a share in the creative power of God. The gift of every human life is precious and unrepeatable. The unborn child is a unique, living human being from the moment of conception. Before conception or fertilisation the sperm and ovum (egg) were cells of the respective parents, but at the moment of conception they fuse to create a single cell which has the potential to grow and develop into an adult human being. This is one of the great wonders of God's creative plan for human life. Every time a child is conceived a miracle begins to unfold.

At conception the characteristics that distinguish each of us from others are established...the colour of our eyes and hair, our sex, our height and even our intelligence potential. Cells from any part of a person's body are always genetically the same. That is, they all contain the same genes which determine bodily characteristics and development, e.g. the colour of a person's hair, their height, the colour of their eyes etc. Examination of an unborn baby's cells show that it is never part of its mother's body in this way. The child inherits genes from both its father and mother and is therefore genetically distinct from either of them. Right from the beginning it is a distinct, living human being. As it develops its various organs are clearly distinct from its mother's. The unborn baby's heart is its own heart, not its mother's. When the brain begins to function it is the unborn baby's brain, not its mother's. Though completely dependent on the mother, the unborn baby is never simply part of her body. It is always a new, individual human life. The unborn child develops rapidly in its mother's womb. It cannot defend itself, and is totally dependent on others, even for life itself. It is our responsibility to nurture and protect the life of the unborn child.

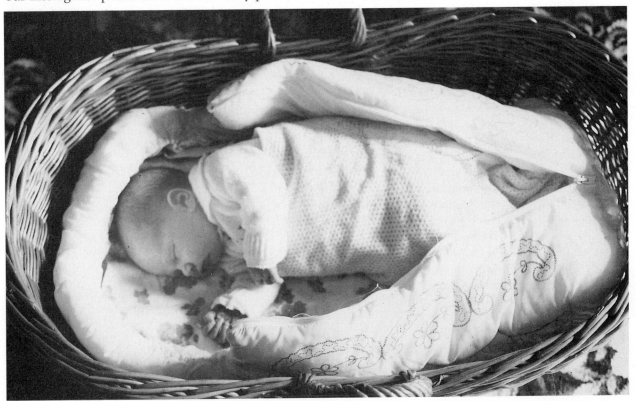

The growth and development of the child in the womb

Month 1

The moment your mother's egg was fertilised, 46 chromosomes with 30,000 genes combined to determine all your physical characteristics: sex; facial features; body type; colour of hair, eyes and skin. Even more amazingly, intelligence and personality – the way you think and feel – were already in place within your genetic code. At the moment of conception, you were already essentially and uniquely 'you'.

Month 2

A wondrous and dynamic chain of events takes place within the womb. In the brief span of 2 months, you progressed from a single cell to a tiny human with all organs present and functioning. The rest of your time in the womb was devoted to refinement, growth and practice. While still in the womb, you began to move, swallow and 'breathe' amniotic fluid, react to stimuli and generally prepare yourself for 'life on the outside'.

Month 3

By 9 weeks, you were as cute as a button – with large eyes, a fine little nose and a mouth which occasionally sucked a tiny thumb. Since you were still small and not cramped for space, you had plenty of room to move. Even though your mother couldn't feel you yet, you had already perfected a somersault, backflip and scissor kick.

Month 4–9

By the time your mother's pregnancy 'showed', you were already fully formed. Now all you needed was time to grow and develop in preparation for birth.

Newborn

'Birth' isn't the beginning of your life – it's just one chapter in a continuing story. In fact, you'll continue to develop, just like you did in the womb, until you reach the ancient age of approximately 23 years!

Quiz

1   You started swimming and doing back flips:
    A   When your mother was six months pregnant
    B   Nine weeks
    C   Eight months

2   If you kept growing all nine months as fast as
    you did during your second month, you
    would have been born as big as:
    A   Arnold Schwarzenneger
    B   An M-1 tank
    C   A pair of overfed elephants

3   When did you most likely feel pain for the first
    time?
    A   When they cut your umbilical cord
    B   When your mother was nine weeks pregnant
    C   After your first lunch in the school cafeteria

4   By the time your mother found out she was
    pregnant, you were:
    A   A tiny speck smaller than a full-stop
    B   A miniature human with arms, legs and a
        heartbeat
    C   A ball of cells the size of a marble

5   Your mother says you started to kick and poke
    her:
    A   Three months into the pregnancy
    B   At four months
    C   Never mind when you started, when are
        you going to stop?

6   Five months into the pregnancy you got a lot of
    hiccups because:
    A   Your mother was pigging out on pickles,
    ice cream, pizza and sardines
    B   You swallowed amniotic fluid
    C   Your diaphragm was being formed
    D   You couldn't find a bag to put over your
    head

7   Before you were born, your skin was:
    A   As wrinkled as a raisin
    B   As waxy as a statue from a wax museum
    C   Both of the above

8   When did you start using your brain?
    A   When your mother was eight months
        pregnant
    B   When she was forty days pregnant
    C   If you still haven't started using your
        brain, go on to the next question

9   When was the colour of your hair determined?
    A   At conception
    B   Three months into pregnancy
    C   Only your hairdresser knows for sure

10   Five months before you were born, your heart
     pumped enough blood every day to:
     A   Overflow a coffee mug
     B   Fill half a tank of a Firebird
     C   Fill an Olympic size swimming pool

11   When did you first start looking like either a
     boy or a girl?
     A   The seventh month of pregnancy
     B   The end of the second month
     C   When the doctor announced to your
         parents, 'It's a ...'

12   If your mother smoked while she was
     pregnant, you may have been born:
     A   Overweight and overdue
     B   Underweight and premature
     C   With yellow teeth and a nagging cough

13   How premature can a baby be born and still
     survive?
     A   One month early
     B   Two months early
     C   Four months early

14   When did you begin to look like your mother
     or your father?
     A   When your mother was six months pregnant
     B   When your mother was four months
         pregnant
     C   Who cares when it happened – does any-
         body know a good plastic surgeon?

The answers to this quiz are at the back of this book.

What is Abortion?

Abortion is the deliberate and intentional killing of an unborn baby. Abortion means destroying the life of an unborn baby, either by killing it in the womb or by removing it from the womb prematurely before it is able to live in the outside world.

The Right to Life

The Second Vatican Council called abortion 'an abominable crime'. The Irish bishops in their pastoral letter, *Human Life is Sacred*, say:

> God's commandment...is that no human being may deliberately take away innocent human life. What life could be more inno cent than that of the unborn child? Deliberate abortion is, therefore, always gravely sinful. The embryo or foetus possesses its fundamental right to life from the moment of conception.

Similar statements have been made by the Bishops' Conferences of England & Wales, and Scotland. In 1959 the UN Declaration of the Rights of the Child stated:

> The child, by reason of his physical and mental immaturity, needs special safeguards and care, including appropriate legal protect- tion, before as well as after birth (Preamble).

The declaration continues:

> The child shall be entitled to grow and develop in health; to this end special care and protection shall be provided both to the child and the mother including adequate care both before and after birth (Principle 4).

It is clear from this Declaration that the life of the unborn child is entitled to be protected when it is growing and developing in its mother's womb. A truly just society should give special protection to the weak and vulnerable members in its community. It should never discriminate against them.

Research

Look up the UN Declaration of Human Rights and the Declaration of the Rights of the Child and compile a list of other fundamental rights of the child which should be safe-guarded and protected.

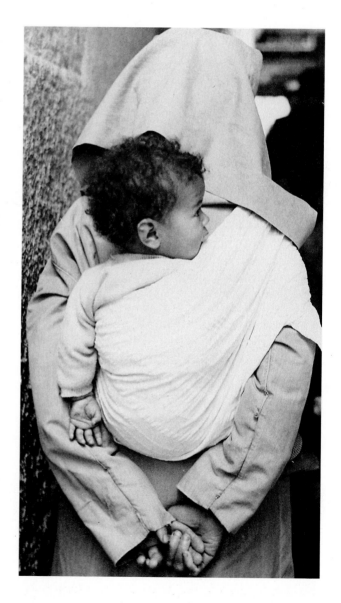

Abortion Act 1967

In 1967 the British Parliament passed a law which stated that it was no longer a criminal offence for an unborn child to be aborted by a doctor if two doctors agree on either of the following two conditions:

1. *That to carry on with the pregnancy would involve a greater risk to the life or the physical or mental health of the mother or of her existing children than if she had it terminated.*

2. *That there was a substantial risk that if the child were born it would suffer serious physical or mental handicap.*

Find Your Group

What rights of the unborn child are denied by the Abortion Act of 1967?

When abortion was first legalised in Britain in 1967 the intention was to restrict the number of women opting for abortion by stating only two conditions under which an abortion could be obtained. However, the Act contained a clause allowing account to be taken of the woman's 'actual or reasonably foreseeable environment', and this allowed doctors to interpret the act in such a way that a great variety of social, financial or emotional problems could be considered as justifying abortion. During the period that the Act has been in force the number of abortions has risen dramatically. The following are some figures of registered abortions in England and Wales:

Year	No. of abortions
1968	23,641
1972	159,884
1989	183,974
1991	191,698

Abortions conducted on the grounds of the risk of grave injury to the mental or physical health of the mother are rare. In 1972, for example, there were apparently less than thirty altogether in England and Wales. The vast majority of abortions, well over 95 per cent, are not carried out to save the life of the mother, or to save her from serious damage, or where babies were conceived through rape, or even where babies are thought likely to be born with severe handicap. In the main, they are abortions of healthy babies of healthy mothers, carried out for social, economic or emotional reasons. However, over the years these two conditions have come to be interpreted in such a way that any number of reasons for wanting an abortion can now be offered and it will be granted. The result is abortion on demand!

In Your Religion Journal

Make a list of the different reasons and circumstances you know of which make a woman opt for abortion.

Legal time limits on abortion

Until recently a woman in the United Kingdom could have a legal abortion up to 28 weeks into her pregnancy. The time limit has since been reduced to 24 weeks. However, whether a woman has an abortion one week into pregnancy or within the 24-week limit, the result is the same – it is still the deliberate killing of an innocent child and is always wrong.

When is the right time?

Arguments which are used to justify abortion are that the unborn child is not human or is not yet fully human but gradually becomes human; that it is not able to think; that it is kept alive only by the life support given it by others. However, human development is a continuous process and so it is impossible to pick a moment during a woman's pregnancy and say that before that time the unborn child is not human.

Discuss

Knowing how rapidly the unborn child grows and develops in the womb, what surprises you about the 24-week time limit?

We don't say a new-born baby is not human because he or she cannot do the things a toddler can, or that a toddler is not human because he or she is not as capable as a primary school child, or that a primary school child is not human because he or she is not a teenager, or that a teenager is not human because he or she is not an adult. An unborn child is clearly a human being at a partic- ular stage of development, a stage through which all of us have passed. To kill it then is to kill a human being just as surely as if it were already a new-born baby, or a toddler, or a primary school child, or a teenager or an adult. If you had been aborted, it is you who would have died. One rea- son for having an abortion is often the risk that a child will be born handicapped. In Britain a recent amendment to the law on abortion has made abortion on these grounds permissible, prac- tically up to the time of birth.

Read this letter:

1 Mayfair Street
London

Dear Cathy,

How are you? I know it has been a long time since I've written to you. I suppose I have neglected writing because I have been so involved with Simon. It is ten months now since we first started going out. I really need your help and advice Cathy, I don't know who else to turn to. The physi- cal side of our relationship seemed so exciting at the time that we didn't think of the possible consequences. That is until I missed my period. Even before I went to the doctor today, I had a horrible feeling that I was pregnant. She confirmed that I was almost nine weeks pregnant. What am I going to do? I can't keep the baby, I'm too young and I've got my whole life ahead of me.

When I told Simon the bad news, he told me that he wasn't ready for parenthood, and that there must be some way to sort out this mess. He suggested that I have an abortion because it is the quickest and easiest solution to the problem and no one need ever know. Maybe he's right. I just couldn't bring myself to tell my parents. They wouldn't understand and they'd be so ashamed of me.

I've read in some magazines that having an abortion isn't as bad as it sounds and anyway it's all over in fifteen minutes. The foetus is only nine weeks old so it's not as if it's a properly formed human being. It probably wouldn't feel any pain.

I've often heard people say it's a woman's right to choose whether or not to have a baby and now I'm beginning to think they're right. After all, it is my body and the foetus is only a part of my body. I should be able to do what I like with my own body.

I know I could never show this baby the love it deserves. It would feel unwanted. It probably is much kinder to terminate the pregnancy now. The doctor suggested that if I didn't want to keep the baby I could have it adopted. But I don't think I could carry the baby for nine months and then undergo the trauma of adoption. Whereas, with an abortion, once I've made the decision to ter- minate the pregnancy that's it, all over and done with and forgotten.

I feel my only choice is to have an abortion. I hope you can understand my difficult situation, Cathy, and advise me what to do.

Best wishes,

Sandra

In Your Religion Journal

Identify the points made in this letter which attempt to justify abortion. For each point you have identified write your own points to oppose it. Why do you think the writer of the letter prefers to use terms like 'foetus' instead of baby, 'termination of pregnancy' instead of abortion? What is your response to the claim that abortion spares society the burden of many unwanted and abused children? Sandra seems very much alone in making this decision. Who else do you think could have been involved with her in making it? Write a reply to this letter, offering the girl advice and support.

Read about the following two situations which are presented in dialogue form. Answer the questions which follow the stories and then finish off the dialogues. What is the main difference between the two situations?

● ● ● ● ● ● ● ● ● ● ● ● ● ●

Discuss

What words would you use to describe how you think Louisa feels? What words would you use to describe how you think Peter feels? What are all the options open to Louisa and Peter? Is there anyone who can help?

Activity

Finish off the conversation between Peter and Louisa.

Role Play

Find a partner. One of you take the role of Peter and the other the role of Louisa. Act out the situation described in 'Going to the Pictures' and bring it to a conclusion.

Going to the pictures

Louisa and Peter have been going out together for four months. They have agreed to meet to go to the pictures together tonight. Peter has been noticing for some time now that Louisa has not been in great form. She's been edgy and uneasy when they're together and doesn't talk very much, in fact most of the time they spend together recently, they seem to spend in silence. This, in turn, leaves Peter feeling uneasy and edgy. As soon as Peter sees Louisa's face he knows that things have not improved. She starts to talk immediately:

Louisa: Peter, we have to talk. Let's give the pictures a miss. Something is terribly wrong.

Peter: Right. Of course. What's up? I knew something was wrong. You haven't gone off me, have you?

Louisa: To tell you the truth, Peter, I don't know what I feel either about you or about anything else right now.

Peter: Why don't you just tell me what's wrong?

Louisa: I'm pregnant.

Peter: You can't be. It can't be true.

Louisa: It's true. I've been to the doctor. I wish it wasn't. But it's true.

Peter: How could it have happened? We only had sex once. I didn't mean this to happen. I never thought...

Louisa: What did you mean, Peter? Do you love me? Or is it all just a bit of fun?

Peter: (getting up and walking around distractedly) Of course I love you. What are we going to do? How will we manage? Have you thought of all the difficulties?

Louisa: Of course I have. I'm fifteen. I want to go to school. I want to get my exams. I want to go to college. You know I want to study art. Of course I don't want to have a baby. But I'm pregnant, I'm pregnant, and I don't know what to do.

Peter: You haven't told anyone? I mean your parents or anyone?

Louisa: No, I'm afraid. Dad would be very angry, I know, and Mam would be upset and worried. What are we going to do, Peter?

Peter: Well, don't think of an abortion. I couldn't bear the thought of being responsible for the abortion of my baby.

Louisa: I've thought of that too. But I know nothing about abortion. I don't know what it entails, how it happens or even where you have to go to have one. I only know that it frightens me. And I don't want that for our baby.

Together again!

John and Sylvia have been going out together for four months. They are meeting tonight. They'll probably have a cup of coffee and then go for a walk. John is not looking forward to the night. Recently things have not been going that well between himself and Sylvia. Sylvia has been rather quiet and withdrawn, as if she had something on her mind and she rarely seems to show her usual good humour any more.

For her part Sylvia is beginning to wish that she could turn the clock back and relive the last few months of her life. She'd always been attracted to John. He was good fun to be with and she was delighted when he asked her to go out with him. Soon she was sure she was in love with John. And then things just seemed to get out of hand. John told Sylvia constantly that he loved her, that she was the best thing that had ever happened to him and that they would be together always.

When they had sexual intercourse Sylvia was shocked afterwards that it could have happened. However, John reassured her that it was okay, and that he simply wanted her to know how much he loved her. Then whenever they were together things just seemed to get out of hand. Sylvia was worried but she didn't want to lose John. And then she missed a period. For days she just hoped and hoped that her period was later than usual for some reason. Then she realised that she would have to go to the doctor. A week ago the doctor confirmed that she is pregnant. It all seems like a bad dream. Sylvia doesn't know what to do or who to turn to. She'll have to tell John tonight.

John: Hi Syl! D'you want a cup of coffee?

Sylvia: Yes please. John, there's something I have to tell you. Something terrible has happened.

John: What's wrong.

Sylvia: I'm pregnant.

John: Don't be ridiculous. You couldn't be!

Sylvia: How can you say that? Of course I could. And I am. What are we going to do, John?

John: Now hang on. What's all this 'we' business? I'm not pregnant. You surely must mean what are you going to do? You're the one who's pregnant.

Sylvia: But John, it takes two. And you said you loved me. You do love me, John, don't you?

John: What's that got to do with it? This is a mess.

Sylvia: It has everything to do with it. This would never have happened except that I believed that you loved me. Do you love me?

John: (angry)

Of course I love you. But you'll have to have an abortion.

Sylvia: Why are you so angry? It's not all my fault. And what do you mean, I'll have to have an abortion? You haven't asked me what I want.

John: Okay, so do whatever you want. Have a baby at fifteen if that's what you want. It's your own life you'll ruin.

Sylvia: But what about the life of the baby? It's our baby, John. And what about you? What do you want?

John: What do I want? I just want out! I'm having nothing to do with it.

Discuss

What do you think John is feeling?
What do you think Sylvia is feeling?
What options do they have?
What do you think of Sylvia's attitude?
What do you think of John's attitude?

Activity

Finish off this conversation between Sylvia and John.

In Your Religion Journal

You are Sylvia or John. Write a letter to your best friend about the situation you find yourself in and saying how you feel.

Research

How would you help a person who was pregnant and on her own and wanted to keep her baby?
Find out what is provided, e.g. agencies, locally and nationally, to help in these circumstances.

1 Mayfair St
London

Dear Cathy,

I tried to write to you on a number of occasions after I received your letter last year. But possibly I was too ashamed to put pen to paper. Your letter was a source of comfort to me and it is only now that I wish I had taken your advice.

You will remember that at the time I wrote to you I was almost nine weeks pregnant. I just wanted the pregnancy to be over. I know you advised me to talk to my parents or even to contact an agency which helps unmarried mothers and offers them support, but I thought I knew best. I wonder now whether I really took the easy option.

At that time my doctor referred me to a gynaecologist who booked me into an abortion clinic. It all happened so fast, I was stunned, not that it made it less traumatic. I was riddled with guilt. I knew at the bottom of my heart that I didn't want to have an abortion, but I felt I had no choice.

I arrived at the clinic, in the afternoon. The clinic was very clean and very sterile. I got the impression that the staff worked hard at being professionally indifferent to the patients. They didn't want to get involved. The whole experience was so degrading. There were five women being prepared. It only took fifteen minutes. It was like a conveyor belt and it repulsed me.

Afterwards I expected to feel relief. Instead I woke up crying – tears stinging my eyes. Crying for myself and the baby I'd allowed to be killed. I suppose this was a natural reaction. Although there was little physical discomfort – just some stomach cramps – I had a numbing ache and my heart was broken.

However, within a couple of weeks I was back to normal. I had to get on with my own life now. I decided to put any remorse or guilt to the back of my mind and hopefully the whole sordid business would be forgotten. After all, what's done is done!

But, really, I was only fooling myself. The choice I made will scar me for the rest of my life. I have to face the fact that on this day a year ago I allowed my child to be killed. I can't help wondering what might have been. I wonder would my child have been a boy or a girl? What would I have called my child?

Oh yes, abortion has set me free. But I will never be free from my guilt – from my grief. I have denied my child a life because it was inconvenient and now I will never know what might have been!

Best Wishes,

Sandra

The bishops speak

In their pastoral letter, *Human Life is Sacred*, the Irish bishops teach as follows:

Abortion

1. The embryo or foetus possesses its fundamental right to life from the moment of conception.
2. Each single embryo, even if invisible to the naked eye, is unique and unrepeatable.
3. Interrupting the process of development in the womb is to take innocent human life.
4. Abortion does not become in any way less ugly or less evil if some state law permits it.
5. The Church is not simply 'against abortion'; she is for life and for human dignity and social justice.
6. All of us, first parents, then society, are obliged to create the best possible conditions for newly-born life.
7. All who have been involved in abortions, especially the woman who has suffered 'agonies of conscience and the tortures of remorse', are assured of the boundless compassion and unlimited mercy of Christ.
8. One of the foremost duties of Christians in society is to work for conditions in which all the children of the nation will be guaranteed equality of dignity and opportunity.

In Your Religion Journal

Indicate what you think are the areas in a woman's life which would be affected as a result of having an abortion.
What advice and support would you offer a woman who has had an abortion?
What advice and support would you give to an unmarried mother who wants to keep her baby?

There is a beauty about the Irish rendering of 'unborn'. The Irish phrase, 'Beo gan breith', means 'Alive but not yet born'.

In Your Religion Journal

Compose a poem or prayer with the title – 'Alive but not yet born'.

Class Activity

Prepare a thanksgiving celebration in which you remember and celebrate some aspects of your life, using music, poems, reflections and readings. Organise a display of your work.

The Right to Die?

Read and act out the following:

Welcome to our radio phone-in programme, 'Voice of the People'. My name is Ivor McIvor and today we will be discussing voluntary euthanasia. I look forward to hearing your comments. Our listeners will have the opportunity to phone in and give their views on whether or not a person has the right to choose when and how to die.

But let me begin by telling our listeners just what euthanasia is.

The word euthanasia has a Greek origin and, in its original form, meant a good and honourable death, which would be painless and pleasant. In medical terms it was taken to mean the kindness offered to a dying person by a doctor in order to lessen the pain and suffering.

However, in recent times the term euthanasia has come to be used to describe a gentle and easy death and is applied to the killing of those who are incurably ill and in great pain and distress.

Voluntary euthanasia is the act of terminating the life of someone painlessly at their own request. Under the present law, voluntary euthanasia is illegal. It is considered illegal to help someone die or to terminate their life at their own request. However, a number of organisations are campaigning for this law to be changed. They claim that people have a right to choose to die a dignified death. I want to know what you think. The lines are now open for your calls to the programme.

But before I take your calls, let's take a short commercial break...

In Your Religion Journal

Imagine you phoned the programme 'Voice of the People'. What is your view on voluntary euthanasia? Give reasons for your answer.

Ivor:	Our first caller to the programme is a member of an organisation which is currently campaigning for legalised voluntary euthanasia.
First Caller:	Hello, Ivor, I was delighted to hear that your programme was discussing voluntary euthanasia. I am a member of the society known as 'Exit'. Our society believes that an adult person suffering from a severe or terminal illness, for which no relief is known, should be entitled, by law, to the mercy of a painless death if, and only if, that is their expressed wish. Obviously, if the law were changed, doctors would then be allowed to help incurably ill patients to die peacefully and with dignity at their own request.
Ivor:	Could you tell me how patients would give their consent?
First Caller:	We propose that people would sign a request form asking in advance for euthanasia in certain circumstances. The doctor should then be free to implement this decision should the circumstances arise.
Ivor:	But surely helping to take the life of another person, no matter how compassionate the reasons and no matter how tragic the circumstances, is still murder?
First Caller:	Well, I don't agree with you, Ivor. To people of good sense it has always been obvious that voluntary euthanasia is not murder. Murder, as you know, is never intended for the good of the victim. Whereas voluntary euthanasia is only shortening the process of dying and comes as a merciful release from a patient's suffering.
Ivor:	Let's take another caller who has a very different point of view on the subject.
Second Caller:	Hello, Ivor. I am a volunteer worker in a hospice and in my line of work I care for the terminally ill and the dying. I am very concerned about some of the comments your previous caller made, so I would just like to draw her attention to a number of points.
—As a Christian I believe that life is a gift from God and only God can take

it away. The right to life is a fundamental human right. Respect for human life must apply 'from the moment of conception to the moment of natural death'. And on this basis then, to take your own life or to co-operate with another person in deliberately shortening their life, no matter how compassionate the motives, is always wrong.

—Those who campaigned to have abortion legalised initially only intended it to be used on compassionate grounds, for example if the unborn child was severely handicapped and so on. But that was only a first step on to a slippery slope and as a result we now have abortion on demand in some countries.

If euthanasia, or mercy killing, as it is often referred to, were legalised, where would society draw the line? First it was the unborn child, now it is the elderly and terminally ill who are under threat. I ask you, who will be next?

Ivor: Yes, you do have a point. Before I take another call, could you just tell the listeners about the work of the hospice?

Second Caller: Well, I go along to my local hospice three mornings a week to help the nursing staff care for the terminally ill

254

and dying. If you ever go into a hospice you will notice that hospices are not about dying but rather about helping people to live as fully as possible until they die.

The nursing staff do a wonderful job, making each patient as comfortable as possible. An important part of our job as volunteers is taking the time to talk and listen to the patients. Pain-killing drugs are given to patients to relieve their suffering but care is taken to ensure that patients remain alert and are at ease with their surroundings. Relatives are also encouraged to get involved. I think the realisation that their loved ones are not in pain and will die in their own time in peace and with dignity helps them to overcome some of their anxiety.

Ivor: So, possibly, if there were more hospices and better facilities for caring for the dying the whole issue of euthanasia would be less relevant.

Second Caller: Yes, exactly!

Ivor: Other listeners who have phoned the programme, but who were unable to get on air, have given us some comments.

If euthanasia were to become legal, no sick or old person would be safe.

The old and fatally ill often feel helplessly dependent on the good will, patience and love of others. They feel insecure, afraid of being unwanted, rejected, a burden. The possibility of euthanasia could only increase these feelings of insecurity.

Legalised euthanasia would soon be used as a means of population control. Older people feel under pressure to do the responsible thing and could easily be persuaded that it is their duty to die.

With the introduction of legalised euthanasia a patient's confidence in their doctor's motives could be affected by the knowledge that they are both licensed and willing to kill.

Discuss

In what way do you think a patient's relationship with their doctor might be affected if legalised euthanasia were introduced?

Ivor: Our third caller to the programme is now on the line.

Third Caller: Hello, Ivor. I listen to your programme every day and I thought this particular topic was relevant to my own situation. I'm a seventy-nine-year-old widow. My husband died three years ago and since then I've been living with my daughter and her family. However, over the last six months my health has deteriorated and I'm now beginning to depend on my daughter more and more.

Ivor: Does your daughter have children?

Third Caller: The eldest boy is fourteen and his two sisters are aged eleven and nine. But they are all very kind and considerate to me. But my point is, Ivor, that if voluntary euthanasia was legalised I would probably opt for it.

Ivor: And why would you do that?

Third Caller: I don't want to become a nuisance or a burden to my daughter. She has her own life to lead and I don't want to tie her down by having to care for me in my old age.

Ivor: Have you spoken to the family about your feelings?

Third Caller: Oh no, I couldn't do that. The family might think I'm ungrateful after all they've done for me.

Ivor: I'll have to stop you there for a short commercial break...

Find Your Group

After hearing the third caller describe herself as a possible nuisance and a burden to the family, write out the reasons why you think an elderly person might opt for euthanasia.

If euthanasia was legalised, what might be the risk of abuse from relatives of an elderly person?

Ivor: Our last call to the programme today is from a doctor.

Fourth Caller: Ivor, I've been listening carefully to your discussion about euthanasia and I would like to point out a few of the reasons why I think euthanasia should not be legalised. Firstly, as a doctor I do not believe that life and suffering should be prolonged artificially by modern medical techniques when natural death is inevitably close. This is also the view taken by the Catholic Church.

Ivor: But you do not agree with the deliberate and intentional shortening of a patient's life through euthanasia.

Fourth Caller: Yes, exactly. I believe it is always wrong either to take your own life or to help another person to terminate theirs. My second point is that if euthanasia were legalised the relationship of trust between doctors and patients could be destroyed. It would only lead to suspicion and fear. Doctors must try to nurture and preserve life.

Ivor: For those listeners who are not familiar with the oath that all doctors must take when they first qualify, it was drawn up by the World Medical Association in Geneva in 1948, and I quote...

The health of my patient will be my first consideration; I will maintain the utmost respect for human life from the time of conception.

256

Fourth Caller: The burden of responsibility for carrying out the euthanasia would fall on the medical profession. As your first caller to the programme failed to point out, the patient who would be seeking euthanasia obviously needs the consent of a doctor who can then decide whether or not to agree to the patient's request. But I ask your listeners, Ivor, what right has a doctor to decide who is unfit to live?

Ivor: Well, it does seem quite unacceptable that hospitals, the traditional centres of healing, may become places where one goes to have one's life deliberately terminated.

Fourth Caller: The sad phone call from the previous listener, who said she would probably opt for euthanasia so as not to become a burden or a nuisance to her family, shows the pressure an elderly person would be under. There is a danger that once euthanasia is legalised it would be offered to the elderly or terminally ill as an option and, as such, pressure could be put on them to opt for euthanasia when in actual fact they want to keep on living.

Ivor: I suppose most of us have encountered old people who complain that they're no use to anybody or that they've lived too long. Usually such people are in need of reassurance that they are still wanted. There is a real risk of abuse of euthanasia, possibly from relatives or friends of an elderly person, who could see it as the easy way out to get rid of troublesome old folk.

Fourth Caller: My last point is that those in the medical profession and society as a whole have to be more willing to serve those who suffer in a way which does not degrade the dignity of the person or their right to life.

Ivor: Thank you for your comments. Before we end today's discussion, I want to leave you with one final

thought. The fact that a particular person does not have long to live or has a life we judge to be more imperfect than our own does not remove their right to life, nor does it remove their right to respect as an individual.

Discuss

What is your point of view on voluntary euthanasia after reading this discussion?

Experience itself is enough to show that no person can be trusted with absolute power over the lives of others, and especially with absolute power over life and death. It is a grim fact that throughout history scientific knowledge and technological power has been used for the enslavement of people, as well as for increasing the sum of human happiness. This is why it is so important that the absolute principle that innocent human life is sacred, and that every human being has its right to life directly from God, and not from any human authority, is upheld. Because he saw this so clearly, Pope Pius XII taught that:

> No person, no human authority, no science, no medical, eugenic, social, economic or moral indication can offer or produce a valid juridical title for disposing directly of innocent human life.

(Address to Midwives, 1951)

The Hospice Movement

The aim of the hospice movement is to care for people who are terminally ill, in such a way as to help them to die with dignity in a loving, caring environment. For those who are terminally ill there can be no cure, but the hospice offers the healing that comes from the love, compassion, care and respect which is offered to each patient who seeks hospice care.

The patient's spiritual and physical needs are taken into account. Help and support are also offered to the patient's family.

Patients are kept fully informed of their physical condition and the most modern drugs and treatments are used to relieve their pain and discomfort so that they can live life as fully as possible for as long as possible.

The History of the Hospice Movement

The word hospice comes from a Latin word which means 'a home of entertainment for strangers...a place of refuge'. In medieval times hospices were places where travellers received food and shelter to enable them to continue their journey. In later years the word hospice came to be associated with the care of people who were dying.

In 1815 the Sisters of Charity were founded by Mary Aikenhead. She believed that the poor deserved the very best medical attention and the Sisters of Charity were the first order to work on the streets of Dublin caring for the poor and the sick. In 1834 the Sisters of Charity opened St Vincent's Hospital in Dublin, the first Catholic voluntary hospital in Ireland.

There is a story which says that one of the novices who was working in St Vincent's got cholera. She was living in the novitiate in Harold's Cross and, because she carried the disease, another fifteen sisters became infected. However, unlike many Dubliners who caught

the disease, the sisters all survived because of the excellence of the nursing. When the order moved the novitiate out of the city to Milltown, Harold's Cross became vacant. This building

Mary Aikenhead

was to become the first hospice in Europe. In 1879 its first patients were welcomed, and six years later the foundation stone for the present Hospice was laid.

Dame Cicely Saunders is recognised as the pioneer of the modern hospice movement. She worked in St Joseph's Hospice in London with the Irish Sisters of Charity in the 1950s.

As a result of her work and her research she has done much to help people come to a new understanding of the type of care needed by those who are dying and by their families.

Hospice buildings are usually bright and cheerful. The hospice tries to be a 'home from home' for the patients – they can bring their own bed linen, and there's always room for their paintings, photographs and other mementos.

Various activities such as painting classes, aromatherapy, bingo and massage are available for those who are able to take part, and when the weather is fine enough, those who are able are taken out for wheelchair walks.

The philosophy of the hospice is 'living to the

Dame Cicely Saunders

end'. Nowhere is the sense of the value for human life more evident than in a hospice. It is no wonder that the value of the hospice is being more and more clearly understood and that their numbers are growing all the time.

In Your Religion Journal

Prepare a short talk for your class on: 'Euthanasia should be unnecessary and is an admission of defeat!'

Class Activity

Debate:
This house opposes the motion that euthanasia should be made legal.

Research

Write a short personal profile on Dame Cicely Saunders, one of the leaders of the hospice movement.
Find out if there is a hospice in your area. Do a project on your local hospice and present your work to the class.

The bishops speak in their pastoral letter, *Human Life is Sacred.*

Euthanasia

1. Deliberately to take one's own life is suicide and is gravely wrong in all circumstances.

2. To co-operate with another in taking his or her own life, no matter how merciful the motive, is to share in the guilt of suicide.

3. Deliberately to terminate the innocent life of another is murder, no matter how merciful the motive, no matter how seemingly desirable the result.

4. In a culture where euthanasia – so-called mercy killing – becomes thinkable, Christians must commit themselves anew to the care of the old and dying.

In the Declaration on Euthanasia, 1980, the following is stated:

> When inevitable death is imminent in spite of the means used, it is permitted in conscience to take the decision to refuse forms of treatment that would only secure a precarious and burdensome prolongation of life, so long as the normal care due to the sick person in similar cases is not interrupted.

Human Love is Sacred

From the moment of birth, we need to feel loved. A new baby feels the love of its parents by being fed and changed regularly, by being handled gently, with great care, by being held and cuddled. Gradually the baby learns to love in return. A baby could survive without the love of parents or other adults but would always find it difficult to feel secure, to trust others, to build relationships.

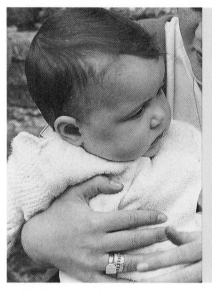

Love is...

No one can be truly happy without being loved and giving love in return. The word 'love' can mean many different things to different people.

It is used in many different circumstances and situations.

Find Your Group

In your group brainstorm the word love. Write down the words you think of when you hear the word **love.** Report back to the class. Which words were used most often by the others in your class as they tried to talk about love?

Love is about **responsible**: It takes account of consequences. To be responsible is to accept that our actions do have consequences, and that we should give due consideration to the effects they may have on others and on ourselves.

Love is about **giving**: It is active, not passive. It is a giving of oneself to and for others.

Love is about **serving**: It involves putting our needs second to those of another person, a readiness to make sacrifices for their benefit.

Activity

Design a 'Love Diary' for this coming week. Record the times when you lived out these qualities of love in your own life.

In Your Religion Journal

Design a poster illustrating the caption: 'Love is...!'

Love is about **respecting**: It accepts that other people may have different opinions or attitudes, and shows consideration for these.

Love is about **understanding**: It is only when we try to understand others that we truly come to love them, even when at times they may be difficult to understand.

Love and Attraction

It may have occurred to you that not everything that people call 'love' fits in with the picture of love you have been considering. This is because the word 'love' is often misused.

There is a kind of 'love' which is merely an attraction to something or someone. In itself there is nothing wrong with such an attraction, but in itself it is not real love. 'Love' which is merely attraction is mostly self-centred. If someone has a love for someone that is merely attraction, he or she will value the other mainly for what they can get from them, for the use they can make of them. When they no longer feel the attraction, or when they no longer have a use for them, that is the end of 'love' of this kind. Real love is quite different. It is more concerned with giving than getting.

Friendship is a kind of love, and we all know the difference between a real friend and a false friend. A real friend is ready to put himself or herself out for you, to stand by you when things go wrong and when being your friend doesn't bring any benefits. In those situations a false friend is nowhere to be seen. A false friend values you for what he or she can get out of knowing you. When your usefulness ceases, so does the friendship.

Throughout our lives we may experience different kinds of love, apart from friendship. Each of them, however, can be the real thing, or it can be simply a matter of convenience or mere emotional attraction, which is fundamentally self-centred and which will not last. The acid test of real love is whether it is prepared to make sacrifices. 'Love' which is merely attraction needs to be combined with an attitude of care, concern and self-giving, if it is to become real love. If we don't realise this, we can be hurt and, just as important, we can hurt other people.

Here are some of the kinds of love we can experience:

- PARENTAL
- ROMANTIC
- AFFECTIONATE
- NUTRITIVE
- SEXUAL

262 Read these accounts and identify which kinds of love are involved in each situation, choosing from the headings on p.261.

Peggy and Caroline have grown up together. They have been close friends since primary school. After leaving post-primary school, Caroline began working in a bank while Peggy left home to study at a university. However, they remain in touch with each other by writing regularly. During their holidays they look forward to spending time together as they enjoy each other's company.

What kind of love do they share?

Cathy is fourteen years old and she is finding life difficult at home. She never seems to do the right thing. Her parents always seem to be scolding her about something – school, homework, or staying out late. Cathy feels they just don't understand her. Last Saturday night, for example, they didn't let her go to the local disco. They said it just wasn't suitable. And so Cathy took the huff all evening and wouldn't speak to them. What always surprises Cathy, however, is that, unlike her friends, her parents don't fall out with her when she is moody or sulks.

What kind of love is Cathy experiencing?

Circle diagram titled "Love is" with segments labelled: Affectionate love, Nutritive love, Parental love, Sexual love, Romantic love.

Activity

Fill in the 'circle of love' by writing out the characteristics and qualities of each kind of love.

Class Activity

Look through magazines and newspapers and cut out articles and pictures which illustrate each kind of love. Make a wall display of your work.

Research

Ever since men and women have begun to write songs and poems, one of the most popular themes has been love. Look at this week's top thirty music hits and compile a list of the songs that are about love.

Patrick is fifty-nine. He lives with his family in a quiet area of the city. He is a respected member of his parish. He has gained this respect by taking the time to care for others. He cares for those who are less well-off than himself. He spends an endless amount of time working for the St Vincent de Paul society, and helping the poor and deprived wherever he sees the need. He gives these people dignity and a sense of self-worth. He shows them respect. Patrick goes about his work in a quiet way, unconcerned about the religious background or home background of those he helps.

What kind of love is Patrick living out in his own life?

Nigel and Sharon have been going out together for four months. They feel as if they were made for each other. Sharon thinks of Nigel all the time and counts the minutes until she's with him again. The wonderful thing is that Nigel feels the same way about Sharon. They find all these special ways to say, 'I love you' – little gifts and surprises. All that matters to them is that they love each other. Their friends agree that they have certainly 'fallen in love'.

What kind of love are they experiencing?

David and Karen have been married for eleven years. They have three young children. They enjoy showing their love and intimacy for each other in a physical way. They have had good times and more difficult times in their marriage. What has helped them through the difficult times is that both David and Karen are totally committed to their relationship. Their love for each other has matured and grown deeper.

What kind of love are they expressing?

Parental Love

Parental love is the very special love of parents for their children. At its best it is characterised by unconditional love. The family is the community of love. It is the very first place that children can learn that they are loved and, in return, learn how to love their parents. In the family also, they learn to appreciate the companionship and care of brothers and sisters.

Parents love their children and show this love by taking responsibility for them. They provide them with their every need – food, clothes and shelter – and also take responsibility for their intellectual, spiritual and emotional growth.

Of course there are some parents who could be more understanding, who could take more interest in their children and who could show more love to their children.

Sometimes children could also be more understanding and more appreciative of the sacrifices their parents have had to make for them.

Love is a gift

When the children and grandchildren of Lorene and Julian Vela come to celebrate with their parents, it is a joyous, noisy event. You can almost see the love flowing from one person to another in this family. They know their family is special. Indeed it is. Lorene Vela was arthritic and in pain at the age of forty when she took in their first child, an abandoned infant. And during the next sixteen years she and Julian, despite poverty and ill-health, adopted or took as foster children a steady stream of unwanted, lonely, loveless children – a six-year-old problem child, an unwanted illegitimate infant, four malnourished and frightened children, children half-starved or sullen – until they had adopted nine and had become foster parents to eleven more. Today, when these children return home as adults, love is there. They learned early in life what a gift it is!

Discuss

Why do you think love is described as a gift?
In what ways can you show your appreciation for the gift of love shown to you by your parents?

In Your Religion Journal

Recall a moment of happiness from your childhood, a moment when you felt loved in a special way.
List and describe five sacrifices that your parents have recently made for your benefit.
How do you feel about the sacrifices your parents have made for you?

Activity

Write a letter to your parents telling them about any problems or worries you may have. Express your appreciation to your parents for all they have done for you.

Nutritive Love

The belief that all people are our brothers and sisters leads us to treat them as we would wish to be treated ourselves. This belief leads us to have a special care for the needy, the poor, the homeless, those who are weakest and most in need.

Through the ages there have been many people from all of the great religions of the world who have put this love into practice in extraordinary ways. The gospels are full of stories which show the love of Jesus for those who were weakest and most in need. In Matthew 25 we read that we will be judged finally according to the way in which we have put this love into practice in our lives:

'Then the King will say to the people on his right, "Come, you that are blessed by my Father! Come and possess the kingdom which has been prepared for you ever since the creation of the world. I was hungry and you fed me, thirsty and you gave me a drink; I was a stranger and you received me in your homes, naked and you clothed me; I was sick and you took care of me, in prison and you visited me."

'The righteous will then answer him, "When, Lord, did we ever see you hungry and feed you, or thirsty and give you a drink? When did we ever see you a stranger and welcome you in our

homes, or naked and clothe you? When did we ever see you sick or in prison, and visit you?" The King will reply, "I tell you, whenever you did this for one of the least important of these brothers of mine, you did it for me!" '
(Matthew 25:34-40)

Activity

Take the caption 'Love is' and use it as the starting point for a poster which illustrates the lives of people who live out this love in extraordinary ways.

In Your Religion Journal

Write about ways in which you have put this kind of love into practice in your life in the past week.

Affectionate Love

Affectionate love is the care and love shown between friends and acquaintances. It is characterised by mutual caring and concern between two people. It involves loyalty, support and a capacity to share and enjoy activities of common interest.

Although we can't choose our family we can choose our friends. We can have friends of both sexes.

Discuss

What qualities do you like your friends to have?
Why do you think this is so?
In what situations can you make new friends?

In Your Religion Journal

How would you define a friend?
Make up five sentences that begin with, 'A friend is...'.

We grow very close to only a few friends in life. Our closest friends know almost as much about us as we know about ourselves — the good and the not so good, the interesting and the boring. A good friend lets us pull off our mask and be ourselves.

In Your Religion Journal

How many close friends do you have?
Write down their names and the things you have in common.
In what ways do you show your love and concern for a friend?

Activity

Try and recall a time in your life when you were at a very low point emotionally, depressed or discouraged, and a friend came along and helped you get back on your feet.

Write a description of that time, taking account of these points:
—   Why were you feeling so low?
—   What happened to cause your trouble?
—   Describe exactly how you felt at the time.
—   How did your friend get involved?
—   What did he or she do to help you get back on your feet?

In Your Religion Journal

Write a brief prayer of thanksgiving for the friend who helped you in your time of need.

Romantic Love

Romantic love is characterised by the kind of love shared between a boy and a girl when they are first attracted to each other. It is the sort of love referred to when we talk of someone 'falling in love'. During adolescence we are made more self-aware by the physical changes which are taking place in our bodies. We mature emotionally and physically and gradually we feel more drawn towards the opposite sex. Boys like to be friends with girls, and girls like to become friends with boys.

Such friendship, however, should remain open and not involve commitments. Out of friendship, romantic love can blossom.

Discuss

Have you heard the expression 'Love is blind'?
What do you think it means?

Romantic love can change and grow to become a deeper and more solid kind of love. This can only happen with time and when people really get to know each other deeply and want to care for each other. Sometimes romantic love may provide roots too shallow for real love to grow.

Read this story:

Karen joined St Michael's post-primary school late in the term. Her father had recently got a new job in the neighbourhood and as a result she had to move to a school in the area.

Karen wasn't really looking forward to joining her third-year class as she thought it would be difficult to settle in so late in the term. But to her surprise, the other students in her class were very friendly and gave her a warm welcome to St Michael's.

One advantage of changing school was that Karen now had the opportunity to take up a language which she hadn't studied before. It was during her first Spanish lesson that Karen noticed Paul sitting two seats in front of her.

Paul was a good-looking boy. He had dark hair and brown eyes and was the tallest boy in the class. He was well known throughout the school for his sporting achievements. After Spanish class, Karen made some enquiries about her handsome classmate. Some of the other girls warned her not to get too interested in Paul as she had tough competition from most of the other third-year girls. So for the next couple of weeks Karen admired Paul from a distance. But little did she know that her life was about to be turned upside down. In the canteen one day she was enjoying her lunch, when she heard someone ask if the seat beside her was free. 'Oh yeah', she said, 'Sit down', not realising that it was Paul. And then all of a sudden, Karen could feel her heart begin to beat so fast she had to take a gulp of water to calm herself. She knew all third-year eyes were on her now just to see what she would do. So Karen decided to make the most of the opportunity which had arisen.

Before she realised, she could hear herself rambling on about past, present and future tenses and the difficulty of learning Spanish verbs. By the time Paul had asked Karen to go with him to the pictures on Saturday night, she had certainly fallen in love. She thought she was on cloud nine. Wait until she told her friends that Paul had asked her out! Going home on the bus from school that day Karen found herself day-dreaming – she was walking up the aisle and Paul was standing waiting for her. They married and lived happily ever after.

For the next two months Karen enjoyed going out with the best-looking and most popular boy of her year. She enjoyed the envious looks from the other girls. She enjoyed being known as Paul's girlfriend.

And then one day she came back down to earth with a bang. Paul told her it was over; that he'd found someone else.

Karen is now in sixth year studying for her final Spanish exam. It makes her smile when she thinks of the 'crush' she had on Paul. She remembers that during those two wonderful months in third year, she didn't even stop and take the time to get to know him. Maybe if she had, things would have turned out differently!

In Your Religion Journal

What does the word infatuation mean?

In what way was Karen infatuated with Paul?

What made it difficult for love to grow in this relationship?

Think of a time when you really liked someone, and then shortly afterwards didn't like him or her. Why was this?

Infatuation

This is falling in love with someone 'overnight', before we really have time to get to know them or to find out whether we really like them. It is being 'bowled over' by someone's looks, popularity, image and so on. We imagine ourselves being with them, perhaps even marrying them because they are the 'ideal' person. This is not real love because it is not directed towards the person as he or she really is. We are oblivious of their faults and failings. We only see the good side, the attractive side which we want to see.

do know someone, but only superficially. Again, we concentrate on the qualities and characteristics which we find attractive and make little or no attempt to get to know the the person fully. We do not really love the person, we love our image of the person. A lasting relationship based on this type of love is doomed to failure. If we really want a true friendship or relationship to grow with another person we must be prepared to spend time getting to know the other person and allowing the other person to get to know us.

Discuss

What is the danger if we don't recognise the faults and failings of another person?

In Your Religion Journal

List three people you admire in the sport/television/pop world, etc.
Why do you admire them?
What do you actually know about them as people?
Do you know them personally and, if so, how well?

Hero Worship/Idolising

Another kind of romantic love is hero-worshipping or idolising another person – seeing him or her as perfect, wonderful, the answer to all our prayers and dreams. In some cases we don't really know our 'heroes' at all. All we have is an 'image', sometimes cleverly constructed by publicity experts. It is all one-sided, glossy and unreal, but very often we are happy to accept it and to continue to build it up ourselves, creating our own image of what our own hero or idol is like without real knowledge or facts. We can also idealise or hero-worship when we

Class Activity Discuss

Bring to class a picture or poster of someone who is considered an idol or hero in our culture, or someone whom an advertiser or a promoter wants people to idolise. Display the pictures around the classroom.

Why are these people idols or heroes?
What do you know about these people's values?
Would you trust these people with a secret?
Does idolising someone fit into the true meaning of love?

Obviously, in real-life situations things are often not as clear-cut as might appear from these descriptions. It is, for instance, easy to see how, in a relationship between a boy and girl, where romantic love is the most obvious type of love between the two, there could also be affectionate love.

Christian Love

St Paul summarised many of the characteristics of love in his first letter to the Christian community in Corinth.

Love is always patient and kind; love is never jealous; love is not boastful or conceited, it is never rude and never seeks its own advantage, it does not take offence or store up grievances. Love does not rejoice at wrongdoing, but finds its joy in the truth. It is always ready to make allowances, to trust, to hope and to endure whatever comes. Love never comes to an end (1 Corinthians 13: 4-8).

In Your Religion Journal

Consider how you would rank yourself with regard to the following (very good, good, fair, weak) and complete the sentences:

(a) **Love is patient:**
I keep my cool when others try to irritate me.
I am slow to get angry and upset with those I love.
I rarely yell or lose my temper.
I am prepared to wait for others who are slower than I am.

My love would be more patient if I....

(b) **Love is not jealous:**
I am not jealous when others perform better than I do, or get ahead of me.
I am not threatened by others' talents.
When I'm overlooked, I don't punish others with my moods.

My love would be less jealous if I...

(c) **Love is not conceited:**
I don't hog the spotlight in the group.
I avoid focusing all the glory on myself.
I try to make others look good and do not boast about myself.
I realise that everything I have is a gift from God.

My love would be less conceited if I ...

(d) **Love is never snobbish:**
I don't look down on others.
I don't need special attention or favours to get me to co-operate.
I do not go around putting other people down.

My love would be less snobbish if I...

(e) **Love is not rude:**
I avoid making crude or sarcastic comments to or about others. Instead my conversation is polite and supportive, and my approach to others is sincere and friendly.

My love would be less rude if I...

(f) **Love is not self-seeking:**
I am not self-centred: I avoid making others fit my expectations. I am not possessive of my friends. I don't always insist on my own way.

My love would be less self-seeking if I ...

(g) **Love is not prone to anger:**
I am not touchy, cranky, defensive or super-sensitive.
I don't lay my bad moods on others: I am approachable, warm, open and easy to get along with.

My love would be less angry if I ...

(h) **Love does not brood over injuries:**
I am quick to forgive those who have hurt me.
I don't fight back or seek revenge.
I forget mistakes others make and avoid holding grudges.

My love would be less brooding if I ...

(i) **Love does not rejoice in what is wrong:**
When someone is proven wrong I avoid self-satisfaction.
I don't take delight in another's failures even if it has made me look good.
When anyone slips up I am there with encouragement instead of 'I told you so!'

My love would rejoice less in what is wrong if I...

(j) **Love rejoices with the truth:**
I welcome honesty and justice even when it shows my weaknesses.
I am willing to give credit and praise whenever it is due.
I am willing to admit my mistakes.

I could rejoice more with the truth if I...

(k) **Love never gives up:**
When my relationship with someone is a struggle I try to keep sharing.
I never miss an opportunity to help someone.
There is no rejection or failure that can make me give up my commitment to love.

It would help me not to give up on love if I...

Love Skills

The Christian life asks us to set out on a journey towards loving others as God loves us – to choose a path towards love. When we make the choice to love we have to recognise and develop the skills we need to live out love in our lives.

In Your Religion Journal

For each of the following love skills indicate ways in which you can develop and improve on them in your own life.

1. Knowledge of another person:

We attempt to understand the other person in depth so that we can respond to his or her real needs.

Joe was very impatient with his friend Jim when he heard Jim say that he didn't want to go to the party at Sharon's house that night. He felt that he was just a spoil-sport or a goody-goody. However, when he took the time to talk to Jim he found out that he had a part-time job in order to help out at home since his father had become unemployed and that, therefore, he had neither the time nor the energy to go to the party.

I can develop this skill in my own life by

2. Practical knowledge:

We develop the skills and know-how that are useful in finding ways to serve others – whether in car repair, in listening or in organising a fund-raising event for people in need.
Gary says to himself before he goes to the DIY store, 'I'd better get things straight. If I make a mess of this plumbing job, Gran will be worse off than she was before she asked me to help.'

I can develop this skill in my own life by

_____

_____

_____

3. Flexibility:

We are able to respond to change in the people we love and to shifts in our relationships.
Len explains to a friend how things are going since his wife began college:
'With Barbara in college now, I have to spend a lot more time on housework and taking care of the children. And she's not as available to me as she used to be. But I want to help. I know how important a college education is to Barbara.'

I can develop this skill in my own life by

_____

_____

_____

4. Handling conflict:

We bring out in the open what bothers us in our relationships and try to resolve problems in a way that respects the value of both persons.
Jane says to her friend Maria, 'When you say you'll be here to pick me up at a certain time I wish you'd stick to that rather than coming half an hour later. It's been irritating me because I worry about whether something has happened to you and because I could be doing other stuff while I'm waiting if I know you won't be here for thirty minutes.'

I can develop this skill in my own life by

_____

_____

5. Patience:

We hang in there with the other person through difficult times, and we respect the other person's needs.
Michelle thinks to herself: 'What a good friend Sam has been, particularly during the time when I was having difficulties with my parents at home. He would phone me regularly to ask how I was coping and to see if I needed anyone to talk to. He showed real concern. He didn't get impatient when I was depressed or worried and didn't expect me always to be in a good humour.'

I can develop this skill in my own life by

_____

_____

6. Honesty:

We are genuine in our caring and do not put on masks to pretend we are something we are not. Jane and her friends are going camping at the weekend. Her best friend Claire will be there too. Jane says to Claire, 'I want you to know before the weekend that I haven't forgotten the last time. I still do not want to drink alcohol. I know that you probably still disagree with me on this but I will not be pressurised.'

I can develop this skill in my own life by

_____

_____

7. Trust:

We let go of our concern about constantly protecting our own interests in a relationship so that the other person can grow.
Dan confides to a friend about what hard experience has taught him. 'I learned my lesson about trust when Melissa broke up with me. I was trying to hold on to her. I wouldn't let her be with other people because I was so afraid of losing her. Now I see that she just felt mistrusted and smothered.'

I can develop this skill in my own life by

_____

_____

8. Trustworthiness:

We can live up to the other person's trust in us. Linda talks with a friend about her relationship with her parents. 'After I got caught shoplifting, I thought my parents would never trust me again. They knew I had lied to them several times too. But instead they told me that they forgave me, that they believed in me, and that I could turn around from this. Now I'm totally honest with them. I wouldn't dream of breaking their trust.'

I can develop this skill in my own life by

_____

_____

9. Humility:

We acknowledge our real situation – our accomplishments as well as our limits and flaws – and recognise that we are like all human beings, no better and no worse. We treat others as dignified and deserving of respect.
Jeremy describes his work at a local shelter for the homeless: 'The people who come to the shelter teach me more about life than I ever learned in school. They're remarkable; they know about endurance, about suffering and trying to cope. I feel fortunate that I've had the chance to know them.'

I can develop this skill in my own life by

_____

_____

10. Hope:

We are ready at each moment to foster new growth in our relationships and are open to new relationships without putting heavy expectations on another person.

Julie thinks to herself about getting to know Jane: 'It's really good fun getting to know Jane, maybe we won't develop a lasting friendship but at the moment I'm enjoying the times we spend together.'

I can develop this skill in my own life by

11. Courage:

We have courage to face the unknown – possible rejection, conflicts, separations, the death of another person, abandonment, and the day-to-day demands of working out a relationship.

Wayne hasn't heard from Mark in over a week. Wayne is a bit sensitive about the possibility of being left out: 'Maybe Mark's tired of getting together with me. On the other hand, maybe I should take the initiative and call him, for a change. That's what I'll do.'

I can develop this skill in my own life by

12. Forgiveness:

We do not hold the other person's hurtful behaviour or wrongdoing over his/her head. We talk about it with the person; then we go forward in the relationship with a generous spirit of forgiveness.

Sally says to her sister Megan: 'I understand what you did and why you did it. I know you didn't mean to hurt me, even though it did hurt. I forgive you and I don't hold anything against you.'

I can develop this skill in my own life by

Find Your Group

Activity

Imagine your parish priest has asked you to write and design a booklet which will be used by other members of the parish as a guideline for living out Christian love in their own lives.

When the Pharisees heard that Jesus had silenced the Sadducees, they came together, and one of them, a teacher of the Law, tried to trap him with a question. 'Teacher,' he asked, 'which is the greatest commandment in the Law?'

Jesus answered, ' "Love the Lord your God with all your heart, with all your soul, and with all your mind." This is the greatest and the most important commandment. The second most important commandment is like it: "Love your neighbour as you love yourself." The whole Law of Moses and the teachings of the prophets depend on these two commandments' (*Matthew 22:34-40*).

Discuss

Why do you think Jesus said that these two commandments are the greatest?

Why do you think he said 'The whole Law of Moses and the teachings of the prophets' depend on these two commandments'?

Loving Your Neighbour

Love usually involves some form of self-sacrifice on behalf of other people. It involves an unselfish spirit of self-giving. We can see it in the actions of Christ who suffered and died for us to show that God really loves us. We can see it in the actions of the 'Good Samaritan' who took the trouble to look after a complete stranger. We can see it in the lives of many people around us who spend time taking care of the needs of others in their families and in their neighbourhoods. It is God's greatest gift. It never ends. Most of us will never be called on to lay down our lives for other people but we can make smaller sacrifices in our everyday lives.

In Your Religion Journal

Suggest a few examples of everyday sacrifices you could make for others which would show Christian love.

Love and Marriage

In some cultures men and women who marry are promised to one another by their parents while they are still infants. Sometimes they may never meet before their wedding day.

In our own culture acceptance of the fact that boys and girls mix, form friendships, date and develop relationships, often from some point during their teenage years, is relatively new. Not so long ago one-to-one dating only took place between a young man and a young woman in their early adult years and then it was almost taken for granted that they would marry.

Boy/Girl friendships

During early primary school years little boys and girls mix and play together freely, without

Marriage ceremony in Thailand

any sense of shyness or embarrassment. They have little sense of any difference between boys and girls and take one another very much for granted. In the more senior years of primary school girls and boys tend to become more self-conscious. Boys mix with groups of boys and girls with groups of girls.

In early adolescence this trend continues and girls get together in groups and boys do likewise – for friendship and support. Changing from childhood to adolescence is often very difficult. Because of the physical changes which are taking place in their bodies young people know that they are no longer children. But neither are they adults yet. It can be difficult to know how to handle feelings that are new, for instance a new sense of attraction towards young people of the opposite sex. Boys and girls who were quite self-confident and easygoing about their friendship can become very uneasy and anxious about friendships with young people of the opposite sex.

Dating

Young people start dating at various ages. Sometimes you may feel pressurised into a relationship involving one-to-one dating sooner than you are really ready for it because it seems to be the done thing, because everybody seems to be doing it or because you might be afraid that you'd be laughed at. Because people develop differently there is no right time or age for everybody to begin dating. The number of young people who end up hurt because of the relationships they have been involved in shows us that young people often begin dating before they are mature enough to handle themselves and their partner in a one-to-one relationship. It is important to remember that boy/girl relationships are not limited to dating. If, for instance, you are in a co-ed school, about half of your classmates will be of the opposite sex. If not, you will meet other boys and girls of your own

The easiest and healthiest way for young people to develop an ease and confidence about friendships with young people of the opposite sex is through group activities involving mixed groups of boys and girls.

age in the area where you live. It is important to build up many open, healthy friendships with young people of the opposite sex. In this way girls can come to understand boys better: the way they think, their interests, the topics of conversation they enjoy and so on. Likewise boys can get to understand girls. Groups of young

276 people can take part in activities and sports together. As they get to know and understand one another better there is less likelihood that they will be awkward or embarrassed in one another's company.

When you do begin dating it is important to keep these things in mind:

— Always treat your partner with respect.
— Engage in activities together which lead to personal growth for both of you.
— Do things which help you to get to know one another better.
— Never do on a date something which you would be ashamed to do if others were present.
— If your partner does something which makes you feel uncomfortable, you do not have to accept it.

What to do and where to go on your date!

When you are going out with someone special it is important to do things which you will both enjoy and which will help your relationship to grow. So it is essential to find out what interests you have in common, but also to leave yourself open to new ideas.

List the following in order of priority, according to your own likes and dislikes.
With your boy/girlfriend you could:
— listen to tapes
— look at a video
— play pool
— watch television
— go shopping
— go to a leisure centre
— go and have a cup of coffee in a coffee shop
— play video games
— sit and talk
— go to a film
— go for a walk
— join a club

Activity

List as many other activities as you can think of which would be suitable for a boyfriend and girlfriend to enjoy together.
Share your list with the class.

Research

Look about in your own neighbourhood to see where young people could enjoy spending time together.

Put a brochure together advertising different places and activities which are available to young people.

While some relationships which begin during teenage years last all through life, most do not. Most people who marry spend time dating a number of different people before they finally meet the person they will marry.

Married Love

1. Married love

   expresses itself in many ways – in the way the partners care for each other, show consideration for each other, are loyal and faithful, to each other.

2. Married love

   expresses itself especially through acts of sexual love.

Sexual love involves a special relationship between two people. Sexual intercourse is the expression of their special commitment to each other, and involves shared responsibility for the children of that love. It can only achieve its true purpose in the lasting commitment of marriage.

Sexual intercourse of its very nature 'belongs' to marriage, and only to marriage.

It belongs to marriage:

(a) because it is the fullest natural expression of what it means to be married – a union of two people in mutual commitment and self-giving love. In sexual intercourse one partner says to the other: 'I love you, you only, forever';

(b) because it tends to strengthen and deepen that union and commitment which is found in marriage;

(c) because it is the means through which new human life is brought into existence, and this entails requirements and responsibilities which can only properly be met through marriage.

In the Irish Bishops' pastoral letter, *Love is for Life*, they say:

Sexual union says 'I love you', in a very profound way. By sexual union, a man and woman say to each other: 'I love you. There is nobody else in all the world I love in the way I love you. I love you just for being you. I want you to become even more wonderful than you are. I want to share my life and my world with you. I want you to share your life and your world with me. I want us to build a new life together, a future together, which will be our future. I need you. I can't live without you. I need you to love me, and to love me not just now but always. I will be faithful to you not just now but always. I will never let you down or walk out on you. I will never put anyone else in place of you. I will stay with you through thick and thin. I will be responsible for you and I want you to be responsible for me, for us, no matter what happens.'

Marriage ceremony in Bangalore, India.

278

Sexual intercourse outside marriage:

(a) loses its true meaning;

Since the unity and mutual commitment of marriage are not present, it cannot express them. Instead, it can be an expression not of the commitment of true love, but of self-interest or even exploitation. Without the commitment of marriage it tends to be an act which speaks of temporary usage rather than of devoted love.

(b) tends to foster attitudes of self-interest and exploitation;

Acts tend to reinforce the attitudes they embody. If sex is used to express true self-giving love, it helps us to grow in love. If it is used for selfish reasons, it helps us to become confirmed in that selfishness.

(c) is irresponsible;

Performing an act which can bring a new human life into the world is a very serious matter. To do this outside the commitment of marriage is irresponsible.

Altogether it is a misuse of God's gifts. Sexual intercourse is meant to be the deeply personal and intimate way in which people can express and deepen the very special relationship which exists in marriage, and in which they can co-operate with God in the creation of new human life. For people who do not have the commitment of marriage, or who are not ready for parenthood, to engage in sexual intercourse is to misuse and cheapen one of God's greatest gifts.

Sex outside marriage

Certain actions have very definite meanings, e.g. when we give someone a bunch of flowers we are wishing the person well, either through saying, 'get well soon' or 'congratulations' or 'good luck', etc. Usually whenever we give anything away to another person the action has something to do with generosity or friendship or concern for the other person. Sometimes, though, it does not. Sometimes the same or a similar action can have very different meanings and can express very different attitudes on the part of the person who is doing the action.

Consider the following:

— Paula gives her mother a present for her birthday.
— John gives £5 of his savings to a charity.
— Simon wants to make a good impression on the new girl in class. He gives her a present.
— Anna is sick and tired of her brown sweater. When her friend Ciara admires it, Anna gives it to her, saying 'You can have it, if you like it so much.'
— Michael is being bullied at school. He is terrified. When the school bully asks him for some money he gives it at once.

Discuss

What are the different attitudes expressed in each of the above gestures of giving?
Which of them best fits in with what giving should be about?

One well-known example of a situation where a certain action was used to mean something other than what it should is the story of the way in which Judas betrayed Jesus with a kiss. A kiss is normally a greeting of friendship among the Jews. Here it was used as a means of betrayal.

Find Your Group
Discuss

Can you think of other situations, perhaps situations in your own experience, where certain acts do not mean what they appear to mean?

Marriage ceremony in San Salvador

Sexual Intercourse

Sexual intercourse is an act which involves intimate physical union. It is meant to express real love, real unity and real commitment. In the case of married people, they made a commitment to one another when they were married. So, in their case, the act of sexual intercourse can mean what it is supposed to mean. In the case of people who are not married and are unready or unwilling to make a real commitment to one another, the act of sexual intercourse must mean something else. In the case of married people, they are saying to each other, 'I love you, you

only, you always.' There are many different ways of saying this. One of the ways they say this to each other is through the act of sexual intercourse. In the case of unmarried people the act of sexual intercourse does not say this. It is an act which seeks pleasure or enjoyment without having made a commitment to the other person.

Find Your Group

What are all the reasons you can think of why people would want to take part in the act of sexual intercourse outside marriage?

Marriage and Law

Each state makes its own laws about marriage. Because it is a sacrament so too does the Church. For a person to be married as a member of the Catholic Church, the Church asks the following:

1) Though a husband and wife give each other the sacrament the priest or deacon must be present as the representative of the Church along with two other witnesses.

2) Both the man and the woman must marry freely and with full knowledge of what they are doing.

3) Both must be capable of living out a Christian marriage.

4) Neither must be already married.

Marriage Customs from Around the World

Arranged Marriages

In certain societies, it is the custom for the parents to choose husbands and wives for their children. A marriage is arranged by the two families rather than by the couple themselves. Often money or gifts are exchanged as part of the arrangement.

In some societies, a gift of money or property is given to the groom or his family by the bride's family. This is known as a dowry. In other societies, a gift is given to the bride's family by the groom and his family. This is called a bride price.

Aneeta's Story

Hitesh and Aneeta have been married for two years, and so far happily. Aneeta is nineteen and Hitesh twenty-three. They met through their fathers who were friends.

'My parents had been looking around for a boy for me for some time and a few of the ones they came up with I said no to immediately. When I met Hitesh I knew as little about him as the others my parents came up with. He seemed nicer than the others, not in a good-looking way because I don't think that's very important. I expected that with all their experience my parents were able to make a better choice than me.

I think arranged marriages often work out better than love marriages, because you have to learn to adjust to one another. You start out with fewer expectations, whereas other girls I know who have chosen their own partner think it's all going to be wonderful and easy and end up disappointed.

I do think though that people must be free to make the choice they want. I wouldn't condemn an Asian girl for running away from an arranged marriage and my children will certainly have a choice.'

Discuss

Do you agree with any of Aneeta's views on arranged marriage. Which do you agree or disagree with? Why?

— A traditional Jewish wedding takes place under a canopy made of silk or velvet, supported by four poles. The canopy symbolises the home which the couple are about to set up. At the end of the ceremony an empty wine glass is put on the floor in front of the bridegroom who smashes it with his foot. The wine glass is broken to remind the couple that happiness is fragile and can easily be broken and that life contains sad events as well as happy ones.

— In a traditional Muslim wedding, before the groom leaves his parents' home for the bride's house he will have money attached to his clothes. He is surrounded by members of his family who will accompany him. This is an integral part of the service before the couple meet.

— A traditional Japanese wedding ends with a feast at the home of the groom's parents. There it is customary for the couple to celebrate and seal their union by drinking three cups of sake (Japanese wine).

Find out if there are any old, traditional customs which were carried out at weddings in your country.

Greek Orthodox marriage ceremony

282   In a speech in York in 1982 the Pope described marriage.

In a marriage a man and woman pledge themselves to one another in an unbreakable alliance of total mutual self-giving, a total union of love, love that is not a passing emotion or temporary infatuation but a responsible and free decision to bind oneself completely 'in good times and bad' to one's partner. It is the gift of oneself to another.

In Your Religion Journal

In your own words explain what the Pope says which makes clear what is special about marriage.

If you were going to get married, how could you try to make sure that your love was not 'a passing emotion or temporary infatuation'? What questions could you ask yourself?

In what way do you think that a husband and wife can express their total commitment to each other?

Find Your Group

Look up each of the following references in your bible.
Which of these quotations about love means most to you?
Choose two. Write them into your religion journal.

(Deut 6:1-9; Deut 7:7-11; Ps 133:1-3; Song of Songs 1:1-3, 3:6, 6:4-8; Is 54:1-10; Mt 5:43-48; Mt 22:34-40; Luke 10:25-37; Jn 3:1-21; Jn 11:1-45; Rom 12:1-21; 1 Cor 13:1-13; Gal 5:22-26).

Activity

Complete the crossword by answering the clues.

Across
1. Love is this... (7)
3. ...and this (1 Cor 13:4) (4)
5. Greek for Christian love (5)
9. A husband or wife – partner (6)
13. To endure with patience (8)
14. A couple become this before getting married (7)
15. St Paul wrote a definition of love in this letter (11)

Down
2. Love rejoices with honesty, justice and ...(5)
4. A couple become husband and wife at the...ceremony (8)
6. Develop in love(4)
7. A kind of love we should all aspire to (9)
8. A couple may refer to themselves as this (2)
10. Human love is this...(6)
11. It makes the world go round (4)
12. Love is not prone to this. Also commanded by the fifth commandment (5)

Called to Serve

We have all been called by God to serve others all through our lives. This call is made clear to us in John's Gospel. In the Jewish world in which Jesus lived there was a tradition that only slaves or maid-servants washed the feet of visitors who came to visit a family or house. The hot, dusty climate meant that people who walked the roads were usually covered with sweat and dirt, so on arrival the first thing visitors received was a drink and water to wash their hands and feet. So when Jesus began to wash the feet of his disciples Peter immediately remonstrated with him because Jesus was going against all the traditions of his time. But Peter was told that unless Jesus was allowed to wash Peter's feet that he could have no part of what Jesus wanted from him. The message for Peter and all his disciples and, indeed, for all those who wish to follow Jesus, is the call to service. If you wish to follow in the footsteps of Jesus you have to put yourself at the service of others. Different people answer this call in many different ways. In fact, each one of us answers it differently at different times in our lives.

Discuss

What are all the different services we receive every day and often take for granted?

In Your Religion Journal

Write about a time in your life when you did something which made you feel that you were answering God's call to you to serve others.

Find Your Group

Discuss

If you were in charge of the world what type of world would you like? Would you bring about changes to the current state of the world? What changes would you bring about? Describe the new world which you would like to see. However, keep in mind the fact that people are not robots. They have free will which is one of our greatest gifts. We have the facility to make choices unlike any other creatures on the face of the earth.
What choices do you have in your own life?
When you are reflecting on your career do you have a choice?

284

I choose to be...
I choose to study...
I choose to play games...
I choose to listen to music...
List some of the choices which you have in your daily life.

Now list some things about which you had no choice. I had no choice about where I was born, who my parents were, the colour of my skin, etc...

Our faith tells us that each one of us is God the Creator's choice.

OUR LIFE IS GOD'S GIFT TO US BUT WHAT WE MAKE OF OUR LIFE, WITH GOD'S HELP, IS OUR GIFT TO GOD.

Look up the following biblical references and read the accounts of the times when people were called by God: Genesis 12:1-9; Exodus 3:1-12; Jeremiah 1:4-10; Luke 1:26-38; Luke 5:27-28; Acts 9:1-19.

Set up a television programme with a presenter who interviews Abraham, Moses, Jeremiah, Levi, Mary and Paul, about their experience of being called and the way in which they subsequently lived out their lives.

Responding to God's Call

Jean Donovan was someone who responded to God's call. Read the following account of the life of Jean Donovan.

Jean Donovan was born in Cleveland, Ohio, in 1953, to a middle-class Catholic family. As a child growing up she did not show any outstanding qualities and could be described as an 'ordinary child'. Her parents recall their daughter's childhood and adolescence with pride because she was always a source of happiness for them.

Having graduated from high school, Jean came to Ireland to study at University College Cork. She celebrated her twenty-first birthday while in Cork and is remembered there as a girl who

showed great zest for life. In 1977, at the age of twenty-four, she returned to the US with a Master's degree in Economics. She subsequently worked as a management consultant with a salary of $20,000. During this time she used to ride about on an old motor bike and was happy, friendly and easy to get on with.

The Cork connection did not die off completely

and she kept in touch with some people she met there. She was influenced in particular by a priest, Fr Crowley, who remembered her as being a typical conventional Catholic, who practised but had not personalised a meaning for her life. In one of her letters Jean wrote: 'I became friends with Fr Crowley when I was looking for direction in my life'. Jean's family now look back and recognise this as the beginning of her road to El Salvador.

The seeds of her destiny, sown during her student years, began to grow, and in her job she began to tell her friends that she was looking for something more. During Christmas 1977 she said she was going to El Salvador and she started a preparation programme for missionary work. In September 1979 she finally achieved her goal and became a teacher of nutrition and child care in the La Liberta parish. In her first letter after ten days she talked of how different it was from home – 'the social structures are so unfair, the Church too is different, many of the priests have been murdered, some shot while saying Mass'.

During her first six months in El Salvador, Jean observed a steep increase in violence. This was particularly true of the diocese in which she worked, a diocese led by a man who became famous as a champion of the rights of the poor, a fearless preacher of justice – Archbishop Romero, whose sermons were heard on radio every Sunday throughout El Salvador. On 24 March 1980, at 5:30 p.m., Archbishop Romero was assassinated while saying Mass.

Jean formed part of the guard of honour beside the coffin, which meant she had prominence in the parish. At the funeral mass on 30 March, there were thousands of people packed into the

square in front of the church when two bombs exploded, causing havoc and injury. Afterwards Jean put her thoughts into words: 'I went through a complete spectrum of faith, from I don't believe there is a God, to there must be a God, to it's going to be much better because I know I'm going to die today'.

Extracts from her diary show what life was like then:

8 May	Things are worse, people are killed every day, tortured and hacked to death. My friends want me to get out. Four more priests assassinated.
21 June	I went out blessing bodies with Sr Ita.
10 July	Two of my friends were murdered outside our house at 10.30 p.m. It's so much harder to fight for your liberty in a non-violent way than with guns.
7 August	Picked up refugee children. Twenty-six in one house cared for by a priest.

On 2 September, in a letter to a friend, Rita, who was urging her to come home she writes – 'I do feel deeply that God has sent me here and wants me here, and I'm going to do my best to live up to that.'

Later that September, Jean came back to Ireland to attend a wedding. At that time, her boyfriend Douglas, Fr Crowley and other friends were trying to dissuade her from returning. When talking with a group of students she told them that she was returning, aware of the danger, and that there was a good chance she would be killed. She believed she had to go back, because life meant so much more to her in El Salvador than in Ireland or the US. It was pointed out to her that even though she was not working for the revolution-

aries, – the army perceived her as doing so – and that was all that mattered.

This point was made by Senator Robert White in a US Senate debate:
'Poor people are more revolutionary than rich people, and when you commit your life to the poor it is perceived as being revolutionary, when in fact you are fulfilling the mission of the Church, which is to work with the poor. This is misinterpreted deliberately to justify the violence.'

This conflict within Jean's mind and heart is reflected in her own words, written in mid-November: 'Several times I decided to leave Salvador. I almost could, except for the children, the poor bruised victims of this insanity, who would care for them? Whose heart could be so staunch as to favour the reasonable thing in a sea of their tears and loneliness? Not mine, dear friend, not mine'. These are the last written words of Jean Donovan, for on Tuesday 2 December 1980, at 6.00 p.m., she and a number of sisters were murdered on a roadside and their bodies buried in shallow graves. The subsequent outcry after the discovery of the bodies led to an investigation which culminated in the arrest of the five soldiers responsible. The following is taken from the official transcript at their trial.
'We were ordered to put on civilian clothes. We waited for and stopped a white mini-bus which we boarded and ordered the driver to drive to a lonely place. We killed the four women after sexually abusing them. We were told to do this because, our commander said, they were subversives.'

When interviewed about Jean, her teacher at riding school could say: 'This was typical of Jean — commitment was always there...in the stables, with the horses, keeping things in order. In fact...commitment with anything she did'.

Making a choice

People answer God's call in many different ways: some in their lives as single people, some in their lives as married people, some as religious and some as priests. Making a choice about your life is a most important decision. Many different options will present themselves: the type of job you'll take on, the study you'll specialise in, whether or not you'll marry, the man or woman you'll marry, how you believe in God and put belief into action.

These are vital decisions. And in them God is present and active. He is present as the one who loves you, who, humanly speaking, has hope for you. He is present also as the one who calls you, who has plans for the world which involve you. In the choices of your life, can you make space for his words, 'Come, follow me'?

Single life

People are single for many reasons. Some because they have chosen to be single, some because their marriage partner has died. Everybody spends part of their lives as single people. Single people are called to serve God and others through the way in which they relate to other people and to the world we live in. They are called to be open to recognising and responding to the needs of others in the places where they work, in the neighbourhoods where they live and in the broader society. They are called to become aware of the need to care for and nurture the earth.

Single people do not have a commitment to a spouse or to children of their own. Therefore, they can have freedom to spend time developing their own gifts and talents and becoming aware of their strengths and weaknesses.

Single people often become very involved in the work of voluntary organisations in their own locality and in groups who are concerned with global issues. They also have time to offer support to other members of their own families in times of sickness or difficulty.

Single people can have many close friends and they have time and freedom to develop deep bonds of friendship.

Research

Interview at least one person you know who is single. Make a brochure designed to help people to be aware of the advantages and disadvantages of the single life.

Married life

In marriage a man and woman make a commitment to live together in love and care for one another for the whole of their lives. They also make a commitment to accept and love the children who are sent to them by God. Married people promise that their love for their partner will be special and will last forever. The sexual love which married people give to their partners is exclusive and their relationship with their partner is different from the relationship they have with any other person.

A married person lives out God's call in his or her life, in the first instance through their love and care for his or her spouse and for his or her children. In a good marriage, where people are secure in the knowledge that they are loved and accepted for the persons they are, they continue to grow and develop as individuals. Married people are challenged to reach outside their own immediate family to help and care for others in their neighbourhoods, and in the broader society where they recognise needs that they can answer. Because marriage is a lifelong commitment people need to spend much time in preparation and reflection before entering into it. A person can

288 have many good friendships and relationships with people of the opposite sex which would not necessarily lead to good marriages. It is a great mistake to rush into marriage at too young an age or without taking sufficient time to get to know your partner thoroughly. However, a good marriage offers the possibility of a ful-filled, happy life, secure in the knowledge that one is loved and accepted by one's partner and that one can contribute to the growth and happiness of one's partner and one's children.

Research

Interview a man and a woman, both of whom are married, though not to one another. Ask them to describe married life — the difficulties, and the joys.

Activity

Make out a brochure aimed at help-ing people to become aware of the good things about marriage and to be ready to take the necessary steps to make marriage a success.

It takes a married couple years to build up their relationship and to develop the qualities that they need if they are to live together successfully for the rest of their lives – qualities such as patience, understanding, trust, honesty, dependability and for-giveness.

In the Church we see the promise of love between a man and woman in marriage as an image of the Covenant that God made with the Jewish people. God promised that he would always be with his people and, in spite of the fact that they sometimes turned away from God and that he sometimes got angry with them, God always remained faithful to this promise.

St Paul compares the love of a husband and wife to the love that Christ has for the Church: 'Husbands should love their wives just as Christ loved the Church and sacrificed himself for it.'

In the Sacrament of Marriage, the community gathers to celebrate the love of a man and a woman and to be witnesses to the promises they make. In the Sacrament of Marriage the Church formally blesses the commitment that the couple make.

What to look for in the ideal partner

It is important to recognise the qualities you are looking for in another person, and which are important to you, before embarking on a long-term relationship.

As you mature, your choice of qualities and values may change and for this reason it is important that you don't date one boy or girl exclusively, but that friendships with the opposite sex should remain open.

Activity

Think of your ideal (boyfriend or girlfriend) partner. What qualities would you like them to have?
Imagine that you have £100 to spend on those qualities which, when put together, will give you that ideal partner. Look at the list on the right where you will see certain qualities at different prices. Look down the list carefully and decide how you want to spend your £100 . You may under -spend if you wish, but you must not go over £100.

STAR BUY

£25 Each
★ A good Christian
★ Attractive face
★ Highly intelligent

£20 Each
★ Friendly, well-liked
★ Thoughtful, caring
★ A shapely figure/well-built
★ Witty, good company

£15 Each
★ Committed to their religion
★ Rich/wealthy
★ Healthy/athletic
★ Honest
★ Popular

BARGAIN BUY

£12 Each
★ Hard-working
★ Well-dressed
★ Home-loving
★ Adventurous
★ Generous

£10 Each
★ Good with children
★ Pop musician/actor
★ Ambitious
★ Well-educated

EXTRA BUY

£5 Each
★ Car owner
★ Animal lover
★ Music fame: pop/classical
★ Politically aware
★ Collects teddy bears
★ Non-smoker

Discuss

Are there other qualities, not on this list, which you think are essential to a good relationship?

Activity

Complete the following quiz to see what you expect from marriage at this stage. As you grow older, your ideas may well change.

Marriage Quiz

The statements are numbered 1–30.
Against each one put either:
U = unimportant
I = important
VI = very important.

In Your Religion Journal

Read over the list. Which ones mattered very much to you. Why?

Are there any things not on the list which matter a lot to you? If so, what are they?

Find Your Group

A couple who have recently got engaged have come to you for advice. What practical preparations would you advise them to make?

What does marriage mean to you?

Each statement begins: 'The person I marry must...'

1   not be a fussy eater;   ❑
2   share my interests in music;   ❑
3   be committed to their religion;   ❑
4   enjoy sport;   ❑
5   budget money carefully;   ❑
6   have a good sense of humour;   ❑
7   be an 'outdoor' person;   ❑
8   never tease or embarrass me;   ❑
9   like children very much;   ❑
10 like my parents;   ❑
11 work hard at our marriage;   ❑
12 not drink alcohol;   ❑
13 be interested in politics;   ❑
14 not interfere with the way I dress;   ❑
15 have a good education;   ❑
16 want to buy our own house;   ❑
17 like to give dinner parties;   ❑
18 want to marry in church;   ❑
19 have a very good background;   ❑
20 be of my nationality/race;   ❑
21 be honest about themselves;   ❑
22 have good table manners;   ❑
23 like discos;   ❑
24 share the housework;   ❑
25 be my best friend;   ❑
26 surprise me with gifts sometimes;   ❑
27 never be unfaithful;   ❑
28 never criticise my family;   ❑
29 prefer my company to any other;   ❑
30 be a good listener.   ❑

Religious Life

Many of the great religions of the world have members who devote themselves totally to serving God through deepening their relationship with him in prayer and through the service of others. They usually live in communities called religious orders or congregations.

In the Christian tradition those who live in such communities are called religious. There are many religious congregations or orders with many different lifestyles. Some religious are contemplatives and they spend most of their lives in prayer, fasting, meditation and physical work of one kind or another. Members of religious orders who are not contemplatives are engaged in all sorts of work: social work, education, medicine, farming, spiritual direction, work with physically and mentally handicapped people, work with emotionally disturbed young people, missionary work, work in Third World countries.

People who belong to religious orders usually spend regular times in prayer every day. They usually live in community and in their work they serve the needs of others, especially those most in need.

Research

1. Interview a religious about her or his life.
   Why did they decide to become a religious?
   What work are they engaged in?
   How do they see themselves answering God's call in their life?
   What is difficult about living in community?
   Are there advantages to living in community?

2. Find out all you can about the life story of the founder or foundress of one of the religious orders, e.g. Ignatius of Loyola, John Bosco, Edmund Ignatius Rice, Catherine McCauley, Nano Nagle, John Baptist de la Salle, etc.

The Priesthood

All of us, through Baptism, have been called to a life of ministry to others, that is to bring God's love into the lives of others through the care and compassion which we show them. In the Sacrament of Holy Order deacons, priests and bishops are called to a particular way of ministering to others in the Church. They are called to be leaders in the community, to make known to people the teachings of Jesus and to show them how to live out these teachings. They are also called to be representatives of the community by presenting the concerns of the community to God. Above all they are empowered to act as the visible representatives of Jesus Christ in the celebration of the sacraments and especially the Eucharist. At Mass it is through the ministry of the priest that Jesus becomes present under the appearances of bread and wine and that we are enabled to take part in the offering of his sacrifice. Through the ministry of the priest Jesus grants us God's forgiveness in the Sacrament of Reconciliation and brings strength and healing in the Sacrament of the Anointing of the Sick. Although, in an emergency, anyone may baptise, it is normally the function of a priest or deacon to do this.

By his additional or episcopal ordination a bishop receives the fullness of the priesthood as a successor to the apostles. He is responsible for the welfare of the whole Church in his diocese, for safeguarding the faith and seeing that it is correctly taught, and for ensuring that the sacraments are properly celebrated. He ordains others as bishops, priests or deacons, and it is usually a bishop who confirms, though a priest may sometimes be delegated to do so.

Deacons have a special ministry of service. They preach, baptise, assist at funerals and marriages, read the Gospel at Mass, assist with the distribution of Holy Communion, and assist the bishop or priests in a variety of ways. Though they are not priests, they are ordained ministers of the Church. All ordained ministers, bishops, priests and deacons, and all who carry out any special function in the Church, are called to exercise their ministry in a spirit of love and service. They are also called to help all the people of God to exercise their own gifts and talents in the service of Christ and his Church. At the Last Supper Jesus performed the task of a servant when he washed the feet of the apostles, thereby showing his followers what they are meant to be to one another. As the leaders of the community bishops and priests are challenged to show the community how to live lives of service for one another.

The Rite of Ordination in the Sacrament of Holy Orders describes the role of the priest as follows:

– To represent Christ in the world;
– To serve the people by being Christ's minister in the Church;
– To continue the work which Jesus started as teacher, priest and shepherd;
– To encourage and enable the Church to grow into a living, caring Christian community;
– To work together with other priests and lay people to build God's kingdom.

Read the following extracts from the address which the bishop makes at a priest's ordination:

Share with all humankind the word of God you have received with joy. Meditate on the law of God, believe what you read, teach what you believe, and put into practice what you teach.

Let the doctrine you teach be true nourishment for the people of God. Let the example of your lives attract the followers of Christ, so that by word and action you may build up the house which is God's Church.

When you baptise, you will bring men and women into the people of God. In the Sacrament of Penance, you will forgive sins in the name of Christ and the Church. With the holy oil you will relieve and console the sick. You will celebrate the liturgy and offer thanks and praise to God throughout the day, praying not only for the people of God but for the whole world. Remember that you are chosen from among God's people and appointed to act for them in relation to God. Do your part in the work of Christ, the priest, with genuine joy and love, and attend to the concerns of Christ before your own.

Finally, conscious of sharing in the work of Christ, the head and shepherd of the Church, and united with the bishop and subject to him, seek to bring the faithful together into a united family and to lead them effectively, through Christ and in the Holy Spirit, to God the Father. Always remember the example of the Good Shepherd who came not to be served, but to serve, and to seek and rescue those who were lost.

Find Your Group
Discuss
What are some of the qualities which people, if they are trying to live according to the role spelled out in the Rite of Ordination, try to develop in themselves?

294 Read the following statements made by priests about what they see as important in their lives.

'I like dealing with teenagers. Their idealism and enthusiasm are contagious and they prevent you from growing smug by constantly challenging your ideas. They enable you to keep an open mind on many matters.'

Fr Stephen Farragher

'Having time for people is the most important thing for me.'
Fr Dick Mohan

'Just to be there when someone needs you.'
Fr Joseph Summerville

'The priest is a person standing for the truth, being free to search for it formally and having the task of transmitting it and helping others to search for it.'
Fr Eamonn Barry

'That was my role, to show the face of Christ to the world.'
Fr Michael Casey

Activity

You have been appointed to decide which of all those who have applied to enter a seminary to train for the priesthood are suitable for this way of life and which are not.
Make out the questionnaire which you would ask the applicants to fill in.

Prayerful Reflection

To do what is good with my life

Lord, I really want to do something good with my life.
I see the needs of the world I'm part of,
     one million poor in my own country,
     people killed each day through violence,
     old people living lonely and in squalour,
     kids of my own age drugging themselves as
     an escape from life.

I know there are needs,
There are people who cannot live
Without the dedicated help of your friends.

I hear your call,
Sometimes a whisper, other times a gentle shove
Inviting me to be your presence,
Through my own personality and my own talents
And with all my weaknesses,
In the world of these people.
But, Lord, I'm afraid.
     I don't know if I can do anything for them.
     I don't know how you want me to follow you.
     Married? single? a religious? a priest?
I'm not sure I can give without losing so much myself.
Faith is what I ask, and light and love:
Faith to believe in your risen power at the foot of your cross,
Light to know the way you're asking me to serve you,
And love to trust that it's all possible.

Donal Neary SJ

Do the Looking Back exercises for Unit Eight at the back of this book.

LOOKING BACK

Looking to the Future

Find Your Group
Discuss

When you think about the future...
What are the things which you hope will happen?
What causes you to feel excited about the future?
What causes you to be uncertain about the future?
Are there things which cause you to feel afraid of
the future?

Activity

Make two contrasting posters, one to illustrate the
caption Towards the Future with Hope, and the
other to illustrate the caption Towards the Future
with Fear.

In Your Religion Journal

Getting a job
Having children of my own
Unemployment
Examinations
Becoming independent
Emigrating
Death

Leaving school
Nuclear war
Getting married
Going to college
Seeing the world
Leaving home
War

Write this list into your religion journal. Number the
items 1-14, putting 14 opposite the event which
comes to mind most often when you think about the
future and 1 opposite the event which comes to
mind least often when you think about the future.

Check with the class

Which event scored highest? Which scored lowest?

Death

Usually when we think about the future, the last thing to come to mind is probably death. It may only be when someone close to us in our family, or one of our friends dies, or at times of tragedy that we think about death at all. Then we often think about death with feelings of fear and uncertainty.

We have no clear idea about what will happen to us after death. And what about the end of the world? When the world, as we know it, ceases to exist, what will happen? Will there be life at all? What form will it take? Where will it exist?

As followers of Jesus, we have his assurance that the future is in God's hands and is safe in God's hands. Jesus has promised that if we live for God's Kingdom in this world, we will live with God forever.

Yet, even if we believe what Jesus has said, because we have never been able to speak to anyone who has died and because we have never had an actual eye witness account of what life is like after death, we sometimes find talk about life after death vague and lacking in reassurance.

If you could imagine what it might be like for an unborn baby to consider birth, you would probably find it would be similar to our anticipation of death. If a baby could think it would probably be terrified of birth. At the moment of birth the baby leaves behind the world that it is familiar with and feels safe and secure in. The world out there is full of unknown fears. However, once the baby has been born and is safe in the security of the love and care of its family it would probably, if it could talk, say that there was indeed nothing to be afraid of.

But even if the unborn baby could hear and if someone tried to communicate to it what life after birth was like it would still be unable to understand. With the limited capacity of the unborn baby to communicate or to understand human speech it would be impossible for it to understand what life is about.

So it is with us when we try to think about and understand what life after death is like. St Paul says:
Eye has not seen, nor ear heard, nor has it entered into the heart of man to conceive what God has prepared for those who love him.
(1 Corinthians 2:9)
So even if it were possible for someone who had already died to try to communicate with us about life after death we probably would not, with our limited human intelligence, be able to understand what they were

Find Your Group
Discuss

Can you remember some of the things adults said to you about death when you were little?
Why do you think it is so difficult to talk to children about death?

Role Play

Find one other person to work with. One of you takes the role of the unborn baby. Imagine that this baby can hear and communicate with people in the outside world. The other person takes the role of someone who is trying to communicate with the unborn baby about what life is like outside the womb. Carry on the conversation which you think might take place.

We all have pictures of Hell, Heaven and Purgatory. They come from the things that we've heard people say about them, the things that we've read, the pictures and paintings we've seen and the films we've watched.

Find Your Group
Discuss

What images or pictures come to your mind when you think about Hell, Heaven or Purgatory?

Activity

Make posters to represent these.

Death for a Christian

Some things we can be sure of!

Heaven

God offers to each of us the possibility of living with God forever in Heaven. The Book of Revelation 21:3-4 describes Heaven in these words: 'God's house is with his people. He will live with them and they shall be his people. God himself will be with them, and he will be their God. He will wipe away all tears from their eyes. There will be no more death, no more grief, or crying or pain. The old things have disappeared.' Every day we choose whether or not we want to accept God's invitation to live with him forever in Heaven. We make this choice when we decide whether or not we want to live a life of love for God and for one another. Jesus said to his followers: 'Do not be worried and upset. Believe in God and believe in me. There are many rooms in my father's house and I am going to prepare a place for you. I would not tell you this if it were not so. And after I go to prepare a place for you, I will come back and take you to myself, so that you will be where I am. You know the way that leads to the place where I am going.'

Discuss

What do you think Jesus meant when he said, 'You know the way that leads to the place where I am going'?
Do you know 'the way'?

Activity

Design a poster to illustrate the caption *We know the Way*.

The decision whether or not we will live with God forever in Heaven is not one that is made at the moment of death. We have been making that decision during our lives as we choose how to relate to God, to the people around us and to the environment we live in.

Read the following story:

The Blacksmith's Vision

Once a village blacksmith had a vision. An angel came to tell him that God was calling him home to the fullness of the Kingdom.

'I thank God for thinking of me,' replied the blacksmith, 'but as you know, the season for sowing the crops is beginning and, as I am the only blacksmith in these parts, who will help these poor people when a horse needs to be shod, or a plough needs to be fixed? I don't wish to appear ungrateful, but do you think I could put off taking my place in the Kingdom until I have finished?'

'I'll see what can be done,' said the angel, as he vanished. The angel returned a year or two later with the same message. This time, however, a farmer was seriously ill, and the blacksmith was trying to save his crop for him, so that his family wouldn't suffer. The angel was sent back to see what could be done.

This happened again and again, and on each occasion the blacksmith just spread his hands in a gesture of resignation and compassion, and drew the angel's attention to where the suffering was, and where his help was needed. Eventually, the blacksmith felt very old and tired, and he prayed, 'Lord, if you would like to send your angel again, I think I'd be happy to see him.'

The angel appeared. 'If you still want to take me,' said the blacksmith, 'I am ready to take up my abode in the Lord's Kingdom.'

The angel looked at the blacksmith in surprise and said, 'Where do you think you've been all these years?'

Discuss

What do you think the angel meant?
Why do you think the angel gave that answer?

The East Face of Muireadach's Cross, at Monasterboice, shows an eighth century interpretation of The Last Judgment. In the centre is the figure of Christ, holding in his left hand the Cross and in his right a flowering sceptre. Beneath is the Archangel, weighing the souls in a scales and thrusting his staff into the head of Satan. On the left arm of the cross are the faithful in heaven and, on the right, the figure of Satan with a trident drives the lost souls to their doom. This kind of symbolism was popular at the time. (See p.303.)

*On this map of Ireland, dated 1513, St
Patrick's Purgatory (Lough Derg) is
prominently shown. It was believed then
that the world ended at the west coast
of Ireland and the last chance a sinner
had of repentance was to make a pilgrimage to this holy place. The tradition
continues to this day and Lough Derg is
one of the most famous pilgrimage sites
in Europe.*

Purgatory

God wants everyone to live with
him forever in love. God also
wants to set us free from anything that could prevent us from
being able to respond to that
invitation. It is easy to imagine
that there may be plenty of
people who have not died separated from God by serious
sin, but who nevertheless still
have faults and imperfections
of which they have not perfectly repented, and who indeed
may be very far from perfect.

Such a person's life would, to
some extent, be influenced by
whatever sin or selfishness they
had failed to break away from.
The Church teaches that God's
mercy is so great and God's
desire to save is so strong that
he will not condemn that person
but will prepare them for life
in Heaven through Purgatory.

God's purification after death
is called Purgatory. Again we
don't know exactly what Purgatory is like or how exactly
God purifies those who are in
Purgatory.

Purgatory is another sign of God's love for us. It reassures us that above all else God wants us to be happy with him forever in Heaven. It is because of the belief in Purgatory that the Church prays for the dead and offers Mass for them. Praying for the dead is a sign of faith in God's mercy and his promise of eternal life. Those undergoing the purification of Purgatory can be helped by our prayers.

Research

In what month are the dead specially remembered?
Which day in the year is specially dedicated by the Church to prayers for the dead?

Hell

God wants all people to be saved from sin and from the effects of sin. He wants all people to be happy forever in Heaven. However, God also gave to people the gift of free will, and he respects each person's right to choose freely how they live their lives. They can choose to live in a way that leads to life or in a way that leads to death.

Jesus showed us clearly how we should live and promised to send his Spirit to help us to live as his followers. Yet some people seem to choose lives of self-ishness, evil and sin. If someone chooses to be completely selfish and heartless and to do what they want regardless of how it affects anyone else then they are choosing not to be with God. God is love. We must have love in order to live with God. To reject the way of love is to reject God.

Hell means being out of God's presence for eternity. The greatest punishment of all is probably the knowledge that a person could be in Hell as a result of their own free choices.

We should not think of Hell as somewhere we can end up accidentally or because of some momentary lapse. It is not possible to be seriously sinful by accident, and we can be sure that God offers everyone the grace of repentance. If anyone is eternally separated from God, it will be because he or she has died refusing to turn back to God and to accept his mercy. Neither can we ever be sure whether or not any particular person will go to Hell even if they appear to live lives that are evil and bad. We must remember that God's mercy is always available to them and that they may turn to God in sorrow even at the hour of death.

At the end of our lives we all need God's grace in order to choose to persevere in his love, or to repent, if we have fallen away from him. Throughout our lives we choose for or against God. The more we choose for God during our lives, the easier our final choice will be. The more we choose against God during our lives, the more we harden ourselves against his mercy.

Lough Derg

Read the following story.

Heaven and Hell

A righteous man was permitted by God to attain foreknowledge of the world to come. In a celestial palace he was ushered into a large room where he saw people seated at a banquet table. The table was laden with the most delectable foods, but not a morsel had been touched. The man gazed in wonder at the people seated at the table because they were emaciated with hunger and they moaned constantly for food even though it was in front of them.

'If they are hungry, why is it that they don't partake of the food that is before them?' asked the man of his heavenly guide. 'They cannot feed themselves,' said the guide. 'If you will notice, each one has their arm strapped straight, so that no matter how they try, they cannot get the food into their mouths.' 'Truly, this is Hell,' said the righteous man as they left the hall.

The heavenly attendant escorted him across the hall into another room, and the man observed another table equally beautiful and laden with delicacies and choice foods. Here he noticed that those seated around the table were well-fed, happy, and joyous. To his amazement, he saw that these people, too, had their arms strapped straight. Turning to his guide he asked in perplexity, 'How is it that they are so well-fed, seeing they are unable to feed themselves?'

'Behold,' said the guide. The righteous man looked and saw that each one was feeding the other. 'In truth,' he exclaimed, 'this is really Heaven!'

'In truth it is,' agreed the attendant. 'As you can see, the difference between Hell and Heaven is a matter of co-operation and serving each other.'

Discuss

What do you think it is that makes the first scene like Hell?

What do you think it is about the second that makes it like Heaven?

Find Your Group
Discuss

Find and read the following biblical passages:

Luke 16: 19-31

Mark 9: 43-48

Matthew 22: 1-14

Matthew 24: 45-57

Matthew 25: 14-30

Summarise what these passages say to us about Hell.

In the following passage from Matthew's Gospel, Jesus told us quite clearly how we will be judged as to whether or not we have prepared ourselves for life with God forever.

Matthew 25: 31-46

'When the Son of Man comes as King and all the angels with him, he will sit on his royal throne, and the people of all the nations will be gathered before him. Then he will divide them into two groups, just as a shepherd separates the sheep from the goats. He will put the righteous people on his right and the others on his left. Then the King will say to the people on his right, "Come, you that are blessed by my Father! Come and possess the kingdom which has been prepared for you ever since the creation of the world. I was hungry and you fed me, thirsty and you gave me a drink; I was a stranger and you received me in your homes, naked and you clothed me; I was sick and you took care of me, in prison and you visited me."

The righteous will then answer him, "When, Lord, did we ever see you hungry and feed you, or thirsty and give you a drink? When did we ever see you a stranger and welcome you in our homes, or naked and clothe you? When did we ever see you sick or in prison, and visit you?" The King will reply, "I tell you, whenever you did this for one of the least

important of these brothers of mine, you did it for me!"

Then he will say to those on his left, "Away from me, you that are under God's curse! Away to the eternal fire which has been prepared for the Devil and his angels! I was hungry but you would not feed me, thirsty but you would not give me a drink; I was a stranger but you would not welcome me in your homes, naked but you would not clothe me; I was sick and in prison but you would not take care of me."

Then they will answer him,

"When, Lord, did we ever see you hungry or thirsty or a stranger or naked or sick or in prison, and would not help you?" The King will reply, "I tell you, whenever you refused to help one of the least important ones, you refused to help me." These, then, will be sent off to eternal punishment, but the righteous will go to eternal life.'

Discuss

Who is the king in this story?

Why were those who had led good lives surprised by what the king had to say to them?

Why were those who had not led good lives surprised by what the king had to say to them?

What do you think is the main message of this story for you?

Find Your Group

Discuss

Have you ever wondered about 'the end of the world'?

What do you think it might be like?

Describe it in words or art or drama.

The passage from Matthew's Gospel is the description which Jesus gave of the general judgment which will take place at the end of time when God will judge humanity. The blessed will be invited to share eternal life for all eternity and those who did not live according to the demands of Jesus will be condemned to Hell for all eternity.

One of the very few things which we can all be sure will happen to us is that one day we will die. It is not unusual that we would spend very little time considering death. Neither is it unusual that when we do think of death we do so with feelings of fear, sadness and even dread.

Sometimes we live as if life in this world was all that there is. Especially for young people, life can seem to stretch out as if it will last forever.

This is the story of how one man reacted when he suddenly faced the reality that one day he would die.

Dynamite King Dies

One morning a man picked up the morning newspaper and to his horror saw his own obituary. The newspaper had reported the death of the wrong man. As most of us would be, he was very curious to find out what people would have to say about him after his death. So he read on. 'Dynamite King Dies', was the caption. He read further and saw himself described as a 'merchant of death'. He had invented dynamite and had made a huge fortune from the manufacture of weapons used for the destruction of human life. However, he found the description of himself which he read in the paper quite disturbing. He realised that he really did not wish to be remembered as the 'merchant of death'.

The event was to change the whole centre of his life. From then on he became someone whose whole life was devoted to work for the development of human life and the creation of peace. He is still remembered today, not as the 'merchant of death', but as the founder of the Nobel Peace Prize – Alfred Nobel.

Alfred Nobel

Find Your Group

Discuss
What effect do you think it would have on you if you were told that you would die in the very near future?

In Your Religion Journal

Write out what you would most like people to remember you for and say about you after your death.
Then write the inscription which you would like to have written on your own tombstone.

A Time to Pray

Leader: Help us, Lord, to accept the inevitability of death.
Give us the courage to live in such a way
that life here on earth is really a
preparation for life with you forever in Heaven.
Give us faith to believe that you want us to live
with you forever in Heaven and that
through the life, death and resurrection of
your Son, Jesus, this salvation is possible
for each one of us.

All: Help us, Lord, to put our trust in you.

Reader: Yahweh, you search me and know me.
You know if I am standing or sitting.
You perceive my thoughts from far away.
Whether I walk or lie down, you are watching;
you are familiar with all my ways.

All: Help us, Lord, to put our trust in you.

Reader: Before a word is even on my tongue, Yahweh,
you know it completely.
Close behind and close in front you hem me in,
shielding me with your hand.
Such knowledge is beyond my understanding,
too high beyond my reach.

All: Help us, Lord, to put our trust in you.

Reader: Where could I go to escape your spirit?
Where could I flee from your presence?
If I climb to the heavens, you are there;
there, too, if I sink to Sheol.
If I flew to the point of sunrise –
or far across the sea –
your hand would still be guiding me,
your right hand holding me.

All: Help us, Lord, to put our trust in you.

Reader: If I asked darkness to cover me
and light to become night around me,
that darkness would not be dark to you;
night would shine as the day.

All: Help us, Lord, to put our trust in you.

Reader: You created my inmost being
and knit me together in my mother's womb.
For all these mysteries –
for the wonder of myself,
for the wonder of your works –
I thank you.

All: Help us, Lord, to put our trust in you.

Reader: You know me through and through
from having watched my bones take shape
when I was being formed in secret,
woven together in the womb.

All: Help us, Lord, to put our trust in you.

Leader: Let us pray for all those who have died,
especially those whom we knew, in this life,
members of our families, our friends,
people who have helped us in some way.

All: Almighty God,
through the death of your Son on the cross
you destroyed our death;
through his rest in the tomb
you hallowed the graves of all who believe in you;
and through his rising again
you restored us to eternal life.

God of the living and the dead
accept our prayers for those who have died in Christ
and are buried with him in the hope of rising again.
Since they were true to your name on earth,
let them praise you forever in the joy of Heaven.

We ask this through Christ our Lord.
Amen.

Reader: A reading from the Book of the Apocalypse (14:13).

Happy are those who die in the Lord!
Happy indeed, the Spirit says; now they can rest
forever after their work, since their good
deeds go with them.
This is the word of the Lord.

All: Thanks be to God.

Reader: A reading from the holy Gospel according to
St John (14:1-6)

'Do not be worried and upset,' Jesus told them. 'Believe in
God and believe also in me. There are many rooms in my
Father's house, and I am going to prepare a place for you. I
will come back and take you to myself, so that you will be
where I am. You know the way that leads to the place
where I am going.'

Thomas said to him, 'Lord, we do not know where you
are going; so how can we know the way to get there?'

Jesus answered him, 'I am the way, the truth, and the life;
no one goes to the Father except by me.'

This is the Gospel of the Lord.

All: Praise to you Lord, Jesus Christ.

Leader: God, the Almighty Father, raised his Son, Jesus
Christ, from the dead; with confidence we ask
him to save all his people, living and dead.

Reader: For our relatives and friends who have gone
before us, and await the kingdom, that they may
have the reward of their goodness.
Lord, in your mercy:

All: Hear our prayer.

Reader: For those who have fallen asleep in the hope of
rising again, that they may see God face to face.
Lord, in your mercy:

All: Hear our prayer.

Reader: For those whose faith was known to you alone,
that they will have light, happiness and peace.
Lord, in your mercy:

All: Hear our prayer.

Reader: For all who mourn for the loss of their loved ones,
that they will find comfort in their sadness,
certainty in their doubt, and courage in their
loneliness.
Lord, in your mercy:

All: Hear our prayer.

Reader: For ourselves, who have assembled here to worship in faith, that we may be reunited one day
with all whom we love, when every tear will be
wiped away.
Lord, in your mercy:

All: Hear our prayer.

Reader: God, our shelter and our strength, you listen in
love to the cry of your people: hear the prayers
we offer for our departed brothers and sisters.
Cleanse them of their sins and grant them the
fullness of redemption.
We ask this through Christ our Lord.

All: Amen.

Leader: Lord God,
whose days are without end
and whose mercies beyond counting,
keep us mindful
that life is short and the hour of death unknown.
Let your Spirit guide our days on earth
in the ways of holiness and justice,
that we may serve you
in union with the whole Church,
sure in faith, strong in hope, perfect in love.
And when our earthly journey is ended,
lead us rejoicing into your kingdom,
where you live for ever and ever.

All: Amen.

Do the Looking Back exercises for
Unit Nine at the back of this book.

Looking Back

When you have completed
Unit One

Do you remember?

What was Jesus' command that challenges us to relate to others openly and lovingly?

Name three groups of people who would be likely to suffer from loneliness.

List three ways we can get to know God.

What is religious faith?

What do we mean by a living faith?

Give two examples of a mystery.

The Trinity is made up of three persons - name them.

What do the words 'to reveal' mean?

What is St Patrick said to have used to teach the people of Ireland about the Trinity?

What do you think?

What do you think is the basis of a good friendship? What would you do to help someone who was lonely?

In your own life

Think about your own image of God. What kind of experiences is your image based on?

Is your image of God continually changing or has it always been the same?

Think about it!

At what times in your life is your faith strongest?

At what times in your life is your faith weakest?

When you have completed
Unit Two

Do you remember?

Where, in the Bible, do we see how the first followers of Jesus put the mission of the Church into practice?

Christ has often been described as having a three-fold mission; what are the three elements?

Describe what an infallible statement is.

During the reign of the Emperor Nero, and for a long time after his death, what was the penalty for being a Christian?

Which emperor made Christianity the religion of the Roman Empire?

List three of the great Fathers of the Church.

Who founded the Franciscan order of Friars?

What are indulgences?

Jesus told one of the apostles that Mary was his mother. Which apostle did he say this to?

Name two places of pilgrimage where Mary is believed to have appeared.

What do you think?

In what ways can you live out the mission of the Church?

Which period in the history of the Church did you find the most interesting? Why?

In your own life

Think about the ways you respond to God's call in your own life.

Is your attitude one of 'Do whatever he tells you'?

When do you find it most difficult to respond to God's call?

308

Do you remember?

In what order were the Gospels written?

What are the three main parts in Matthew's Gospel?

Jesus used a type of story to teach his message. What are these stories called?

List two examples of the images used by Jesus to describe the Kingdom of Heaven.

According to Matthew, how many times do you have to forgive your sister/brother if she/he sins against you?

What is the name of the prayer that Jesus tells his followers to pray in Matthew's Gospel?

What do you think?

Matthew portrays Jesus as a teacher. Do you think this is a good image to use? Why/Why not?

Write out the most important message for you in one of the following:

(a)   Jesus' teaching about the Kingdom of God.
(b)   Jesus' teaching about children and the Kingdom of God.
(c)   Jesus' teaching about forgiveness.

In your own life

What do you know about Jesus?

Where did you get this information?

What could you do to get to know Jesus better?

Think about it!

Who in today's world do you think would be included/excluded from the Kingdom of God?

Do you remember?

Who were the Jewish people waiting for at the time of Jesus?

Who were the people who prepared the way for the Son of God?

Give two examples of these people.

What is the purpose of the season of Advent?

Who is the 'Word' in John's Gospel?

What does the word 'Bethlehem' mean in Hebrew?

What king was born at Bethlehem?

Who shares the Church of the Nativity in Bethlehem?

What do you think?

In your opinion, what is the importance of the Magi in the Christmas story?

What do you understand by the term 'incarnation'?

Do you think that Christmas has lost its original significance and meaning? Give reasons for your answer.

In your own life

In what ways can you identify with the Magi's role in the Christmas story?

Think about it!

Christ's presence in the world is shown through us. How do you show Christ's presence in the world?

When you have completed Unit Five

Do you remember?

What caused the decisive split between the Eastern and the Western Churches?

List three principal Orthodox countries.

How many sacraments does the Orthodox Church have?

What do Orthodox Christians call the Blessed Virgin?

At what age do Orthodox Christians receive the Sacrament of Chrismation (Confirmation)?

What are icons?

What do Muslims usually add when they speak or write Muhammad's name? Why do they do this?

How many pillars are there in Islam? What are they?

Name two of the places where Muslims go on pilgrimage.

What is the name of Islam's sacred book?

What is the title given to Muhammad by Muslims?

What do you think?

How do you think closer unity between the Roman Catholic Church and the Orthodox Church could be achieved?

What do you think is the most valuable aspect of Islam? Give reasons for your answer.

In your own life

If you were a follower of Islam, what do you think you would find hardest? Why?

When you have completed Unit Six

Do you remember?

What is the purpose of the season of Lent for Christians?

The season of Lent lasts 40 days. What is the significance of the 40 days?

What do the ashes used on Ash Wednesday remind us of?

Describe three situations of injustice and say how justice could be restored to these situations.

Who published its Declaration of Human Rights in 1942?

Give three examples of a human right.

Give one example of an Old Testament prophet of social justice.

Give two examples of stereotyping.

What types of groups are most likely to suffer from poverty?

What do you think?

If you were asked to give a definition of justice, what would it be?

What do you understand by the term 'relative poverty'?

What do you think are the main causes of poverty?

In your own life

In what ways can you help people, with whom you come into contact, who suffer from one of the following:
(a) stereotyping; (b) discrimination; (c) poverty.

Think about it

If there are people with advantages there have, therefore, to be others who experience disadvantages. How true do you think this statement is?

When you have completed Unit Seven

When you have completed Unit Eight

Do you remember?

What do we, as Christians, celebrate during Holy Week?

What is the name given to the Sunday before Easter?

What event in Jesus' life does this Sunday celebrate?

What feast were the Jewish people celebrating during the days leading up to Jesus' death?

What was the significance of Jesus washing the feet of the apostles?

What sacramental promises are renewed at the Easter Vigil?

What does the paschal candle symbolise in the Service of Light at the Easter Vigil?

Where was Jesus when he was arrested by the Roman soldiers?

What do you think?

How do think Jesus felt in the garden of Gethsemane?

How do you think Peter felt when he had denied, three times, as predicted, that he knew Jesus?

Why, in your opinion, is Easter Sunday the high point in the life of Christ's followers?

In your own life

Are there times in your life when you have experienced loneliness and isolation?

Do you think the Resurrection has anything to say to the human experience of loneliness?

Think about it!

The cross is a significant symbol for Christians. Why do you think this is?

Do you remember?

List three things that threaten human life.

Give an example of something that reminds us of the sacredness of human life.

When does life begin?

What do a person's genes determine?

What is abortion?

What two conditions allow a person living in Britain to have an abortion?

What is euthanasia?

Describe the difference between love and attraction.

List three different kinds of love that we can experience.

What does the term 'infatuation' mean?

Why is the washing of feet associated with Christ's call to service?

In what ways did Jean Donovan respond to God's call?

Give two examples of the ways in which people answer God's call.

What do you think?

Do you agree with the conditions and the time limit set down by British law to provide for the situation where a woman wants to have an abortion? Why/Why not?

In your own life

Do you experience love as a gift? Why/Why not?

What do you think are the benefits of learning about love skills?

In what ways do you answer God's call?

Think about it!

Think about times when you have lived by Jesus'
teaching, 'Love one another as I have loved you'.
How easy or how hard did you find it to do this?

**When you have completed
Unit Nine**

LOOKING
BACK

Do you remember?

How does Jesus describe heaven to his followers?

What do you understand by the term 'purgatory'?

In Matthew's Gospel, what images does Jesus use
in his description of the judgment that will take
place at the end of time?

What do you think?

What do you think will happen at the end of time?
Why?

Why do you think people are afraid of death?

What would you say to comfort somebody who
was dying and afraid?

In your own life

'I tell you, whenever you did this for one of the
least important of these brothers of mine, you did
it for me.'

What do you think Jesus meant when he said this?

Give an example of how you could show that you
lived out what Jesus said in this statement.

Answers to Quiz Questions on p243

1 B. Around the time your mother learned
she was pregnant, you could swim a
mean backstroke. Your favourite technique was a little backwards walk,
leading with your head.

2 C. It's a good thing you slowed down after
the second month, or your birthweight
would've been 14 tons.

3 B. By nine weeks all the structures necessary for pain sensation are functioning.
You would try your hardest to avoid the
source of pain.

4 B. About eight weeks after conception, all
systems were go: skeletal, nervous, digestive, circulatory and respiratory. The
only job left was to refine what you
already had.

5 B. At only a couple of months you started
to shake, rattle and roll, but you were
too little for your mother to notice. By
four or five months, however, she swore
you had a black belt in karate.

6 B. Not only does amniotic fluid make a
cushy 'water-bed', but it's also full of
glucose (sugar). Swallowing the fluid
was good practice for your digestive system and made for a healthier baby.

7 C. About half-way through the pregnancy,
you had lots of nice skin but not much
fat to fill it out. That's why premature
babies look wrinkled—they need more
'meat on their bones'. The wax-works
effect was caused by the vernix, a thick
whitish cream which covered your skin
to protect it from the amniotic fluid.

8 B. Foetal electric brain waves have been
traced as early as the sixth week. What
do you suppose you were thinking
about?

9 A. At conception, each parent contributed
15,000 chemical 'instruction sheets' (or
genes) that determined not only what

you look like, but also your health, talents, tastes, athletic abilities, intelligence, allergies, and more.

10   B. Four months after conception you were pumping 6½ gallons of blood each day through a body about as long as your hand is now. And it was your blood, not your mother's – you never shared her circulatory system. You may even have a completely different blood type!

11   B. You were either male or female from the point of conception, but it took about forty-six days for parts to be recognizable. Thanks to modern science, parents can now see the sex of their unborn baby with the help of an ultrasound machine by about four months. At last, they can answer the age-old question: 'What colour should I paint the nursery?'

12   B. A smoking Mother sends nicotine, carbon monoxide, carbonic acid and wood alcohol right down the line to her baby. Smoking two packs a day reduces a baby's birth weight by 10%– which can seriously reduce the infant's chances of survival.

13   C. With modern technology, babies as young as five months after conception, weighing only fourteen ounces, have survived premature birth. You would need a lot of medical help, but would fight like a champion to hold on to life.

14   B. During your fourth month, you grew to the grand height of six inches and began to resemble your parents. You also had a trait that may interest the FBI someday – fingerprints.